Life as Observed from the Middle Seat

JANICE TUTTON FINGADO

Life as Observed from the Middle Seat

Published by JF Designs
Tucson, Arizona

ISBN: 979-8-9911801-0-8 (paperback)
ISBN: 979-8-9911801-1-5 (ebook)
LCCN: 2024917473

To all the women who dare to dream

Contents

Part 2

Author's Note

So, you've decided to take up the challenge and write your memoirs because you think you have something to say. In an essay by Lucas Mann titled "By Heart," he questions if the reality of the writer's subject is worth discussing. Who cares? Who cares? As you start writing about things that happened, you discover that if you write about an event and tell it like it truly was, you're going to hurt someone's feelings. I decided that if I'm going to write details of what I think are worthwhile, I want to write the truth as I lived it. Do you admit that things weren't always rosy? Do you mention something unpleasant about a relative who is held in high regard by the rest of the family? Do you ruin somebody's reputation when you discuss their real motivation? Do you admit to your own mistakes, and express your (now) heartfelt regrets? Will your recollection of an event differ from theirs? How far do you go?

As I started clearing my mind of unhappy events, unfortunate decisions, serious mistakes, questionable relationships, I realized I was sitting on a minefield. I discovered in talking to other memoirists that they have all faced this dilemma.

But the book shouldn't substitute for a psychologist's Barcalounger, with a nearby box of Kleenex. I worried: How far do I go?

I got the answer in a literary magazine. The author addressed the question when she responded, "Are you writing fiction or nonfiction?" So. That was it. I had to tell the truth, the whole truth, and nothing but the truth. Hopefully, as you read excerpts from my story, you will find that the whole truth also contained many happy moments, many funny moments, pride in hard-won accomplish-ments, and gems of wisdom scattered here and there. I have tried to create a com-fortable balance between humor and sadness, excitement and boredom, learning and growing, and I hope that at the end of each page, I've also created a desire to turn to the next one.

One of my friends asked me, "How did you fit ninety-seven years in a reason-able-sized book?"

By pushing the Delete button more often than the Enter.

Acknowledgments

This book would never have been published had it not been for the following people and their support.

Members of the Rillito River Writers Group in Tucson, Arizona, who suggested that writing a book is different from writing an email, and that compliments ("You should write a book!") don't necessarily mean that you *can* write a book. It's a steep learning curve from one to the other, but each critique was seriously considered, and the laughs we shared made it fun.

My family. I had hesitantly suggested that instead of just jotting little notes for my grandchildren to read after I was gone, I might actually concentrate on my own experiences and make a book out of them. Their rueful smiles only made me more determined. I have changed their names in the book to protect their anonymity. And innocence.

My husband, Fritz (posthumously). He would have had a fit if he'd known my intentions. I met him by chance, married on hope, survived the gift of a vacuum cleaner on our first anniversary, and became his Designated Packer on all our travels. The man who taught me to grow up by not only explaining the cultures of many foreign countries but also taking me there to observe them for myself. He was a teacher extraordinaire.

Alejandra Velazquez, who made all the tech stuff look so easy while being a patient perfectionist.

My friend and neighbor Ann, whose many years in the publishing business provided me with the advice I needed and the courage to keep at it. Thank you.

To David Fitzsimmons, cartoonist and columnist for *The Arizona Daily Star*, who generously allowed me to use his cartoon of me on the front cover and gave me the idea that a cartoon cover would make the reader laugh and thus make the book more appealing.

To all my friends, everywhere in this wide, wide world, who assured me that they thought it was a great idea and that they would buy the book when it got published: Thank you. Your belief in me was the shove I needed.

Preface

When I decided to begin writing my memoirs for my grandchildren, I realized they would just be little vignettes of my life abroad, my travels, and the thoughts and observations I'd made along the way. I had to have a title for this collection of thoughts.

Since a lot of the ideas occurred to me while we were flying at thirty-nine thousand feet from one adventure to the next, with my husband in the window seat and a corpulent man in the aisle seat who fell asleep as soon as we reached cruising altitude, I realized I had the title of my future book.

Join me on a journey which I call:

Life As Observed from the Middle Seat.

Fasten your seat belt and raise the tray to an upright position.

Introduction

And the Winner is ...

In July 2005, I was reading the morning newspaper on the balcony of my condo in Kelowna, British Columbia, Canada. I glanced down at the beautiful view of the lake and the park from time to time, thinking how lucky we had been to buy the condo when we did.

I saw a small item in the paper announcing that two studios were becoming available at the nearby Rotary Centre for the Performing Arts. Any artist of any venue was invited to submit their résumé for consideration and adjudication. I stopped reading and sat there, numb, remembering my past.

After my husband's death in May 2005, I spent my days doing what every new widow does. I got copies of the official death certificate from the lawyer's office. I sent them to Social Security, Medicare, all the airlines, and several banks, and updated the accounts to reflect just my name. I did the same for the credit card companies, insurance companies, utilities, subscriptions, club memberships—the list was endless. I wrote to the land title company, changing ownership of the condo to my name with our daughter as co-owner. I updated my will, gave her power of attorney, access to our saf-deposit box ... it went on and on. Finally all the paperwork was finished and I began to wonder what to do with all those blank days facing me.

My thoughts returned to that day a few years earlier, when the Rotary Centre for the Performing Arts had opened. We had toured the building while we were out for a walk and were impressed with the new entertainment possibilities so close to our apartment. I remarked to Fritz how I would love to have a studio in the Centre, make my jewelry there and sell it instead of just doing the exhausting craft shows. He turned on me and vehemently said, "Don't even consider it! Your place is at home." He was so upset at the concept of me showing any sign of independence that he didn't speak to me for a couple of days. I never mentioned it again.

But now, was it possible? At seventy-eight? To start a career? What would it entail? What would my family in Tucson think? How much would it cost? I had never worked for pay before. I had never run a business; heck, I didn't even know how to write out a check! What was I thinking?

I had always wondered whether *if* I'd had an opportunity, *could* I have become a professional jeweler instead of just a kitchen-table hobbyist? Could I have had a career? Were my designs worthy of consideration? How did one write a résumé? What had I accomplished that counted for a résumé?

For fifty-nine years I had been a wife and a mother. Wife of a respected businessman. Absent mother to my daughter because of all the years spent living in foreign countries. She'd graduated from Stanford, earned her BA in Houston, gotten her doctorate in Tucson—all on her own—and was now an honored clinical psychologist.

Did anyone even think of me as being my own entity? Who was this seventy-eight-year-old Janice Fingado?

Doubts assailed me over the next few days, though the idea kept nagging. I began making lists, Pro and Con. Under Con, it was easy to come up with items: possible costs; figuring out how to learn to run a business, collect taxes, get insurance on the studio; rent to pay for the studio; having to turn up on time every day—it was a business. Possibility of failure. Loss of face. Sort of. Not having that much "face" to begin with, I could live with that. But what if my jewelry didn't sell? What if I didn't measure up to the other artists there? How could I overcome my lifelong shyness and talk to strangers every day?

What would I do in the studio if I did get chosen? Oh, forget it, I would never be chosen.

The Cons were many, the Pros only one: to be recognized. I decided to add stars to each item on the two lists: one star for least important, five stars for most important. The Con stars far outweighed the single Pro. But I placed ten stars in front of the Pro.

Then there was the alternative. It consisted of one sentence: *I can sit back with my feet up and read every murder mystery on the shelves of the Kelowna Public Library.* Hmmmm, that did sound attractive. But it also sounded a little pedantic. I had this gnawing feeling that I wanted to *do* something! To prove something.

Okay, back to the Cons. If I did it, if I won the studio, and then it didn't succeed, what was the worst that could happen? Financially it would cost me $350 to pay some moving men to move all my machines and equipment back over to the second bedroom of the condo, where they would again compete for space with the computer. I had enough money in the bank, so that wasn't a problem. I would just be back to square one: back to the murder mysteries.

Finally, the answer to all my questions was the one the little gremlin whispered in my ear: "The only failure you can have is the failure to try." That settled it. The Pro won.

I walked over to the Rotary Centre, which was just across the large parking lot of the Skyreach Arena, home of hockey games and big-name concerts. From my living-room window on the fifteenth floor I had watched the limousines disgorging Elton John, the Three Tenors, Michael Bublé. It would be a three-minute walk to work every day; hey, a second Pro! I told the receptionist that I was thinking about applying for the studio opening but had never made a résumé, and how did you write a good one?

That is when I made an important discovery: If you admit right from the start that you don't know how to do something, people are kind and helpful. She handed me the list of requirements and encouraged me to apply. They had never had a jeweler in one of the studios, and she thought it would be wonderful. I toured the studios already in operation: two painters, a sculpture co-op, a studio for the spinners and weavers, a large potter's studio, the dance studio and music room, plus the two vacant studios. The tenants were all so friendly and welcoming—perhaps because I did not represent any competition to any of them, but I preferred to think it was because they actually saw me as a plus to the arts building. They told me how much rent they paid and promised to answer my questions. The ceramic artist next door to studio 203 showed me the ceramic beads and the batik fabric she made, and indicated she would love to have me as her neighbor. I went home feeling more confident and excited, but realized that my age and inexperience would probably count against me. I felt I needed a hook.

I took those two negatives and turned them into a positive. I wrote my résumé describing the jewelry courses I had taken in Switzerland, Brazil, England, and Tucson. I mentioned the craft shows I had competed in. I added some photos of my work. Then I threw in the last paragraph:

I admitted frankly that I was seventy-eight and had never held a job but was willing to teach classes in the studio. Because I'd lived in various countries, I had learned to speak conversational German, Portuguese, and Spanish and would not be afraid to speak to international tourists visiting the Centre. (Kelowna was considered a tourist destination due to its many wineries and four-season sporting activities.) I would be willing to hold the studio open nights when there were concerts or plays taking place in the theater auditorium so that the guests could tour the studio during intermission. I intended to hang a large world map on the wall with pins showing all our travels and residencies. I would give out free semiprecious stones to the school groups that went through on Career Day and show the students on the map where the stones came from. My punch line was: "Don't you think it would set a good example to older women like myself for the Rotary Centre to show that dreams don't have to die, that you are never too old to start a new venture, a possible career?"

They agreed.

There were twenty-four applicants for the two studios. Over the next two months they winnowed it down to three, of which I was one. We were called in before the entire board of directors and interviewed. I was nervous but was one of the two winners. The other winner was a sixty-eight-year-old digital photography artist, so apparently the idea of having older artists appealed to the directors.

I was over the moon and scared to death.

I was also imbued with enthusiasm.

My mantra became the poem by Jenny Joseph.

When I am an old woman, I shall wear purple.

(She goes on to say all the funny things she will start doing once she's an old woman. Then she says that maybe she should practice a little now, so that people who know her won't be shocked when she starts wearing purple.)

I installed shelves and lighting to spotlight my jewelry. I bought a heavy, solid desk to use as my teaching table for the students, and moved my workbench, a couch, a coffee table, and bookshelves over from my apartment. A sink, small refrigerator, and microwave completed the back wall. *I painted the walls purple.*

On October 1, 2005, I opened Studio 203 at the end of the second-floor corridor. I stood outside and gazed at it in awe; it was the most beautiful thing I had ever seen.

The service manager hung a simple stainless-steel sign over the glass door at the entrance.

JFDESIGNS 203

The most exciting, fulfilling four years of my life started that day.

But I was born seventy-eight years earlier on a cold, snowy January 13, 1927, in Ithaca, New York.

I made friends of all my students and loved the camaraderie of my fellow artists. I learned to write manuals for my courses. I learned to take clear photos of each piece of custom-made jewelry and write up concise descriptions for my website. I enjoyed greeting Swiss tourists with "Gruezi, miteinand!" and seeing their faces light up. I was the subject of three magazine articles on artists in the Okanagan. There were two full-page newspaper interviews (one headline in bold letters proclaimed "Janice gets her first job at seventy-eight.") Since the interior decorating of several of my houses had resulted in their being published in *Sunset, Better Homes and Garden, Architectural Digest*, etcetera, I added that as well. The director of the Rotary Centre admired my dedication and long hours in the studio and the fact that I contributed so freely of my time to civic activities held at the Centre. The happiest moments came when I would be walking a student out at 8:30 p.m., after a class, and she would turn and say, "I can't wait until next week!"

Three years later, as I sat in the audience of the auditorium of the University of British Columbia in Kelowna, British Columbia, in February 2008, listening to the familiar Oscar-style awards for the First Annual Okanagan Arts Awards' eight winners, the joy and pleasure of the past three years culminated.

Best Actor, Best Musician, Best Teacher, Best Dancer, Best Performance …

… and when they came to the seventh category I heard, "And the winner of Best Designer of the Year is … Janice Fingado." One of my students had nominated me, and the director had seconded it. A video began playing on the huge screen at the back of the stage, showing me working in my studio and describing how I had started a career at the age of seventy-eight. As I shakily made my way up the steps to the lectern to accept the large bronze trophy, I thought back on all the questions that had assailed me three years earlier. I gave a little speech of gratitude to the judges and, holding the trophy high, told the audience, "Never give up your dreams!"

When I drove home alone that night, I sat in the car in the parking garage for a few minutes, gathering my thoughts. I reflected on how lucky that young girl from Ithaca, New York, was, and how far I had come.

All the many experiences that had formed me, molded me into the woman I was, ran by in a lightning-flash scenario.

On the day I was born, my mother wrote a nursery rhyme in my baby album. It was to teach children the days of the week while forecasting their future:

Monday's child is fair of face.
Tuesday's child is full of grace.
Wednesday's child is full of woe,
Thursday's child has far to go …

Come, take my hand. Join me on the journey. We've a long way to go.

Part 1

1

Auburn, the Prison City?

Auburn has had to live under the moniker of the "Prison City" ever since the monstrous stone fortress was built in 1816. Strangely, it was built right in the center of downtown, although it was probably on the outskirts at the time.

In the early nineteenth century, many Americans believed that industrialization and dramatic demographic, economic, and political upheavals had "conspired" against the traditional controls of family, church, and community. From their perspective, these moral guardians could no longer adequately control disorder. They saw crime as the product of social chaos. Necessary to its eradication was a structured environment in which deviants could be separated from the disorder of society and the contagion of one another. Their solution was to create the "penitentiary"—a new institution for reforming offenders and, ultimately, restoring social stability. That is why the "Auburn System" became so popular and was adopted by many other prisons across the nation.

The Auburn System was introduced by the Quakers, who modified the schedule of prayer, contemplation (*penitentiary* comes from the Latin *penitent*, to feel repentance), and humane conditions with hard labor. Over the years, the plan grew lax and corrupt. The prisoners were compelled to work during the day, and the profit of their labor helped to support the prison. Prisoners were segregated by offense; additionally, they were issued clothing that identified their crime. The traditional American prison uniform, consisting of horizontal black and white stripes, originated at the Auburn prison. The prisoners had their heads closely cropped and walked in lockstep, keeping step, with their heads bowed. Females (first committed to Auburn in 1825) were relegated to an attic and excluded from regular work and exercise. Later, they did become part of the workforce in a large sewing machine workshop.

There was a communal dining room so that the prisoners could gather together for meals, but a code of silence was enforced harshly at all times by the guards; the inmates worked and ate together, but in complete silence.

Letters were banned, and the chaplain was the only occasional visitor. Flogging and other corporal punishment enforced the rules. Such regimentation was thought necessary to restrain the rebellious nature of the offenders. After numerous suicides, instances of mental illness, and attempted escapes, the governor of New York terminated the classification system and the experiment in solitary confinement. Eventually, overcrowding made the silence system unenforceable.

The Auburn prison was the first prison in the United States to receive the electric chair. Many executions were performed in Auburn; the first one took place in 1890. The most important one was Leon Czolgosz, American laborer and anarchist, who fatally shot President William McKinley on September 6, 1901, and was executed in Auburn on October 29, 1901. No long, drawn-out appeals back then!

The electric chair was moved to Sing Sing, another prison in Ossining, New York, and used until the Supreme Court decided in 1972 that its use was unconstitutional. By that time, 614 men and women had been executed, including Julius and Ethel Rosenberg on June 19, 1953, for conspiring to pass atomic secrets to Russia. They were the first Americans to be executed for espionage. Although the ideas of the Auburn System have been abandoned, the prison continues to serve as a maximum security facility and is one of the most secure prisons in the continental United States

I'm glad I lived a life of conventional purity. That code of silence would have killed me.

Auburn, the Rest of the Story …

Auburn is at the north end of Owasco Lake, the index finger of the Finger Lakes region of Upstate New York. It was only a few miles from the Erie Canal, which opened in 1825 and allowed local factories to inexpensively ship goods north or south. Auburn was destined to grow.

Auburn's climate could differ considerably: very hot, humid summers and severely cold winters. The inhabitants claim they have only two seasons: winter and the Fourth of July. Growing up there, I never gave it a thought. Our boots squeaked in the snow as we walked to school in the winter, and we lived in our bathing suits as soon as school let out the end of June. In researching Auburn, I became aware of the famous places in Auburn notoriety (aside from the infamous prison) as well as many very famous people who came from there. "There" is the key word. They mostly became famous after leaving, but I would like to think that Auburn left its mark on their psyche.

The two best-known historical figures associated with Auburn are William H. Seward and Harriet Tubman. Seward served as a New York state senator, the governor of New York, a United States senator, and a presidential candidate, and then he was secretary of state under presidents Abraham Lincoln and Andrew Johnson. Gosh, you can't really get more famous than that, can you? As secretary of state, he negotiated the 1867 purchase from Russia of Alaska—which became known as "Seward's Folly," but I believe he has been exonerated for that craziness. He lived in Auburn from 1823 until his death in 1872.

The Seward Mansion, at 33 South Street, is one of Auburn's earliest surviving examples of the Federal style. William Seward was the son-in-law of Judge Elijah Miller, who built the house. Seward lived in it all the years he worked in government. Brigham Young, noted leader of the Mormon faith, was one of the carpenters to work on the home's original interior. It includes two carriage houses and a horse stable on its property.

Seward was deeply opposed to slavery; the abolitionist party was strongly supported in Auburn. In the 1850s, the Seward family opened their Auburn home as a safe house to fugitive slaves on the Underground Railroad.

In 1859 Seward sold a plot of land to abolitionist Harriet Tubman, who used it to create a safe haven for her family and other black Americans seeking a better life in the North. Harriet Tubman's house was a couple of blocks south of where my mother lived after my father died. Tubman moved to Auburn in 1859, where she fulfilled her dream of opening a home for elderly African Americans, and lived there herself until her death in 1913.

Seward's house is now a historical museum, and both it and Tubman's house are on the National Register of Historic Places.

Behind the Cayuga Museum stands the Case Research Lab, the birthplace of talking movies. Yes, indeed; the talkies were invented in Auburn. Willard and Theodore Case converted a greenhouse into a scientific laboratory and invented a very sensitive light bulb that could react to variations in sound waves. They invented a sound film system, recording test film in the carriage house behind the mansion, and called it Movietone. In 1927, Charles Lindbergh's flight from New York to Paris was the first sound film and caused a sensation.

Could Shirley Temple be far behind?

Auburn has had a long association with professional baseball; a general in the military, Abner Doubleday, was credited for creating baseball. In late 1901, Auburn became the headquarters of the National Association of Professional Baseball Leagues, which is now known simply as Minor League Baseball. The next time you're sitting in the bleachers enjoying a game, give a moment's thought to Auburn.

On the walk to high school every day, I would pass the large metal statue of Thomas Mott Osborne on his marble pedestal, set in a semicircle of trees. He was known to Auburnans as a prison reformer. But to me he stood for the Morse code. His name was the example given when in the Girl Scouts I had to learn the entire Morse code and be able to tap messages out on the sender in order to achieve my badge in communication. Thomas Mott Osborne was T — (one dash),

M — — (two dashes), and O — — — (three dashes). E, I, S, H were the four dots.
Now, years later, I still do the Morse code: I make necklaces in code with secret
messages. Round silver beads for the dots and silver tube beads for the dashes.
They spell out "You are loved" or "Forever yours."

In 1936, Theodore Case sold his sound system to Fox, and the Willard-Case
Mansion to a group organizing a museum headed by Walter Long for "$5 and a
box of cigars." And shortly after, a young girl by the name of Janice Lucy Tutton
began studying art under Dr. Long, as we called him. Every Saturday, I would
go to the carriage house behind the Case Museum and learn how to sketch with
charcoal or soft pencil. It was there that I made the sketches of my grandparents
which I still have today—a bit yellowed with age, but every line a true likeness
of two wonderful people.

The Early Years

In retrospect, Auburn was the perfect place to be brought up, Prison City or not. Back in 1927 it had a population of 35,000, a large library in a mansion, enough doctors and dentists, a good hospital, and friendly neighbors who, like you, left their doors unlocked. Good schools; you could walk to everything, and banks gave you bonuses of glasses and dishes for every deposit of $100 or more. I have a complete set of wine glasses with silver rims, thanks to the Genesee Bank and my mother's faithful deposits. People sat on each other's porches and talked of an evening while kids played on their swing sets and trapezes and held "circuses" for the indulgent parents. All of the lakes had state parks, waterfalls, hiking trails, and idyllic picnic spots. Right on the water's edge was the large Enna Jettick Park, which was the amusement park. It boasted a large carousel of magnificent carved horses, a clubhouse, changing rooms, a picnic area, a roped-off swimming area with a high diving board for diving exhibitions. There was a ballroom for dancing. The ballroom had one of those large crystal revolving balls that sent sparkles all over the walls and floor. With the live orchestra, it was a romantic way to spend a Saturday evening, even for high school students. The miniature paper umbrellas they put in our cokes added to the sophistication.

The Cottage

My grandparents (Dad's parents) owned a camp right on the lake near the park. We could watch the park's fireworks every Fourth of July from our seawall. We would move, lock, stock, and barrel, to the camp the day after school ended in June and remain there all summer. The house was two stories, with four bedrooms and a sleeping balcony on the second floor and a living room, dining room, bedroom, and kitchen on the ground floor. Many of our out-of-town visitors chose the outdoor sleeping balcony so they could sleep under the stars on a soft warm night. The camp had a nice flat lawn all the way down to the seawall, a natural for a croquet court. My sister and I had to pull up the wickets every night as dusk settled so no one would trip over them in the dark on the way to the deck chairs waiting on the cement seawall at the lake's edge. Phyl and I became adept at replacing the wickets the next day, flipping the croquet mallets the required lengths of the pole handles to determine the correct distances between the wickets. What? You didn't know there was a mathematical rule to the layout of croquet? Mercy.

There was nothing more peaceful than sitting on the seawall after supper and watching the lights on the other side of the long, narrow lake blink on.

I discovered clay areas in the shallow pools near the shoreline and loved digging up the gooey mess of clay to shape them into shallow bowls, decorated with carvings or layered decorations, left to dry in the warm sun on the seawall. If I had had a ceramic oven, I could have had quite a business.

Sounds incredibly beautiful, doesn't it? I'd better throw in a "but" here so you don't get completely carried away. The house had no plumbing, so it truly was a camp. To get water in the house, we had an old-fashioned pump in the kitchen. You had to pump the handle up and down and "prime" with water to get it to draw water out of the lake, which was clean enough to drink. We bathed from porcelain bowls in each bedroom, which also came furnished with chamber pots for use during the night. There was an outhouse at the end of the backyard. A luxurious one: it was a two-seater. (I never did figure that one out!) I'll never forget the summer when wasps decided the outhouse was the ideal location for a very large nest, which I discovered when they began to attack me and I made a screaming run back to the cottage without any panties on.

The Garden

The family Grandpa worked for, as the head gardener, had an estate at 63 and 65 South Street, now called King's and Queen's Court. It was built in 1913 for Frederick and Flora Ward Fay. The Fay Mansion had nineteen fireplaces, marble pavement, family and separate freight elevators, gas lights in all the rooms, seven baths, steam heat, a full bath, washing sinks, indoor gasoline pumps, electric lights, and bays for four touring cars. There were cottages for the staff who maintained the mansion. It now houses twenty apartments.

My grandfather was in his element and proceeded to grow prizewinning roses, delphiniums, and cucumbers three feet long. He won blue ribbons at every flower show he entered.

His employers later bought the estate next door: 91 South Street. Built in 1849, Roselawn is one of the few remaining intact estates in the city. It had servants' quarters which are now townhouses, and the mansion was converted to apartments in 1939. Grandpa managed and maintained the fabulous gardens at Roselawn for many years.

The Family

It was during these years that their children came along: first William (Uncle Bill), then (Aunt) Ada, and finally Gordon Nekrews Tutton, my father.

Grandpa must have retired around 1929 because I don't remember visiting those estates on South Street, just walking past them and peeping in.

I was born in Ithaca, New York, in 1927 while my dad was in his last year at Cornell University studying mechanical engineering. He and my mother, Lucy Heffron Tutton, moved back to Auburn when he graduated.

A Humble Man

Grandma and Grandpa led a Rockwellian life: They sat glued to the Emerson radio in the front room; it held pride of place, with their chairs placed on each side of it and a little table in front of it to hold their cups of tea.

Grandma made their own beer, and batches were always fermenting in the cellar with the aroma of hops wafting up the stairwell whenever the door was opened. Grandpa lived to within three weeks of a century, and he always claimed it was Grandma's daily bottle of beer that kept him so healthy. I maintain it was the gardening. They were simple people who took every day as it came with equanimity, measured only by the growth of the cucumbers in the backyard.

Grandma cooked on a monstrous coal stove where you kept the coals glowing, lifting the round plates with a hooked handle to add more coals into its belly for the baking. Every Christmas Eve, the entire family gathered at Grandma and Grandpa's house; all the aunts, uncles, and cousins scattered around the Finger Lakes. We enjoyed a lavish English feast with roast beef, Yorkshire Pudding, mince pies, and plum pudding, steamed many hours and served with a hard sauce. (Lots of brandy, for those of you unfamiliar with the typical holiday dessert.) With so many little kids running around, opening presents was festive and good fun.

Grandpa never relinquished his heritage. He was an Englishman first, foremost, and forever. He paid homage to Queen Elizabeth when she came to the throne in 1952. He would sit for hours in front of the radio listening to the news, especially during the war, and you could feel his pride when something royal was reported, or his concern when the Germans were bombing London. When Grandma died in 1950, he moved in with my mother and father, who had moved to the lake by then. He passed the days serenely, looking at the beautiful view of the lake with the boats passing by. Rocking contentedly in his chair, his eternal pipe in his fingers, he was the image of a Norman Rockwell painting.

In 1952, on our first trip to Europe after the war, my husband and I dropped off our five-year-old daughter with my parents in Auburn and flew to Europe. We visited my husband's relatives in Germany and then on to Spain, where he had grown up.

At the end of the trip, we had three extra days. We decided spontaneously to fly over to England to squeeze that in, too. Luckily, the first day we were in London, the queen opened Parliament, and I made sure I was standing on the curb as her entourage went by in the gilded carriages. So impressive to see: the Horse Guards with their high fur hats and red coats, on their satiny black horses. It was the first official act after her coronation. She had ascended the throne on February 6, 1952, upon King George's death.

We arrived back in Auburn a couple of days later to pick up our daughter, by now completely spoiled. After giving her some gifts from the places we had visited, I went to greet Grandpa and said, "Hold out your hand, Grandpa." When

he did, looking curious, I dropped some English coins into it. I smiled enigmat-
ically, saying, "Guess where I was yesterday, Grandpa." He looked at the coins
and then it dawned on him that they were English. He looked up and in an awed
whisper he said, "M'gawd. Jan, didja see the queen?" I gleefully told him that
indeed I had. She was in the golden carriage, wearing her crown. I was six feet
away as she waved her backward-hand wave and smiled. At me.

You would have thought I had given this simple, decent, humble man the
world. It was the equivalent of kissing the Pope's ring. His granddaughter had
been blessed by his queen.

Our House

My sister and I were brought up in Auburn in a beautiful Federal style house
at 147 Franklin Street, which is listed in the Registry of Heritage Houses in the
United States. My mother and father bought the house in 1928, the year after I
was born.

John Cogswell, a farmer, built the house and lived in it from 1813 to 1835,
when his daughter Harriet married William P. Brown and took up residence until 1842. The house was typical of that era: red brick and white shutters. This early
farmhouse was built with local handmade brick.

The doorbell was a gong which banged against a round black metal plate
when you pulled the doorbell outdoors. A white railed staircase led directly to
the upstairs, while a long hallway opposite the stairs contained the telephone
stand with a chair. We actually sat down and talked to people. It was a party line
with four families tied to it. Not that that encouraged conference calls; if the line
was busy when you picked it up to make a call, when the person talking heard
the click, they would hang up so you could make the call. Then the operator
would come on with "Number, please." Our number was 2044-J. I was so shy
back then that the idea of talking to a stranger to make a call terrified me. I ended up with a lifelong phobia of talking on the phone. I later learned that it was a
genuine obsession called "phonophobia."

Every Sunday evening, we gathered in front of the radio and laughed ourselves silly: first with Jack Benny, then George Burns and Gracie Allen, Fibber McGee and Molly, and Amos and Andy. The den held large, comfortable reading chairs with good lights, and one easy chair in particular became my haven; with my legs over one arm, and slouching in the chair, I would go through my allotment of seven library books per week. Reading was my joy, my contentment, and my path to the outside world. I read all the Bobbsey Twins and Nancy Drew, along with *Little Women, Wuthering Heights*, the Brontes, and adventure travel odysseys. I read my way through high school and always got As on my book reports.

The Dishwashers

It was my sister's and my chore to do the dishes every night, and washing them was an anathema for me. Every night the argument went, "It's my turn to dry!" "No, it's not; you dried last night!" "No, you did!" It was only the quiet arrival of our mother at the door of the kitchen that would shut us up.

Off the kitchen and two steps down, my dad had built a sunroom. It was all glass and looked out on the extensive gardens. He loved sitting there with the evening paper (*The Citizen Advertiser*), an ice-cold bottle of beer, some saltine crackers, and odiferous Limburger cheese. And the radio. He always listened to Lowell Thomas for the news. Sort of a Norman Rockwell painting, but all was well in the United States back in the thirties and forties. We had a nice, not luxurious, house, and Dad turned in his Buick every two years for a new one. I still remember that "new-car" smell after all these years.

Dad

My dad had a wonderful sense of humor. He was the best storyteller ever. Since there was no internet back in the forties, I have no idea how he came across the stories, but the office staff always looked forward to their lunch hour, especially if "Tut" was there to tell a joke or two. Although he did not speak any foreign languages, he had the ability to tell a story in any dialect, and you would have sworn he had been born and raised in Italy, Germany, Poland, or Israel.

He did it by singsonging the phrases, making the words guttural, or sometimes merely raising an eyebrow. He could be funny without uttering a word.

My father

My dad was office manager for the Shoe Form Company in Auburn. They made shoe and leg forms out of clear and flesh-colored plastic and sold them to shoe stores across the country to display shoes and sandals in store windows. And to show off the new sheer nylon stockings which were just being introduced at the end of the war. Women were going wild about the nylon stockings with seams down the back, which were replacing the thick cotton stockings and the silk stockings that developed "runs" in them after only a few trials. All the shoe stores bought the forms. My dad was the person who went to various shoe conventions across the United States. The biggest ones were in Saint Louis and Chicago. He enjoyed Chicago the most because he loved his steaks at the Stockyards restaurants. One convention was memorable because Dad racked up more sales than any other plastic forms representative there. How? He braced two of his transparent leg forms in their toe holders at his booth, the legs standing straight up, filled them with water, and bought some goldfish at Woolworths. Well, *everyone* stopped by his booth to watch the goldfish swimming up and down the legs.

When he returned from a shoe show, my sister and I would meet Dad at the door with, "What did you bring us?" He always brought us something unusual. One year our gifts were Bakelite pins: a new form of plastic. A bluebird for Phyl, who had blue eyes, and a robin for me because I had brown eyes. My brown robin pin is now listed as Collectors' Vintage. (At least it doesn't qualify as antique yet!)

We were longtime Methodists, belonging to Trinity Methodist Church over on Genesee Street. Dad and Mom were greeters in the lobby, handing out the programs enumerating the hymns to be sung at that week's service. Phyl and I belonged to the Sunday school class, as did my mother and father, although theirs was more the study of the Bible and ours were fables from the Bible meant to teach us morals. Our Sunday school teacher was determined to keep us on the straight and narrow. I never missed a Sunday, and at the end of thirteen years (all my school years from kindergarten through high school), I got a gold star. No, not a *gold* star. A stickum paper gold star. For thirteen years of attendance. Now I ask you … really? A little trophy would have been nice.

At ten o'clock every Sunday, we all attended the church service and listened to the minister's sermon. Well, the three of them sat in the audience. I was dressed in my black choir robe and sat at the side of the platform with the rest of the choir.

I was occasionally asked to do a solo, which scared the daylights out of me. I had a quavering voice, but pure, and the choir director always liked to make me perform.

My parents always invited the minister to our Thanksgiving dinners. They included our distant relatives, aunts, uncles, and cousins we rarely saw from around the Finger Lakes region, and lonely members of Dad's office. We never had fewer than twenty-two around the extended dining-room table and the card tables set in the corners for the kids. What a job my mother did, preparing for that dinner. BMW. Before microwaves.

The minister accepted with alacrity and made a point of asking for more of my mother's homemade mincemeat tarts. He once included them in the blessing. "We thank you, Lord, for what we are about to receive, and especially Lucy's mincemeat tarts." She made the mincemeat from scratch, and always added a generous dollop of brandy into the batch before bottling it up to can it. Did he know about the brandy—our teetotaling pastor? Dad just smiled and passed him the tray.

The Playhouse

When my niece Nancy, in Portland, Oregon, recently sent me a booklet she had serendipitously found at a garage sale about heritage sites in Auburn, New York, I wasn't surprised to see that the house where I grew up was now listed as a heritage house. What did surprise me was the paragraph they devoted to the playhouse that my dad had built at the bottom of the garden, stating that the owner, Gordon Tutton, had built it in the 1930s for his two daughters, Janice and Phyllis. The playhouse was located behind the goldfish pond just before the woods leading down to the creek that bordered the boundary of the extensive backyard.

Our garden deserves a mention or two. As I've written before, Grandpa had been a gardener over in England and was highly respected by the family for whom he worked. They had taken him to Marseille every summer, where they owned a large villa, to manage that estate as well. My dad had Grandpa's genes—as do I—and his love for gardening meant that any flower show awards that didn't go to Grandpa went to my dad. The upper half of the garden contained a fenced-in dog run connected to the garage for our English setter named Bing, Dad's hunting dog. He had documented papers on his lineage, and his full name was Cayshire Warhorse Bing. Our black cocker spaniel, Turvey (brother to Topsy at my grandparents'), lived inside the house and was our pet. The lawn, which was relatively level, had beds of annuals and perennials bordering both neighbors' houses. It was divided from the lower garden by a steep rock garden all the way across which held coral bells, succulents, bulbs, "hens and chickens," and creeping flowers, interspersed with large boulders and brick steps leading down to an arch of climbing roses (my wedding photos were taken in the arch). At the right side of the rock garden, Dad built a brick patio with a brick fireplace, for grilling. He loved his steaks.

The lower, larger garden sloped to the goldfish pond at the end, with a sundial in the center and flower beds of hollyhocks, delphinium, and roses down both sides of the lush green lawn.

Dad had just completed redoing the dining room in our house. One didn't "renovate" in those days, you redid something. He installed pine planks on the floor, fitting all the notched strips himself (he used wooden pegs, not a single nail was used) and finishing with many coats of hand-rubbed wax. Then he decided to build two china cabinets in the front corners of the dining room to hold the many antique serving dishes my parents had inherited from Dad's English parents. I still have the exquisite glass-domed footed cake plate, which rings like a clear bell when you flick it with your fingernail. The china cabinets were made of pine paneling and were triangular to fit into the corners of the room, large enough to accommodate all the extra leaves in the Thanksgiving table.

Dad had some of the planks and paneling left over, and that would never do. He started building a secret construction at the end of our garden, and no one figured it out until it was revealed to Phyl and me that summer. Dad had built a playhouse. It was the size of a large shed but had a sloped roof, with shingles, a large single room, with pine floors, and two miniature china cabinets in the corners, for our dolls' dishes. Mom made curtains for the windows, and we had a little rug on the floor. Plenty of room for our dolls' cradles, a tiny high chair, and a doll carriage. It had a large front porch with a railing, which held a small table and four chairs where we held innumerable "tea parties" with our two dolls and us sitting at the table. The cups of imaginary tea our parents drank! With the creek gurgling down below, and the goldfish hiding under the lily pads, no little girls ever had such a treat as we had, playing board games and reading in that playhouse. We were the envy of the neighborhood.

I don't remember my quiet, reserved parents ever spontaneously hugging me as a child.

But Dad built a playhouse.

The Impersonator

The church had many social occasions: Christmas caroling and the Nativity pageant with the children portraying angels. Garage sales. Choir concerts. The ice cream social held every summer in our backyard was a highlight. The churns of homemade ice cream on the tables, made with the fresh fruits of summer, were delicious, and the candlelit paper lanterns Dad hung up, lighting the garden, made it a beautiful evening.

The big fun thing was the Sunday school Halloween party. This was for the adults, not the children. The adults indulged in their fantasies and dressed in outlandish costumes, then had a buffet supper and sat around enjoying each other's creations. One year, my mother arrived at the Halloween party alone. When they asked, "Where's Tut?" she replied, "Oh, he had to stop at the office first, but he'll be right along." They were all sitting around, gossiping, when an unusually gorgeous lady arrived, dressed in a red satin evening gown. She had long hair and was wearing a black eye mask. Never said a word, but took a place on one of the folding chairs and joined the group with a smile. When she sat down, the slit in her evening gown revealed a shapely leg in a sheer nylon stocking, with a high-heeled black pump. Crossing her legs, she swung her leg up and down casually. This went on for some time, entrancing the men and making the women very curious. Who was she? Then someone started chuckling and asked, "Tut, is that you?" Dad reached up and removed the mask, and unfastened the third leg which he had been manipulating with a cord, and the joke broke up the party as everyone howled with laughter.

In the basement of the Methodist church. Can you imagine?

Lucy's Story

Since I've written quite a bit about my dad, it's time to give Mom her due. At first glance I wondered how to make an entire chapter up, because she was just, well, Mom. She cooked, cleaned, was a helpmeet to my father and worked beside him, and never said boo. Then I began remembering … Sunday dinners were always special. I mean, special. Roast beef with Yorkshire pudding, fresh vegetables, homemade bread or Parker House rolls, and always fresh apple pie, to which Dad added a slice of cheddar cheese, and we got a ball of homemade vanilla ice cream. Sometimes a whole roasted chicken with com on the cob that they had picked from a nearby farm that morning. Sometimes at Christmas, plum pudding. And always mashed or scalloped potatoes. And this was after church every Sunday. It might have been a day of rest for our Lord, but not for my mother. Never any homemade exotic foreign foods: Spaghetti came from a can, and I don't think we had even one Chinese restaurant in Auburn, but macaroni 'n' cheese was made from scratch. Soups were also made the old-fashioned way, simmering for hours from bones of whatever she had roasted on Sunday. Special treats were cold leftovers, sandwiches of turkey after Thanksgiving, with homemade cranberry relish. Bread and butter pickles and relish she had canned during cucumber season. Wonderful jams and jellies made the previous summer. She canned everything: tomatoes, pickles, peaches, whatever was in season. The enormous enamel kettle was always bubbling away, canning something with the hinged glass lids waiting to be snapped into place. Nothing was frozen back then. These were the times when you had a block of ice delivered to your icebox, which the iceman brought in with huge tongs, sawdust still clinging to it.

It's a wonder Mom had time to do anything else, but she sewed clothes for my sister and me. They weren't always in style. My prom dress was a quickly thrown together thing, because my boyfriend didn't invite me till the last minute. Was he waiting for something better to come along? In Auburn? The skirt was a red silk material, gathered at the waist, worn with a white blouse with a squared neckline of the same red material. All the other girls were dressed in satin and lace. What she loved to do was sew clothes for our dolls. So many clothes for our rubber baby dolls, and so many for older dolls that required elaborate dresses. She knitted for them, too, and really, the dolls ended up with fancier wardrobes than we did. Barbie dolls came out in my daughter's generation, and Joana's Barbie and Madame Alexanders were dressed to kill. Mom was such a professional knitter that she was asked to manage the yarn department at the Big Store, the large department store in Auburn. She headed it up for years, selling yarns and patterns, and giving knitting classes to the women of Auburn. If you couldn't figure out a cable in an Aran Isle sweater, Lucy was the one you asked. She loved challenges but was bored with just plain knit and purl sweaters. My dad kidded her that she had twenty-five different projects lying around the house, unfinished, that she had put aside once she had figured out the pattern. To show her customers all the possible designs they could make up, she knitted five-inch squares of each one. Later my sister gave me the big bag of them. I selected a contrasting color and crocheted them all together in a lovely afghan. It was fun sitting under the afghan and looking at each square, one different from the other. She taught me how to knit when I was about six, and for many years I never bought a sweater or a scarf. I always knitted my own, and when I married, I made complicated Norwegian-designed sweaters in blue and white for Fritz. She also taught me how to recognize and "pick up" dropped stitches, a talent I recently put to use with one of my students who was knitting a baby blanket for her daughter. She couldn't get over how I found the missing stitch twelve rows down and brought it back on the needle. On our travels later on, if I was in New Zealand, or Germany, or Switzerland, I would buy enough of their unusual yarns or colors and send them to Mom. She always took pride in showing them to her customers and telling them where they had come from.

Mom took me to visit her father once. Only once, although he lived nearby. He had remarried after his wife died. My mother was only a few years old when her mother died. The stepmother was the personification of the "evil stepmother." She didn't like the kids at all. Mom's older sister Hazel brought her and their brother up. My mother didn't talk about her youth, not a word, and being a young child, I didn't much care. It didn't register with me. I'm sorry now that I didn't delve a little bit more when I got older. She easily fitted into Dad's family, and that was enough for her.

My sister was two years younger than I.

Christmas was always a big deal involving lots of homemade ornaments for the Christmas tree (oh, how many red and green strips of paper I glued together in long ropes of circles). I think it was Mom's way of compensating for the loss of Christmas celebrations when she was a child. I don't know when popcorn strings became universal, but not in my time. Popcorn was a treat that we ate, not wasted on Christmas trees. The long silver tinsel strings were added one at a time until the tree shimmered. A silvery star ornament from Czechoslovakia was the last to go on the tip of the tree. Then the plate of cookies and glass of milk for Santa was put on the table near the tree. He must have had a voracious appetite because all the cookies were gone Christmas morning; the crumbs attested to the fact. Made perfect sense to us that Santa was fat. We were up with the rooster, going in and bouncing on our parents' bed, entreating them to come down and open presents.

One Christmas threatened to become a disaster. I remember it vividly. When we were little, maybe six and four, or five and three, in that never-never land of beginning to question if there was a Santa Claus, or if it was our parents. A few days before Christmas, my mother was rushed to the hospital where she had her appendix removed. Dad said, "Don't worry, Santa knows where Mom is, and he'll deliver the presents to her room." My mother looked so sad, Phyl and I had our doubts. Dad suggested we write to Santa, explaining the problem and giving him the address of the hospital. He mailed it for us. Now I have to confess something. Mom and Dad had a big walk-in closet, unusual back in the thirties. It was filled with all their clothing but also held all the I-don't-know-where-to-put-this stuff. We figured out that maybe some of our Christmas presents might be stored in that closet. If curiosity killed the cat, our house would have been strewn with a lot of dead felines. When Dad went out every evening to go to the hospital to visit Mom, Phyl and I would hightail it to their bedroom closet and start poking through all the boxes. And lo and behold, what did we find? A big box, and inside was the most beautiful baby doll we ever saw! We were so astonished that we would carefully take the doll out of the box and play with it, reverently touching its rubber arms and legs with little fingers and toes.

And miracle of miracles, it peed. Yes, it was the first DyDee doll; when you fed it a little bottle of water, it "wet" its diaper. Well, we were so innocent, Phyl and I, that we decided it had to be a present for our cousin Dottie, because there was only one. She lived in Geneva, so our reasoning was a bit far-fetched. We thought Dottie was the luckiest girl on the planet. Each night we carefully tucked the doll back in its box and hid it again. Dad bought a small tree for my mother's hospital room, and on Christmas morning he said, "Let's go wish Mom a Merry Christmas." We grabbed up our gifts for her, and as we entered her room, she was sitting up, smiling. And there next to her little tree with the lights on were two big boxes that we recognized at once. Phyl and I looked guiltily at them and at each other, and Mom and Dad knew something was strange. We burst out that we had found only one and thought the doll was for Dottie. We had been playing with it all week.

Well, I thought Mom was going to split her stitches, she and Dad were laughing so much. Phyl's doll had blue eyes, mine had brown. That was the year we found out that No, Virginia, there is no Santa Claus. But there are great parents who manage to turn a disastrous Christmas into a very merry one.

When the war came, Mom got a job at the American Locomotive company, a large factory in Auburn which had contracts with the air force to manufacture aluminum parts and engines for aircraft. My mother became a genuine Rosie the Riveter. She spent her days on a high scaffold and welded together sections of the planes' nose. Not bad for a petite woman of five feet who never weighed more than ninety-eight pounds. Mom was very proud of her war effort. I'm glad that I was named Janice Lucy Tutton. During those years she riveted, my mother hired a Polish lady, Stella, to work in our house, keeping it clean, doing laundry, and being there in the afternoons when Phyllis and I got home from school. Stella taught me a few words of Polish which I remember to this day, but only phonetically. "Yak sha mahsh?" "Dawbria." (How are you? Fine!) Mom and Dad sold the house on Franklin Street after both Phyl and I married, and built a house on the lake. It had a long dock which held a raft at the end of it where the kids could dive from, and two boats, Dad's motorboat and Ed's cabin cruiser. Ed was my sister's husband. Dad loved taking the boat out on the lake, fishing, and was looking forward to a sportsman's paradise when he retired, fishing all summer and deer hunting in the fall. Sadly, he died three months after retiring; that was cruel. Mom continued living at the lake with her cat. My sister and her family visited her often. Phyl and Ed's son, Michael, bought the house next door, so weekends were festive, with picnics and hamburgers cooked on Dad's grill. They took care of Mom when her rheumatoid arthritis became so crippling. I felt so guilty that the burden of her care fell entirely on Phyl's shoulders because I was living in Switzerland at the time. Fritz never considered a visit other than our paid annual home leave. Everything cost a lot back in the mid-sixties. Mom kept every one of my postcards and letters, telling her about all the places we had visited and lived in. She managed to garner the courage to visit us and flew from Syracuse to New York to Zürich. We drove all around Switzerland. She couldn't get over the foreignness and marveled at the beauty. She had a wonderful time shopping for watches for everyone in the family, and I was worried that she would tell the customs in New York how many she had bought and pay a lot of duty. She came in under the allowed amount, but the officer did ask her why some of the watches were in the toes of her packed shoes. When we were living in England, she visited us there, and we took the train to Shepton Mallet, where Dad's parents had come from. She was thrilled to see the church they had been married in. She loved hearing the English accents. I think she felt that she was paying homage to Grandma and Grandpa, who had taken her into their family. Her English mementos were silk scarves from Liberty of London. In Zürich on her last day as I was helping her pack her bag in our apartment, I began crying and said I felt so guilty that I couldn't be in Auburn to help. I told her not to worry about any part of inheritance for me, but to give Phyl my share, because she deserved it.

Mom touched my arm and just said, "You're my daughter, too, Jan." With those simple words, she gave me grace.

2

High School Years

Not much happened during my years in high school. I was increasingly shy, and never held my hand up even when I knew the answer. In sports I was always the last one to get chosen for the baseball team, but I was excellent at archery. I was head of the team, and we came in eleventh in the state—of thirty-five participant teams. I loved being in plays, but mostly it was as prompter, so I hid out just under the front of the stage with the dialogue in my hands, whispering the words when one of the actors forgot his place. One play, I had the leading role, and it required a kiss at the end. (Was that the beginning of Hallmark movies?) I remember the boy's name: Bob Brown. I felt sorry for him; the kiss was a very fast one. On both our parts. I did have a boyfriend in my senior year, but he waited till the last minute to invite me to the prom. My mother hardly had enough time to sew my dress. In my yearbook I was forecast to go into politics. How strange that I was interested in that back then. But I had high ideals, and politics was still looked upon as an honorable profession.

What Is Love?

There are several types of love, which include love based on friendship, selfless love that is focused on others' well-being, love based on mutual enjoyment without commitment, and romantic love. Love is a nourishing emotion that grows stronger the more you experience it. The more positive experiences we have with someone, the greater the bond we develop with them, which is what sustains a loving relationship. When you recognize that you are in love with someone, meaning you are grown-up now and have grown-up feelings, you wonder what the future will bring. It doesn't always work that way.

This initial feeling of love usually occurs in your teens, and I'm not referring to spin-the-bottle kissing games. I'm speaking of when you know that this one young man stands out as different from all your previous boyfriends as someone special, someone you want to be with, and if anyone is going to touch you, please let it be him. When your lips brush, you get this sudden urge to take it further.

Back in the forties, when I reached my last year in high school, I experienced that emotion, and the memory of it has remained all my life as the purest love I ever had. When I think of loving someone, I remember John.

But sometimes loving someone is also knowing when to abandon all hope of this kind of love. When circumstances demand a painful decision.

First Love

In 1943, some sixteen-year-old boys were gathered from all around New York State based on their accomplishments and school grades. They were sent to Auburn for two years before they were due to enlist, to receive officers' training. The program was called ARSTP, which stood for Army Special Reserve Training Program. They were considered officer material. They were housed in the seminary, which had been moved to larger quarters. The mayor's wife called my mother to ask if I could get together a group of high school girls to come to the seminary to attend dances they would hold for these young men. I managed to get enough names from the senior and junior classes in my school. Thus began the youthful version of the USO and Stage Door Canteen. I helped out in the kitchen of the seminary, dishing out treats through the pass-through as the boys would line up. Then they spent the night dancing with the girls, the music handled by a DJ. Since the young men were the crème de la crème and there was adequate supervision, our parents couldn't object. That first night was exciting: all these new boys to dance with! Then John was in front of the window to collect his plate of food. He wasn't the handsomest that evening, but he was the most charming one there. His smile was magic. Later, when he asked me to dance, he was a good natural dancer and conversed easily. He called the next week. We began dating, but our dates were not just a movie. No, he would come to my house and help me with a book report due for English class. He had read all of them, and he made all kinds of suggestions I wouldn't have thought of. He asked penetrating questions and got me thinking in other directions. He was from New York City. We would go for walks; he would tell me about life there. His kisses were warm and loving. By the end of the first year, I graduated from high school. The seminary boys went back to their homes for the summer. I went to the senior prom with my high school boyfriend, platonic. John called me on the phone often. In the fall I entered the Rochester Institute of Technology. John entered Ohio State University for the second year of his ARSTP. We exchanged letters regularly. Our affection ran deep.

The end came shortly before Christmas break. John flew to Rochester, and we spent the weekend in a hotel. Two beds. He talked very seriously about marriage and how it would never work.

John's father was a well-known rabbi in the Bronx. He was expected to marry a Jewish girl. He was wise enough even then to know our love would lead to a life of despair for me, and our love was not enough protection.

We said goodbye.

During Christmas back in Auburn, I became seriously ill and spent two weeks in the hospital. I was diagnosed with mononucleosis. I knew it was heartbreak.

Love came a second time for me when I was nineteen and Fritz was thirty. Again, it was someone I looked up to, who seemed perfect in every way. I spent every day hoping that he would love me as much as I worshipped him. I strived to be the perfect wife. Loving someone means we should abandon our obsession with perfection. There was only one Audrey Hepburn, and Princess Grace, and Paul Newman, and they're all dead. To love someone is a very subjective condition. Unlike any other word in the world, it means something different to each person. Like our fingerprints, individual and unique. When I think of loving someone, I think of John.

After the war, John became a doctor, a pediatrician specializing in childhood cancer. He was president of the American Red Cross for several years. He married a Jewish girl.

In 1978 he was convicted of murdering his wife with a shotgun. He said it was in self-defense when his wife attacked him with a knife during an argument. He served two years and was released. He was reinstated to practice medicine. He remarried.

Addendum: Now, in retrospect, I find myself wondering, "Did John really love me?" Or was he toying with me until he could get on with his life elsewhere? My poor opinion of myself, so inexperienced, so naïve, brings back the doubts I had of myself all my life. It was only after I had accomplished things on my own—only then did I begin to believe in myself. But that doesn't change how I felt when I was an innocent teenager. John was my first love, the first indication of what loving someone could feel like.

Even the Greeks had trouble defining love. They recognized there were several different kinds of love.

- Latin ludus or playful love, flirting.
- Eros, or sexual passion, frightened the Greeks. It was almost a substitute for love itself.
- Philia, or friendship. The love shared by soldiers and parents for their children.
- Agape, love for everyone, selfless love.
- Pragma, longstanding love. Mature love between long-married couples,
- Philautia, love of self. There are two kinds of self-love: narcissism (we all know who has a serious case of that), being self-obsessed and focused on personal fame and fortune; and a wider love to show a wide range of friends. Now you know why the airline attendant advises you to put your own oxygen mask on first.

These contrast with our focus on a single romantic relationship. You have to ask yourself: How do you feel?

Three years later we saw each other quite by chance in a park in Syracuse. My husband and I had been married for a year, and I was a very eight-months pregnant. John was with a girl. After a bit of conversation and one more glance, we said goodbye again.

RIT

I applied for college at the Rochester Institute of Technology after I had graduated high school in 1944. I was thirteenth in a class of 125. It didn't change its name to RIT until the following year. When I was there it was still the Atheneum and Mechanics Institute. I chose to apply there because Rochester was near Auburn, and I could get back and forth from home by Greyhound.

When I was talking to my father about a profession, he suggested studying to be a dental hygienist; it was an always-needed profession and paid well. I couldn't bear the thought of having to stick my hands in another person's mouth for the rest of my life, so that was out of the question with an "ugghh." I decided to concentrate on becoming a buyer for a department store, and that was a specialty at RIT. You attended classes the first month, and then they had you work in a department store for a month as a clerk and learn how to approach customers. I wanted to be a dress buyer, but they put me in cosmetics. This was approaching Christmas and was so busy. I worked from 9:00 a.m. to 9:00 p.m. and was exhausted. The rudeness of some customers dismayed me.

I finished out the year, one month in class and the next month in Siblings, a large department store in Rochester, but decided retailing was not for me. And the pay was lousy. During the summer I got a job at the Big Store in Auburn, which was also a department store, but by the fall I had taken a six-week course at the New York Telephone Co. as a service representative and took orders for phone service and maintenance. The pay was good. I had my own desk; Dad was very pleased. What an ordeal for someone with phonophobia.

I had a serious boyfriend at RIT, and we announced our engagement to my parents. No ring. Dad was totally against it, saying, "Are you out of your mind? He's a photographer!" I wasn't completely convinced, myself, so when he dropped out of RIT, I figured it was for the best.

3

Growing up in Barcelona

In 1914, Fritz's father, Reinhardt, was an engineer with the municipal tram company in Mexico City for several years (he filed several patents for improving the tram system) before sending for his future wife. Margarethe arrived by ship in Veracruz from Germany in 1913, and they had a civil marriage immediately after she landed. They took an apartment in Mexico City, and shortly afterward, she was pregnant with Fritz. That was the time when Pancho Villa was becoming active and a civil war had broken out in Mexico, with President Woodrow Wilson sitting passively in Washington and not taking any active role. As time passed, the tram company became very concerned about the safety of their foreign employees. They decided to evacuate the wives and children to the States. Because Reinhardt's wife was now eight months pregnant, he was designated the leader of the group and would accompany seven of the wives and a few children back to Veracruz to board a freighter which was sailing to New Orleans. The rest of the husbands would remain in Mexico City. They got on board the freighter, but the Pancho Villa forces fired canons at the ship as it zigzagged out of the harbor. One of the stewards was injured as the women huddled together in the dining room. The ship managed to get to New Orleans, and Reinhardt got all of the wives and children on buses and trains to their relatives before he and Margarethe continued on to New York City by train. There, they would continue to Barcelona, Spain, where Fritz's father had been given the franchise for Carrier Air Conditioning and was going to open his office and business right away in

Barcelona, the up-and-coming area in Spain. The Catalans, with their reputation as the workers of Spain, were the entrepreneurs, businessmen, always ahead of the Madrileños. This was 1914, just after Dr. Willis Carrier had invented air-conditioning, almost unknown in most of Europe. However, Fritz chose to arrive on June 2, 1914, in New York, a bona fide American. He slept in the bottom drawer of a bureau in their hotel for three weeks until the doctor assured Margarethe it would be safe to go on to Barcelona.

Fritz grew up in Barcelona with his parents and brother, Gerhard (Gerry), seven years younger. They had a comfortable life, in beautiful homes, the last one being three stories, with several servants and lovely gardens. On the roof, his father had installed a permanent telescope, and Fritz spent many hours looking at the stars while his father described the constellations to him. His father actually discovered a new star, which was registered Fingado and assigned a number. They had a grand piano in one of the rooms, and Fritz followed his mother's wishes that he study the cello while she accompanied him on the piano.

Fritz studied cello at the Casals Music Studio, where Pablo Casals had already attained the distinction of being a renowned cellist and in great demand for concerts. The classes were given by one of Casals's students, but the maestro Pau Casals himself gave Fritz his examinations. Fritz lugged the huge instrument in its case on the trolley every week to get to his lesson.

The two boys attended the Deutsche Schule (German School) because the parents wanted them to be bilingual, and they spoke German with them while the boys spoke Spanish with the servants and their friends on the streets. Fritz formed lasting friendships (into his eighties) with the students in his class, who stayed together as they worked their way up the grades. When they were teenagers (ah, as teenagers everywhere!) they took chances sneaking out of the house at night, meeting with friends and going into the red-light area of Barcelona, just for the thrill—then sneaking back without getting caught.

When Fritz was fifteen, he was enamored with the new idea of flying; in 1929 it was a fledgling business. He ate, drank, and slept flying. He would go out to the airport of Barcelona—just to watch planes coming in. He offered to clean out the toilets on Lufthansa planes for free in order to get free flights back and forth to Frankfurt whenever they had a seat available. In 1930 he was given the honor of helping land the *Graf Zeppelin* (rigid airship) in Barcelona on its initial flight from Germany to Spain to Brazil. Captain Eckener, who commanded the airship, leaned out of the gondola with a megaphone, directing Fritz on the ground to translate his orders given in German for Fritz into Spanish for the ground crew to grab hold of the dangling ropes.

After graduating from high school in 1931, he attended medical school in Freiburg at his mother's request, until the first class in anatomy required him to dissect a human hand, at which point he withdrew from the medical school and returned to Barcelona. His father pointed out that he had two choices: he could take up engineering in order to take over the Carrier distributorship in Barcelona from his father, or he could shine shoes on Las Ramblas, a pedestrian zone in Barcelona.

He opted to study engineering in Weimar, not because he was interested in becoming an engineer, but because the Ingeneurschule in Weimar had a huge flight training school, and he thought he could squeeze in flight classes in between the engineering studies. Fritz convinced his parents to let him enroll in Weimar. This idea backfired on him, however, because shortly after he arrived in Weimar to begin his studies, Hitler took over the flight training school in order to train pilots for the air force he was building up, and it was no longer available to civilian students.

Fritz attended the engineering school in Weimar, Germany, so that he could take over his father's now-successful and thriving air-conditioning business when he graduated. But that was in 1932, and the civil war was raging in Spain, so his parents fled again, to Germany this time, and then his father went on to the States, where Carrier employed him in New Jersey, where they had a factory. It was always the intention of his parents and brother to return to Spain when the civil war ended.

Between 1932 and 1937, Fritz studied mechanical engineering in Weimar but took advantage of every opportunity he could to take occasional private flights. One trip that he recalled later was a flight in a small plane from Weimar to Düsseldorf, accompanying Hanna Reitsch, who was flying to her home. She was the famous woman pilot who would later fly into Berlin during the very last days of the war in 1945 to try to rescue Hitler from the Russian advance, landing dangerously on the rubble-filled street near his bunker. By then Hitler and Eva Braun had already committed suicide.

Hanna was studying medicine when Fritz accompanied her, and he remembered quizzing her on the flight on the names of various bones for a test she was taking. She got them all correct.

While in Weimar, Fritz attended the Nuremberg rallies, watched Leni Riefenstahl filming them, and enjoyed seeing all the pomp of the parades in the mornings, but was disgusted to observe the same soldiers as uncouth drunks at night in their encampments. He wrote about this in his letters to his parents in Spain. Shortly afterward, his landlady fearfully told him one day that the Gestapo had come to his rooming house and demanded that he go immediately to their headquarters. When he was shown into an office, an official was sitting at the desk with one of Fritz's letters in front of him, with various sentences underlined in red. He shouted at Fritz that he must stop this malicious propaganda at once, and if they ever caught him writing such lies again, he would be sent to one of their "re-education" camps, a forerunner to the concentration camps. The official *Sieg-heiled* him and let him go.

When Fritz graduated in 1937, it was getting very dangerous to remain in Germany. But there was also a civil war going on in Spain, and his parents and younger brother had fled to Germany the previous year. His father had lost all of his equipment and business in Barcelona when Franco confiscated it. Carrier had helped his father emigrate to New Jersey from Germany until he could return to Barcelona and open his office again. His mother and brother opted to reclaim their home in Barcelona until the father could return. With his father in New Jersey at the Carrier plant there, Fritz reserved a cabin on the SS Hamburg to join up with his father in New Jersey.

The Exit

Back in that era, it was common for passports to be issued as family passports because it was assumed that wives and children would only travel with the husband or father. Therefore, Fritz had always traveled on his parents' passport, which was German. Since he was American by birth, he went to the American Embassy in Berlin and applied for a US passport in order to sail to New York on the SS *Hamburg* and enter the States. That was complicated because the birth certificate he had, did not give his first name, only "boy Fingado." His parents had left the hospital before they had selected his given name. The Embassy had to receive the corrected document from the hospital in New York City, which he had to have notarized by his parents and updated on the record of his birth. This would take three months. Red tape existed back in 1937, folks.

In the meantime, because he used a German passport while in college, he was ordered by the German government to be conscripted into the German army. He tried to convince them he had American citizenship, but if your parents were German, you were considered to have dual citizenship and would have to serve. Since he knew that as soon as his American passport arrived, he would leave immediately for the ship, he decided not to argue, but refused to join the army, joining the Luftwaffe instead. With hundreds of other conscripts, he was sworn in. And because he still loved flying, he proudly wore the uniform of the air force. feeling like he was a flier. He had a photograph taken of himself in his uniform to send to his parents, even though his duties only consisted of manning searchlights when planes flew over.

After two months, the long-awaited and highly anticipated message came from the Embassy that they had received the corrected birth certificate and had issued the passport. The only requirement was that he had to show proof that he had turned in his German passport and thus given up his German "citizenship" to a delegated authority.

He had a few days leave coming, so he put on his civilian clothes, as if he were still a student, and rode his bike down to the Black Forest. Picking a small town, he entered the police station. He approached a heavyset policeman engaging him in conversation, then said, oh, by the way, he was making a tour of the Black Forest, and he was afraid he might lose his passport or have it stolen. He wondered if he might leave it at the police station for safekeeping, as he would be passing through again in a couple of weeks to pick it up. And would the officer mind signing that he held the passport in case he wasn't on duty the next time Fritz came in? (I thought this was so clever of him.) The officer wrote out a receipt and signed it, handed it to Fritz, and Fritz pedaled quickly back to Weimar, took a train to Berlin, gave the Embassy the receipt, picked up his US passport, and managed to get to Hamburg in time to board the ship. It turned out to be the last passenger ship that would leave Germany before the war started.

He joined his father in New Jersey.

Fritz was one of the few people selected to work in the Carrier pavilion at the 1939 World's Fair in New York because of his language diversity. Air-conditioning was still a novelty, and the pavilion was very popular. It was in the shape of an igloo.

Canal

While talking to the public about air-conditioning in the Carrier igloo, the executives noted how proficient Fritz was, and Carrier sent Fritz to Colombia, South America, to open the office in Bogotá.

In 1941 Fritz had been contacted by Carrier's headquarters in Syracuse, in response to a request from the US government for someone knowledgeable to tour the facilities of the Panama Canal and determine the security of the locks. They wanted to know if the air-conditioned cells in the underground bunkers could be sabotaged and make the Canal unworkable in the event of war. Because Fritz was the closest-positioned Spanish-speaking air-conditioning specialist, Carrier sent him to Panama where he analyzed the situation and reported back to Carrier. He was traveling on his American passport.

On his return to the airport of Bogotá, he was arrested, accused of being a German spy, and held; he was not allowed to return to his apartment. He was shocked and bewildered. Fritz was permitted to call the American tenant he shared the apartment with, who called the American Embassy, and an official visited him. No explanation was given to the Embassy.

Arrested

He was declared persona non grata, not allowed to enter Colombia, and sent back to Panama. From Panama he was flown to Texas, to a prisoner of war camp, which was very traumatic for an upright person who had always lived by the rules.

While in the internment camp, he met a German, Jochen Rehm, and over the next two years they became fast friends. Jochen had inherited a large coffee-roasting company when his father died and had just completed a coffee-buying trip in Costa Rica. He was going to return to Germany when his mother warned him not to come back, but to seek asylum in the US. When he landed in Texas, he was arrested for possibly being a German spy and sent to the same internment camp as Fritz. Germans and Italians were already being rounded up and sent to camps in various areas of the States, much like the more notorious roundup of the Japanese citizens after Pearl Harbor.

Jochen was repatriated to Germany in 1942, but Fritz went on to a different camp in Oklahoma. While there he worked for an American dentist who treated the internees when needed, translating for him. Both Fritz and Jochen admitted that life in the camps wasn't too bad, because the German detainees were good cooks and got sufficient food, which was not the case in Germany by then. Carrier tried to intervene with lawyers during the two years, but to no avail. They hired a famous attorney in Texas at the time, J. D. Connally, to argue Fritz's innocence and the fact that he was an American citizen. Connally went on to become state attorney general, senator, and governor of Texas. He was riding in the car behind the Kennedys when the president was assassinated in 1964. Connelly was unable to get Fritz released.

No one could ever explain what the reason for Fritz's detention was, but years later when we visited Washington, DC, we went to the State Department and asked to see his file.

The file was titled "Fingado, Fritz, Citizenship: None. Last of USA."

Much of it was redacted but we did discover that Fritz's roommate in the apartment in Bogotá worked for the FBI (which Fritz knew), and when the American Embassy was allowed to send his personal effects to him at the POW camp, only the photograph of Fritz in his Luftwaffe uniform was missing.

We deduced that his friend had gone through his bureau while Fritz was in Panama, found the photograph, and reported that he was possibly a spy working for Germany, probably sending information on the workings of the Canal locks to Germany.

Fritz was released in 1943. He tried to enlist in the Navy, but Carrier had re-classified him as A-1, necessary to the war effort. Carrier sent him to the Chicago office for two years; then he returned to Syracuse, and that was when the magic event of our meeting on the train led to our marriage.

But that is the next chapter.

4

Kismet or Karma?

Kismet is defined as fate or destiny.

Karma is defined by *Merriam-Webster Collegiate* as the force generated by a person's actions to perpetuate transmigration and in its ethical consequences to determine the nature of the person's next existence.

I had spent the weekend of April 10, 1946, in New York City. A casual friend from high school had called me to say he was shipping out after having completed basic training in New Jersey, and would I like to spend his last weekend in the States living it up in New York City? Wow, that would be exciting. I figured separate hotel rooms and maybe seeing a play or, at the least, walking around Times Square.

Strangely enough, my parents must not have objected too strongly to the idea, because I was given permission to go. I was nineteen, living at home, and working for the New York Telephone Company. No boyfriends, as all the high school boys in my class had been inducted, having graduated in 1944.

I took the Twentieth Century Limited train down to New York from Syracuse on that Friday and must have met up with Dick at some prearranged location, maybe Grand Central Station, under the clock. My first queasy feeling came when there was only one room reserved, and the desk clerk smirked knowingly as we headed to the elevator. Never mind, it would probably have twin beds. Dick was in uniform, I naively reassured myself, and we had never dated; his best friend was my boyfriend in high school. All went well, we sightsaw New

York, and when it was time to sleep, I cautiously climbed into the same bed (no twin beds) where Dick never touched me the entire weekend. (I wouldn't have known what to do if he had, and I don't think he would have known what to do, either.) *It was most chaste.* No discussion.

On Sunday afternoon I kissed him goodbye at Grand Central, wished him good luck, and climbed back on the train. It had been a fun weekend, and I thought I had done my patriotic duty for the army. Even if it had been sort of a strange weekend.

Years later, at our forty-fifth high school reunion, Dick and I met again; I was with Fritz and he was alone, explaining that he had "come out" years ago and had a partner. Well, that certainly explained the nonintimate weekend, if not why he had asked me in the first place. My parents had probably been able to tell.

I sought out the car number on my ticket, then the reserved-seat number. The war was still on, and train seats were reserved back then. The porter showed me to the pair of seats, and I saw that the window seat was occupied by an older lady.

The train pulled out right on time, and about twenty minutes later, as I was engrossed in my book, I heard a male voice above me: "Excuse me, but I believe you are occupying my seat." I looked up, saw this doppelgänger for Cary Grant, and realized that he was speaking directly to me. I stuttered, "I don't think so," and hastily pulled out my ticket to show him. It was correct. Then he showed me his ticket, and *it was printed with the same seat and car numbers.*

He laughed and reassured me, "Never mind, I will go back to the Club Car and have a drink." By then, I had been completely charmed by the handsome Cary Grant look-alike, right down to the cleft chin, and had detected a slight foreign accent, so all I could say to myself was a heartfelt "Darn!"

Maybe this is where karma enters. I was an innocent—in every way (okay, make that "virgin")—young girl from a small town in Upstate New York, unsophisticated, naive, trusting, and still holding onto the dream that you met Prince Charming, got married, and brought forth 2.5 children in a cottage with a white picket fence. I stared out the window for a long time as the train moved through towns and countryside and the lights came on in the dusk.

In Albany, the lady next to me disembarked, and I momentarily entertained the thought of making my way back to the Club Car, but realized I hadn't a clue as to what to say if I saw him there. So good training took over, with a few parental rules, and I remained where I was. With a big inner sigh.

After the train left Albany I returned to my reading, and suddenly, *there he was again*, this time asking, "Did the lady leave?" I hastily moved over to the window seat, and told him, "Now you can have *your* seat."

He introduced himself, Fritz Fingado, and said he was working for Carrier Air Conditioning in Syracuse, so would be getting off there too. He explained that he had received a cable from his brother in Barcelona that *their mother had died the previous Sunday*, and all week he had been upset. He finally decided to leave Syracuse for the weekend, for a distraction. He had taken the train down to New York where he had worked during the World's Fair. He mentioned that he was thirty, had been brought up in Spain, but had German parents, thus the "Fritz." I explained that I had been seeing New York with a friend from high school who was being sent to England to join a regiment there, that I lived in Auburn, and that I'd had one year of college at the Rochester Institute of Technology. The more he talked, the more dazzled I became. I began to think how strange it was that two clerks in the railway stations of Syracuse and Auburn had printed out two identical tickets for the same seat. Couldn't imagine how someone with that background could possibly have any interest in me.

But he did. As he dropped me off to catch the Greyhound bus to Auburn, he had my name, address, and telephone number. He called me at work a few days later and asked if he could come over. And as he began driving the thirty-five miles between Syracuse and Auburn every week to take me out to dinner or a movie, we began a four-month courtship that ended on September 14, 1946, with our marriage in the Episcopal Church in Auburn.

I knew that my transmigration (the spiritual movement of the physical body to the soul) from my uneventful, unremarkable, blameless life up until then had prepared me for the Karmic Next Existence. *All the coincidences had to have been directed by a powerful, if not understood, Source, Kismet.*

It would last fifty-nine and a half years.

This is the photo Fritz left on our piano
the first time he came to Auburn to date me.

The Vow

However, it was hardly surprising that after he proposed, we set the wedding quickly, for September. The twice-weekly drives were time-consuming and costly. The relief on my parents' faces was apparent when they realized the airplane buzzing would mercifully end when he took me to live in Syracuse.

Fritz did the correct thing and formally asked my father for my hand in marriage.

Dad took me out to lunch and asked if I was sure I really wanted to do this.

In 1946, if you were not married by the age of twenty, you were considered an old maid. Remember, I was only nineteen, and Fritz was thirty. Considering my choices in Auburn, I didn't see much of a future ahead for me. I assured Dad that I definitely wanted to marry Fritz, that I found him so interesting, with so many talents in languages and his having lived abroad; I felt that I would have a very good, secure life with him. I sealed it by reminding my father that Fritz already had a good job, was making good money, and what more could he ask for in a son-in-law?

I think Dad might have mentioned that he would like a hunting or fishing companion, but he knew that was not going to fly. And in reality, the "good job" argument was very convincing.

The answer was yes, and the following week, Fritz arrived with the ring. It was a quarter of a karat, but Fritz assured us that while small, it was a perfect quality. In retrospect, that should have told me something. As he placed it on my finger at dinner, my mother suddenly jumped up and left the table, crying. She never explained why it was such an emotional moment for her. Perhaps comparing it to her own betrothal? It was a joyous occasion for me; my happiness was complete.

Although we were Methodists, we selected the Episcopal Church to be the site of the wedding. I can't think why; maybe the Methodist church was already reserved for the date we wanted. The rush of the wedding plans and details quickly filled my every waking moment. There were none of the elaborate plans girls tend to make today. One didn't agonize over the seating plans, or whether the color scheme of purple napkins was good with the country club's decor. There was a need to keep the expenses low: My parents could not afford a luxurious wedding, and Fritz's family now consisted only of his younger brother in Barcelona. There would be a relatively small reception at my house after the ceremony in the church.

There was still a dress to make, invitations to print, the meeting with the new minister, the reception to plan, the bridesmaids to arrange, their dresses to decide on, and the honeymoon destination to choose.

I was floating around on cloud nine, wondering how I had snagged a glamorous, handsome, European sophisticate with an amazing background instead of ending up with a garage mechanic or a plumber. Not that I had anything against mechanics or plumbers; it was just that I had met a god on a pedestal who for some inexplicable reason had seen something in me and swept me off my feet. I felt as if both glass slippers fitted perfectly.

I telephoned my girlfriends, one from high school, the other from my single year in college who lived in South Dakota, and they agreed to be my bridesmaids. I mailed them the Vogue pattern for their dresses. My sister, Phyllis, would be maid of honor. Fritz had two friends for ushers and a close friend as best man, all from Carrier, of course. A seamstress was called in to make the dress because there was no wedding shop in Auburn; if I remember correctly, the materials, the pattern, and her labor cost thirty-five dollars. I borrowed the veil and headdress from my cousin who had recently married.

Fritz was arranging for all the bouquets (orchids) to be sent from Colombia, South America, where he had lived for two years, but left all the other details to me. Note: They arrived a week late, and my father had to arrange with a florist the afternoon before the wedding for roses. Well, every wedding has to have a crisis, right?

My mother would make finger sandwiches and desserts, with punch, so we would not require tables and chairs. The wedding cake would be made by a grocery store. People would just stand around out in the back garden. We would all be praying for good weather.

The rest of the plans went forward, with relatives arriving from around the cities near Auburn and helping my mother get all the food ready. The rehearsal was the day before and consisted only of the minister showing Fritz where he and his friends would enter and stand. Then he showed us the vestibule where my father and I would wait till we heard Mendelssohn on the organ. A few short words about the vows and it was over.

We went our separate ways for what was to be the final celebration of Singleness. Fritz had chosen a restaurant for his farewell to bachelorhood with his buddies, and was shocked when my bridesmaids and I walked into the same restaurant.

We hadn't intended to crash his party, but with only three or four restaurants to choose from, we might have made it a little less carefree than he had hoped for.

Saturday, September 14, shone brightly, so our prayers must have reached God's ear. I remember a favorite aunt arriving at the house with a smile, telling me, "Happy the bride the sun shines on!"

I began to feel nervous. The panic attack I had had over the missing flowers for me and the bridesmaids had faded, but I was feeling wedding nerves. We drove to the church for the 2:00 p.m. service. We could hear the organist playing musical pieces as we hid ourselves in the vestibule while the guests filed in. The ushers asked them, "Are you friends of the bride or groom?" My ex-boyfriend from high school and all his friends answered groom, just as a joke. Maybe they felt Fritz's side would be empty. Or maybe they were showing their sympathy? Anyway, they occupied his side of the church.

While waiting in the vestibule with my father, the panic suddenly truly set in. As I heard the organ playing music, my panic grew into a genuine fear. My God, this was for real. How could I go through with this? What was going to happen? I wasn't ready to be married. I didn't know a thing about sex. I had never done anything more lewd than play spin the bottle. Good lord, how had this happened? I felt sick to my stomach.

And then a strange thing happened. To calm myself and get through it, I said to myself, "It's OK. If it doesn't work out, you can always get a divorce."

I cannot put into words how shocked I was that as I was preparing to walk down the aisle to marry the man of my dreams, a fantasy that had come true, such a thought could have entered my mind. I was in a church! Prepared to give my enduring love to my husband, and all I could think of was "divorce"? I was aghast.

I hastily offered God my plea for forgiveness; I promised Him I would never think such a thought again, I swore I would never defile a church again with such an evil thought. And then I made a vow with God: If He would accept this transgression, and forgive me, I would wipe the word divorce from my vocabulary. It would never exist for me. I felt a calmness settle over me.

The wedding march blasted out loud and clear through the open door of the vestibule. Dad offered me his arm, he smiled reassuringly, and we took our places behind the maid of honor and the bridesmaids. We began our measured walk down the aisle.

And no matter what happened or was said or was done for the next fifty-nine and a half years, divorce was never an option. I kept my vow.

The rest of the vows were typical for that time. "Do you, Fritz, swear to love, honor, and care for Janice, as long as ye both shall live?" "I do."

"And do you, Janice, take Fritz as your wedded husband, to love, honor, and obey until death do you part?" "I do." I kept that one, too.

Fritz

One of the reasons I found Fritz such a fascinating person: He had been everywhere, done everything, knew so much; everything about him was different from the boys I had dated during my high school years. I was nineteen when I met him, so I had not had a lot of experience. Above all, I could not comprehend how this exciting man seemed to enjoy being with me. I had never been outside of Auburn, except for the nine months I had attended the Athenaeum and Mechanics Institute in Rochester, New York. I had studied French for four years in high school, but, if asked, could probably only say, "bonjour" or "merci." Fritz spoke four languages. I had studied Latin for three years (does anyone take Latin in high school anymore?) but found it only helped me define English words. My circle of friends was not large, just two girls who were Brownies and Girl Scouts with me, and later my bridesmaids. Fritz had friends in all parts of the globe; he had lived in Spain, Germany, Colombia, New York. He was comfortable anywhere speaking or understanding any given language. My only vice was reading, and that was an addiction. I wore thick glasses. I could follow music on the piano, after seven years of lessons, but never learned to play anything from memory. He played the cello and accordion. He took lessons on the cello but learned to play the accordion by listening to the jazz records they smuggled into their college quarters. He knew all the American songs by heart. I was a quiet nineteen-year-old who laughed readily at jokes and was fairly intelligent. He was a world-traveled thirty-year-old with a steady job.

Many years later I finally figured out the connection: Think Pygmalion. But at the time, he seemed like a miracle that had entered my simple, quiet life.

Pygmalion

Pygmalion was a sculptor but detested women, finding them deceitful and promiscuous. He decided to carve the perfect woman and chipped away at a block of marble until the perfect figure of a woman evolved. Then he prayed to Aphrodite to bring him a woman like her, and when he went back home, he kissed the statue and found her lips warm and the rest of her perfect body alive, and he fell in love with her. I believe that Fritz found in my innocence, the chunk of raw marble, the challenge that Pygmalion had, to create the perfect woman for himself.

Haiku Thoughts on Pygmalion

Like the raw piece of stone

Awaits the strike of chisel

And the kiss of life

After we met on the train, he began driving thirty-five miles from Syracuse to Auburn to take me out to dinner or a movie.

The next week on our dinner date, I told him he had nearly given my mother a heart attack on Sunday when he had buzzed the house and wiggled his wings.

I have a small addendum to the story Fritz told me on Hanna Reitsch: When we were living on the Costa del Sol during the seventies, Fritz got a message from Willy Messerschmidt to come for coffee and cakes at his home a short distance down the coast from ours at the finca. We had heard that Messerschmidt had retired to Spain. I haven't any idea how Fritz had come to meet him, but it was probably also in Weimar. He spent a pleasant afternoon talking planes with the famous warplane designer.

On our dates, Fritz often told me anecdotes about Hitler. Fritz had seen him often in person. In Weimar, Fritz had reserved seats in the first balcony of the Opera House for opening night premieres. His seat was Erster Rang, Erster Reihe, Erster Sitzplatz (first balcony, first row, first seat). Therefore, on the far left side, he looked directly across at the Royal Box opposite, where Hitler (a Wagner fan) would sit with his entourage whenever he was near Weimar. Hitler enjoyed these musical forays and was always jovial with his group of followers. He would turn around in his seat to point out things on the stage.

Fritz also attended the famous 1936 Olympics in Berlin. He managed to secure a job as a translator for the Peruvian team. I don't recall their sport, but they had the decency to lose in the first two levels, and left to go back to Peru. Fritz cleverly managed to join the American teams and rode each day in their bus from the Olympic Village out to the Olympic stadium. It was on the bus that he met Jesse Owens and chatted each day with him. When Owens won the 100-meter race and then went on to get four gold medals overall, Hitler ignored all the African American team members. He refused to shake hands with them and continued his glowing comments of Aryan accomplishments.

While at the Olympics, Fritz also became acquainted with the American rowing team, which later became the subjects of a famous book and movie titled *The Boys in the Boat*. Hitler also refused to honor their win.

Fritz went to the two Nuremberg rallies and was able to remember many details about the mesmerizing Führer who held the thousands in the palm of his hand as they Sieg-heiled him all through the speeches. Fritz also watched the famous photographer Leni Riefenstahl, who filmed the rallies as documentaries for Hitler.

Fritz said Hitler always started speaking in a quiet, measured voice, almost a whisper, and gradually increased the volume until he was shouting and the audience was cheering him on. Fritz admitted that even he was drawn in by the magnetism. By the time he graduated in 1937, his eyes were opened to what Hitler was doing with the invasions of Czechoslovakia and Poland.

Fritz realized that it was time to leave.

Many, many years later I finally figured out the connection: Think Pygmalion. But at the time, it seemed like a miracle that had entered my simple, quiet life.

Fritz had joined the Carrier Flying Club with some of his friends at work. The members had purchased a Piper Cub and took turns flying it. He flew over my house during our Sunday dinner and buzzed so low we thought a plane was going to crash. We got up and ran outside. We saw the plane waggle its wings as he circled overhead, we waved our arms, and then he headed back to Syracuse. Give him credit: He did know how to get a girl's attention.

Free as the Wind

Fritz loved gliding. He was a licensed small-plane pilot and, back in the 1930s, took his first glider flight in Germany and was hooked. He loved floating silently over the hills and valleys of whatever country he was in, catching a thermal and tacking in a different direction to make the flight last as long as possible on just wind power. To be able to control the flight on the elegant, elongated wings of the aerodynamic simplicity of the glider was incredibly exciting to him.

He took gliding lessons and got his license in Duxford, England, a town near Hitchin, where we lived. A small plane took the engineless glider up and would release the cable when it was high enough to fly on the thermals. In Wales the glider was perched on the top of a high hill, with a truck down in the valley poised at the start of a runway. The glider was attached to the truck with an elastic bungee cord. When the pilot signaled he was ready for liftoff, the truck would gun its engine, race down the runway, stretching the bungee taut, and the glider would rise, higher and higher until the truck reached the end of the runway and he would push a button to release the cord on the glider. It would catch a thermal and could move from area to area until the pilot decided to land on the runway. Fritz flew gliders in England and Wales, in Canada from the Kelowna airport (joining the Glider Club there), in New York State, and in Arizona at the Marana airport.

Flying a glider, he was in his personal realm: silent, looking down on the world, king of everything he surveyed, and in complete control. Perfect.

When Fritz was living in Bogotá, Colombia, managing the office there for Carrier in 1940, he dated a lot, but mostly it was like they do today: go out to parties in groups. There was no one in particular that he favored. When he heard about a ship that was going to cruise down the Magdalena River to the port city of Barranquilla, he thought he deserved a vacation and it would be a fun thing to do; maybe he'd meet some young women. Imagine his chagrin when he boarded for the week's cruise and discovered that all his fellow passengers were nuns.

When we took our first cruise on the *Crystal Symphony*, Fritz was convinced it would just be "a bunch of snobs." The first day at sea we had lunch on the Lido deck buffet, enjoying the lavish presentation. At the end of the line there was a group of stewards waiting to take your tray. The waiter asked if we wanted a booth inside or a table out on the Lido deck. Fritz preferred a booth inside. The waiter placed our dishes in front of us, then asked Fritz what he wished to drink. He said, "A glass of lemonade but not the kind that was already mixed in a jar." The waiter looked shocked and protested, "Oh, of course not, sir, we make it fresh each time." When he returned with it, Fritz admitted that it tasted very refreshing.

The next day we decided to do the same thing, and when we had made our delectable choices, the same waiter took our trays, saying, "This way," and led us to the same booth as yesterday. As Fritz sat down, the waiter made a little bow and asked, "Would you like your lemonade, Mr. Fingado?"

My goodness, he had memorized the booth, the lemonade, and Fritz's name, which was on a name tag the first day.

Later when we returned home, I heard Fritz talking about the cruise to some friends. "You should take a Symphony cruise," he said. "Worth every penny!"

When I Became a Barber

I learned to cut Fritz's hair when he bought an electric clipper to trim his neckline, and I became quite adept at it. I'm sure the people in his office never realized that he did not go to a barber at all. One year, as a joke gift, I took a square yard of white cotton fabric, cut one side up the middle to a circle I cut out in the center of the square, sewed bias tape all along the cut edges, and made a barber's smock or cape, which I fastened around his neck with a piece of Velcro tape. On the front of it I embroidered with my sewing machine "Shave and a haircut, two bits." He liked it.

During the thirteen years we lived in Phoenix, Fritz developed a liking for Dairy Queen ice cream, and whenever our daughter was in the back seat, after a piano recital, or a shopping trip, or a school play or a good report card ... you get the idea: any occasion would do ... we would suddenly veer off into a Dairy Queen. He maintained that every car we ever bought came with a built-in magnet under the hood which automatically took over. I think we owned the earliest form of GPS. "You have reached your destination."

Our Daughter

Our daughter was born in July 1947, in Syracuse, New York, while my husband was working at Carrier headquarters. Fritz was sure the baby would be a boy so as to carry on the name Fingado, and we had chosen the first name Ricardo. We didn't know the gender in advance in those days. She stayed without a name for four days in the hospital until the head nurse became impatient and said, "Mrs. Fingado, this baby has to have a name before you can leave." It was difficult to come up with a name that sounded right with "Fingado."

That same day, Fritz had received a cablegram from Costa Rica, from the wife of the ambassador there. She had been one of his Barcelona classmates and was sending him her congratulations. When he said her name, it sounded well with Fingado, and with that settled, we were allowed to leave.

Joana was perfect and good-natured. I started sewing little gowns out of many-times-washed pillowcases for softness and eventually graduated to sewing all of my daughter's clothes. I sewed for her right up to the wedding gown.

Joana learned how to swim well and became very adept at all the strokes after we joined the racquet club and she became part of the swim club there. They used to go over as a team every summer to Del Mar and swim against other teams in California, in the open ocean, occasionally with sharks nearby.

She graduated salutatorian of her class. We were so proud of her. She was accepted at Stanford.

5

Homage to Al Beadle

Desert Modernist 1927–1998

Al Beadle was known as an uncompromising architect who embraced International Style modern architecture. He designed austere modular "Beadle Boxes" with floor-to-ceiling glass walls. But, oh, what Al conjured up inside those glass boxes.

When Fritz was made manager of the Phoenix office for Carrier in 1951, he brought refrigerated air-conditioning to the Valley of the Sun. We hired a realtor to find us a house we liked. So, how did we make the connection to Al? Driving around Phoenix, we were growing frustrated when we saw a "Sold" sign on a small ultramodern house and told our realtor that was exactly what we were looking for. She lost a sale, but introduced us to Al Beadle, and that was the first house he had built in Phoenix since moving there in 1951. Because Fritz had gone to college in Weimar, Germany, from 1932 to 1937, he was familiar with the Bauhaus style. He and Al had a mutual base in their design ideas, and we liked his no-nonsense approach. He developed his style throughout the fifties, sixties, and seventies, when he was being compared to Neutra, Mies van der Rohe, Oscar Niemeyer, Corbusier, and others. Beadle brought the geometric symmetry of his glass boxes to the harsh climate of the Sonoran Desert and allowed the barren desert to create magnificent vistas for his clients' enjoyment. How did we form our mutual admiration society? I often reflect on how Fate or Destiny (whatever you believe in) plays a part in the direction our lives take.

Al designed our first house in 1952. I'm sure that the fact that Fritz was familiar with the Bauhaus style had a lot to do with our mutual enjoyment and respect. Despite Fritz's desire to keep the house a carefully-shaded building from his air-conditioning standpoint, he conceded to Al's contention that floor-to-ceiling glass walls were the design factor we wanted. They each gave in a little: Fritz got clerestory windows on the west wall. And Al got his glass walls everywhere else. They both felt they had "won." That first house appeared in several magazines: *Sunset, Better Homes and Gardens, Architectural Digest,* etcetera. I would like to believe that it meant more to Al when Fritz and I came to him in 1958 to tell him that some people from California wanted to buy our house; it was not for sale, they had just driven by and liked it. We told Al we wouldn't sell it until Al assured us that he would build a second one. That expression of confidence and admiration of his talent gave Al the confirmation he sought.

Even after he was published widely and recognized internationally, Beadle never felt that he could rest on his laurels. Al was included in the Case Study Program in *Arts and Architecture Magazine* and the Architectural Record Houses of the Year. His works are part of the permanent collection of New York's Museum of Modern Art.

According to a synopsis of Al's career written by *Gnosis* during the preparation of a video of Al's houses, "there is little in the way of drawings and renderings noting Al Beadle's work. He made no great effort over the years to preserve his own records, believing that the designer's intent and final statement exists 'in the building itself.'"

That is why I was so happy to donate the photos, floor plans, magazine articles, and renderings of our two houses to the architectural archives at Arizona State University. I gave a speech at the Copenhagen store in Mesa in 2021 and presented all the rolled-up drawings and hand-painted sketches he had made of his floor plans, which I had lugged all over the world every time we moved to a new location.

I hope I've been able to share some more insights into Al. Anyone who ever met Al Beadle has never forgotten him. There are countless people who admired this principled man. Even the disgruntled ones, who had their feathers ruffled, acknowledged his brilliance, his uncompromising principles and ethics, and his commitment to his art. To understand his ethics further, please google *the two Fingado houses* to see all the designs and actual photographs of the construction of our houses. It's a thorough article.

A few years ago, I began writing my memoirs and joined a writing group. Occasionally we tried our hands at poetry. I decided to challenge myself and write a Haiku poem about living in a Beadle Box. Haiku is Japanese poetry wherein you have to complete a thought, feeling, or concept in just three lines. Remembering Al, I wrote,

Glass walls enfold me
freeing my spirit to fly
beyond the unseen.

That may not make any sense to you, but I'll bet anything that Al would have understood.

Dallas

The war had ended in 1945, shortly after Fritz and I met on the train that April. We were married in September, and Joana was born in Syracuse, New York, in July, 1947. Don't bother counting on your fingers; it was ten months.

When she was a year old, Fritz was offered the job of assistant branch manager in the Dallas, Texas, office for Carrier Corporation, the air-conditioning company his father had worked for in Spain. Fritz had been in the research and development division in Syracuse. He was excited about getting out of the factory into the field where he felt the action was.

From 1948 till 1952 we lived in Dallas. We rented a house in Grand Prairie, a suburb of Dallas. It was neither Grand nor on a Prairie, just an economical solution to more expensive Dallas. But after a year of commuting into the city, we found a lovely ranch-style house in Dallas, on a hill overlooking White Rock Park with the nearby White Rock Lake. The house had been built by a builder for himself, so it had many beautiful extras, but he needed the money, so he put it on the market. It cost $14,900, and when your annual income was $6,000, it seemed like a huge decision. At least to Fritz. He returned from the bank after signing for a mortgage (our first and only one) with a green face and, I could tell, a sick feeling in his stomach. It was only many years later when I realized that the green face was not because of taking on such a debt, but because buying a house represented his loss of freedom. He was now a married man with a wife and child. And now a house. Gone forever his carefree bachelor days.

The house was lovely and just the kind of place an up-and-coming assistant branch manager should have. He liked his job, he liked his boss, and eventually came to like the house. We would wheel Joana in her pram down in the park amidst the pecan groves. When she was three, we bought a sailboat in partnership with one of the fellows in the office. Well, Fritz and the other fellow took the boat sailing. It seemed as if I spent the weekends caulking the wooden boat. It was eighteen feet long, made of wood back then, not fiberglass, and it seems that those boats were in continual need of caulking. Caulking entailed buying long twists of cotton which you poked in between each crack of a curved stave with a putty knife as you worked your way down the side of the boat. So, Saturdays I caulked. Bob sailed afterward, and Sundays, Fritz sailed. I usually went along, holding Joana, while trying to avoid getting hit by the swinging boom. I'll never forget one Sunday when we had Carrier visitors from the factory in Syracuse. Fritz took them sailing, along with Joana, all dressed up for the dinner we were having later at home for the guests. Imagine my surprise when, a couple of hours later, they showed up at the house sheepishly, with Joana in tow, all wet and bedraggled. She had fallen overboard when Fritz was making a turn near the dock, and the boom knocked Joana over the edge when Fritz shouted, "Coming about!" to warn that the boom would swing to the other side of the boat. Her blond pigtails were covered with mud, as were her shoes and little seersucker pinafore. The water was shallow there, and they were able to get hold of her and haul her back on board. I was sort of happy to sell that boat when we left Dallas for Phoenix a year later.

In general, Dallas was a good experience and the Texans were extremely friendly people. Joana began to talk like a Texan, with a slow drawl and a soft *I*, "ah." Fritz was promoted to branch manager of the new Phoenix office. If there was anyplace more in need of air-conditioning than Arizona in 1952, we weren't aware of it. It was a plum job, and we got to keep it for thirteen years, all the years Joana was growing up and attending school.

After we had been in Phoenix for a while, we received a notice from the Red Cross asking if Fritz might be the relative of a woman in Germany. The Red Cross was trying its best to reconnect relatives with survivors of the war. It was from his aunt in Freiburg in the Black Forest.

Fritz had only spoken to me of his immediate family in Spain. He had mentioned that he had relatives in Germany but did not know if they had survived. His father and mother and younger brother Gerhardt had fled Franco's Civil War from Barcelona in 1937 to a refugee center on the Rhine. When Fritz graduated from Weimar Engineering School, they warned him not to return to Spain, it was too dangerous. It was also dangerous for him to remain in Germany because the Germans were demanding he serve in the army due to his German citizenship. While he sought out his American birth certificate through the United States Embassy in Berlin, he pacified Germany by joining the Luftwaffe for two months. As soon as the embassy notified him that they had received the birth certificate from the hospital in New York where he was born, they issued his American passport, and he booked a ship from Hamburg to New York.

In the meantime, Carrier had managed to get his father, Reinhard, out of Germany, and his father was in an apartment in New Jersey, where Carrier had a factory. Fritz quickly joined him there. His mother, Margarethe, did not want to come to the United States (she did not speak English), preferring to remain with relatives in Germany until it was safe to return to Barcelona with Gerry (Gerhard), who was seven years younger than Fritz. They were able to move back into the house they had owned, but all the furniture was gone. Fritz and his father moved up to Syracuse, Carrier's headquarters. Reinhard died in 1938 and is buried in Syracuse. Fritz's mother died in 1946 and is buried in Barcelona. It was on that weekend in New York that we met on the train returning to Syracuse.

Fritz had lost track of his German relatives. So, when the Red Cross was able to locate him, he was pleased to write to his aunt Liesel Weissbrod and hear that she was a dentist, that his Aunt Lotte was a nurse in Neustadt (north of Hamburg), and that another aunt had died during the bombing of Dresden. They were all sisters of Fritz's mother. We arranged through the Red Cross to send them packages of items they needed: soap, canned food, etcetera. The Red Cross had the packages all made up. On his father's side, he found his father's sister, Aunt Nora; her husband, Armin Kohlund; and his two cousins, Dietlinde and Ingrid. Aunt Nora and Uncle Armin had been enthusiastic Nazis, but politics was never mentioned in the infrequent letters we exchanged.

Another matter engulfed Fritz during our first year in Phoenix. He had decided he would like to go back to Germany to see these relatives, although he feared they would ask him for money since he was the rich American. The more he thought about it, the more important the trip became. He booked a flight for the two weeks in summer when he had his vacation.

When he had sent in his passport to get it renewed while we were in Dallas, he was refused because he was still a declared enemy alien from when he was turned into the FBI by his roommate in Bogotá who had discovered the photo of Fritz in his Luftwaffe uniform, standing next to a small plane. He had spent two years in a prisoner-of-war camp, which was on his record. His passport application was refused.

After we moved to Phoenix, and Fritz "found" his relatives, he had ordered the flight tickets and two Eurailpasses, and he was panicking. He wrote to Senator Barry Goldwater's office in Washington, explaining the situation and asking him to intervene. As the weeks went by with no news, Fritz was getting desperate. Then one day, two weeks before we were scheduled to leave, we received a telegram from Senator Goldwater stating in telegraphic minimalism, "Passport issued. In the mail. Glad to be of help." I guess I don't have to tell you who got our vote in 1964.

First Visit to Europe

The plan was to go to Auburn first, and drop off five-year-old Joana to be spoiled by my parents, who had not met her except when she was born. Then we would go back to Kennedy and fly to Frankfurt for the long-anticipated reunion with Fritz's relatives. We would use the Eurailpasses to go to all the destinations, from the northernmost town in Germany all the way down to Barcelona, then back again to Frankfurt Airport to fly home. A Eurailpass was for a fixed amount of time, but gave you the flexibility of getting on and off wherever you wanted, without making separate reservations each time. It was for first-class compartments and was valid throughout all of Europe, so we could go down the French Riviera into Spain, all on the same ticket. We validated ours as we stepped on the train at the Frankfurt airport to go first to Neustadt to visit Aunt Lotte.

In spite of all the expectations of meeting the relatives after such a long denouement, it was then that I made an important discovery about my husband. The reunions were not his first priority. Travel was. Not the goal. Not the relatives or friends to connect with, but just a quick "see and be seen" visit with perhaps a few minutes of reminiscing, and then his urge to be on the way again surfaced.

Clearly, it was not the destination but the journey itself. He was happiest sitting in a train station or an airport waiting to board and then hearing the conductor blow his whistle for the *all aboard!* Or the roar of the jet engines at the end of the runway. It was a siren's sweet call to him, his mythical Lorelei.

The actual Lorelei was a steep slate rock at a bend in the Rhine River that produced an eerie echo. Legend has it that a beautiful siren sat on this rock, combing her long golden hair, and singing, luring all those who sailed past to their watery deaths.

As we journeyed south, the overnights came in whatever small town we were approaching when we got hungry or tired; I rather enjoyed the spontaneity of it. We would hop off with our luggage, find an inexpensive hotel near the Bahnhof for a quick departure the following morning. In the evenings, we would tour the town center, eating in typical restaurants. It was a shock to see the amount of damage and the destruction of buildings in Germany eight years after the war. The rubble had been cleared away. but bullet holes pockmarked many of the buildings. I think Fritz had expected the Germans to be so efficient that with all the restoration money the United States poured in after the war, the country would have been restored to its pristine quality he had admired so much. The relatives spoke about the hardships they had endured, but Fritz generally directed the conversations to the present. Both of Fritz's cousins were again employed by the Freiburger Opernhaus: Dietlinde a singer in the chorus, and Ingrid a dancer in the Ballet Corps. They got us tickets for whatever opera or operetta they were playing in at the time of our visit.

It was there I became acquainted with the happy musicals of the German operettas, a love affair that continues to this day. We would buy the tapes of whatever we had seen, and I loved the music so much, I memorized the lyrics. One way to learn German.

In Nice, he introduced me to my first experience with France. I couldn't believe my eyes at the topless beaches all along the Riviera. And the Speedos on the men! In Texas, it was still boxer shorts for men, and one-piecers for women. My, we were conservative!

When we reached Barcelona, he wasted no time calling his friends from the Deutsche Schule. He had kept in touch with a few of them, and those friends had immediately reached most of the rest of his class of thirteen students. We got together several times for tapas and wine, or the famous thick hot chocolate with churros. It struck me that he enjoyed the visits with his schoolmates more than the ones with his relatives.

It was sad for him to see the damage also in his beloved Barcelona. But most of the historical buildings were intact, and we explored the famous cathedral in the old section, the unusual modernism of the Sagrada Familia, the house where Picasso's life works were exhibited, and the houses of the modern architect Gaudí.

Barna, as the natives called it, was just generally run-down, a little shabby, a little "tired," but Fritz loved introducing me to the charm of walking down the Ramblas, taking in all the artists, flower stalls, and baby animals for sale. I loved it. He showed me his two houses where he had grown up. They had been luxurious three-story mansions when they lived there, with several servants, but had been turned into apartments after the war. We were pleased to see that one of them had been renamed Villa Joana, the same name as our daughter.

On the final link on our Eurailpass, we passed over the Pyrénées into Andorra, the little principality between France and Spain. Andorra had served as a smuggling haven during the wars, but was now a peculiar little-known tourist attraction. Speaking a mishmash of Spanish, French, and Catalan, it has maintained its unique quality of each country down through the years. What a wonderful place to escape to!

Then finally we pulled back into the Frankfurt airport, and looked forward to getting back home and telling Joana about all we had seen. But she was eagerly chatting away to us about all the exciting things she had done: fishing in a boat with Grandpa, making cookies with Grandma, and rocking with Great Grandpa in his rocking chair.

Can't beat that! Fritz had discovered the lure of Travel, and we had the best babysitters ever! Is there any doubt about what happened next?

The Pink Lincoln Delivery Truck

We took our first vacation to Europe after the war, in 1954, from our home in Phoenix. This was Fritz's first trip back to Europe since he had escaped from Germany in 1937, so it was a very special time for him to visit his aunts, uncle, and cousins in various parts of Germany, and then take the train on a Eurailpass down to Barcelona to visit many of his old schoolmates from the Deutsche Schule years.

It truly was not the goal, it was the journey itself.

Our trips to Europe took on a new level of frequency, as he would first declare to me that it was time to visit Aunt Lotte and Aunt Liesel in Neustadt or Freiburg. Then would come the ordering of two Eurailpasses for two weeks, and we would fly off to Frankfurt. After initiating the passes right at the airport, we would chug up to Hamburg and on to Neustadt where Aunt Lotte lived. That was on the North Sea, as far north in Germany as he could get, so that he could take the train for two weeks southward. Aunt Lotte had me to thank for those visits, although she never knew it, because ten minutes after Fritz said "Hallo!" he was ready to move on. I told him that he had to spend at least a full day with her.

Fritz's idea of the perfect vacation was to pay for a two-week Eurailpass and then see how many cities he could visit as he rail-clicked on to the southernmost point of Italy or Spain.

The trips became more frequent over the years; some years we even squeezed in a second trip. As a result, it strained our finances.

But then Fritz came up with a new idea. He had seen an ad somewhere about having an import-export business and being able to deduct travel costs on your income taxes. Of course, he couldn't do it because he was manager of the Phoenix office for Carrier. *But I could run it.* I, who had had no business training, would be the owner of Impex, and we could make trips to Europe, buy ethnic items, and have them shipped to our house, and I would sell them to the tourist shops in Scottsdale. He bought a book on importing, ordered some business cards, and voilà, I would now buy samples on our vacations and drive out to Scottsdale two or three days a week, peddling my samples from store to store, always making sure to get back to Catalina High School in time to pick up our daughter each afternoon. Then he would write up the orders in Spanish or German and wait for the orders to arrive. On the next trip to Europe, we would visit an alpargata factory in Barcelona, buy new samples of rope-soled shoes in different sizes. Or visit a jewelry factory in Toledo, Spain, to buy the hand-etched gold-inlaid jewelry pieces. The "business" soon expanded to handwoven baskets in Toluca, Mexico, providing Fritz with a good reason to travel to Mexico.

Because of my innate shyness and inexperience in how to write up orders, the first couple of years were difficult for me. I hated the paperwork involved. But Fritz was ecstatic that he now had a further excuse to travel, and was extremely satisfied that he was able to deduct all the airplane tickets and Eurailpasses on his income tax form every year. As I became more experienced, I gained a little self-confidence, although I have to admit that when I was making an initial call on a new client, I would sit in the car for a few minutes before I could get up enough courage to enter and make my spiel.

Sitting in the car was pleasant. Fritz drove a Mercedes for his own car, but he had purchased a used Lincoln Town Car as a second car for me to use. I couldn't believe it when he drove it home from the dealer: It was light pink, with a gray-blue roof. And it was *huge*. I couldn't see how I would ever find a parking space long enough to parallel park. Taking the driver's test was a nightmare. The air-conditioning worked, but cut off every time I stopped for a red light.

I had established a good friendship with the owner of the Basket House in Scottsdale, Sax Pettit, who always invited me to come back to his office in the back of the store while he looked at my samples and decided what to order. He had merchandise imported from all over the world. I think he had seen on my first visit to the store that I didn't have a clue about how to run a business, and he was very patient, making suggestions as to how to fill out the invoice.

One time I was delivering some merchandise to him. He immediately noticed that I was very nervous and upset and asked what was the matter. I explained that I had just delivered a large order of rope-soled shoes to a boutique, and the owner claimed she hadn't ordered them. (She was having financial troubles, I learned later.) I had shown her the order, and she triumphantly pointed out that she hadn't signed it and would not take delivery. Sax sympathized, "Well, now you've learned that not everyone is honest." Then he gave me another order and made a point of signing it in big letters. I eventually got rid of all the shoes at a sacrificial price to a store in Laguna Beach. It hurt that the woman had been a personal friend, which is why I hadn't asked her to sign the order.

Sax would chat with me about the business and where I had been, and then he would get down to ordering: $800 worth of Toledo jewelry and $500 worth of baskets. He asked me once which pieces of Toledo I would recommend he order, and I started to answer, "Oh, I love this piece and that one there, and—" when he interrupted me and said, "Janice, I don't want the pieces you like; I want the ones which will sell the best." Another lesson learned.

Then when the baskets arrived from Mexico, I would stuff them all in the back seat of the pink Lincoln, in the trunk of the car, on the floor, and even in the passenger side of the front. I would drive out to Scottsdale and down the little alley behind the Basket House and honk. One of the salespeople would come out, open the delivery door, and call in to Sax, "Sax, your pink Lincoln delivery truck is here!" It was the big joke at the Basket House.

Changing Seasons

Write about what you love most about your favorite season:

When the subject about seasons came up in our writing group and the above title was suggested, I knew I could not use that title for the chapter. Because for me, the answer was just the opposite. I knew that I did not like living with one season all the year round, and that I had learned that in order to breathe, in order to feel complete, in order to have the excitement of not knowing, in order to *appreciate* seasons, I had to experience them all.

I grew up in upper New York State and if you want to experience lousy weather, just move to the Syracuse area. Twenty-foot snowdrifts in winter were the norm; rusty undersides of cars were the norm, caused by salting the roads. Sliding our way to school over icy sidewalks, in heavy boots, was the norm. Hearing the clatter of dump trucks lifting their loads of coal and aiming it through the cellar window into the bin below was the norm. Shoveling it from the bin into the open fire door of the furnace was the norm, but only for my father. Cleaning out the ashes from the fireplace if you were lucky enough to have one, and remembering the s'mores you had all enjoyed the night before. Riding down the snowy hill behind your house on a sled or toboggan, falling off before you reached the creek. Ice skating at the Hoopes Park pond and being the last one to get picked so you were always the "whip" at the end of the long line of skaters. Having the cold air freeze the hairs in your nose, even if you pulled the knitted scarf that your mother made, up to just under your eyes.

Ah, yes, was it any wonder, the excitement that awaited us when Carrier made Fritz the manager of the Phoenix office in 1952? NO MORE SNOW, NO

MORE BLIZZARDS, NO MORE SHOVELING OUT! Thus began thirteen years of bliss. Planting petunias in your flowerpots in January. Scattering wild poppy seeds all over the backyard so you could enjoy them from the patio. Watching the tourists in their shorts and sandals while possibly donning a long-sleeved sweater ourselves because we were now genuine Arizonans and didn't get out *our* shorts until March. Swimming in heated pools at friends' houses and at the racquet club that we joined. Hiking, riding our bikes, outside all the time.

Fritz's business expanding while people became acquainted with the comfort of air-conditioning. Entertaining the Syracuse Factory executives who decided the best time to take surveys in Arizona was January. And seeing the sunny blue skies, with white, fluffy clouds floating around the mountains, day after day after day. And we still got to take *our* vacations in the summer to escape the suffocating heat. Ah, yes, just a minor inconvenience to get out of all that snow.

When our daughter graduated from high school and Fritz joined the international division of Carrier because of all his languages, our friends started commiserating with us. "Switzerland? Oh, my goodness, how will you stand it, going back to cold weather!" "Oh, my goodness, you'll be miserable!" "All those MOUNTAINS; you'll have to take up skiing!" "Hope you'll find a place that's *heated*." "You'll have to buy all new clothes for the different seasons."

And that was when I discovered the absolute wonder of watching different seasons arrive. Is there anything more hopeful than to see the little green leaves opening on the lilac bushes? And later, to smell those lilacs? They lined the street we lived on and we could smell them all the way home from the tram. No driving cars through drifts — the streets were scraped, the sidewalks shoveled by 7:00 a.m., and the trams ran all day long till midnight (when all good Swissies were tucked in bed). Trains ran to every little village all across Switzerland, so you could take a weekend vacation. And, of course, winter was "Fondue Zeit" when you got to dunk the bread chunks in the melted cheese-wine specialty. In a "stube" where "gemuetlichkeit" reigned. And the lovely apartment we rented had hot-water radiators in every room, clean and quiet. The Swissies enjoyed their own country so much. Fritz and I loved sitting in a train compartment with three or four Swiss people who always let us have the window seats while they sat back with pride, uttering another "Schoen!" (Beautiful!) every time they passed another snow-covered mountain. (We joked that if we had a franc for every *Schoen* we heard in Switzerland, we'd be wealthy.) They loved the winter for the sports it provided. They waited eagerly for the Spring Green to arrive, because that was a new beginning. They loved the summer for sailboating on the lake and slowly enjoying the wine and long meals on the terraces jutting out over the lakes. And the cable cars … so beautiful to shimmy up a mountain in the summer in a cable car, take in the magnificent views, and hop out at the top to enjoy an "eiscafé" and then hop back on, descending through mountain meadows with the huge cowbells ringing out their clarion calls through the clear air. Then we would start seeing the leaves turning red, orange, yellow in huge groups through the dark green pine trees. We usually took our home leave then, went back to Auburn or Phoenix to visit family and friends, or sometimes add train trips throughout Europe. Fall in Europe is colorful, pleasant, and a nice time to see everything from the top of Finland down to the end of Spain or Italy when opera season is on everywhere.

So, can you understand, now that I'm back in enduringly hot Arizona once more, I find myself remembering nostalgically the passing of the seasons and how they can broaden your lives, with anticipation?

It is thus with our lives as we approach the end. Any new experience, new friend, new activity now brightens our outlook like the sudden appearance of a tiny green leaf on a bare tree. Learning something new (spring), listening quietly to songs being sung from our youth (summer), walking slowly along the green paths of Valley Manor (fall) and greeting friends. Perhaps our walks are a little slower (winter) and the thought of a cable car terrifies me, but each new day is like spring, with the hope and eager greeting; it invites me to come along.

An Unusual Privilege

While we were in the Zürich office, Carrier had been awarded the contract to air-condition the Sistine Chapel. Fritz was to oversee the cleaning and installation of the machines. The walls and ceiling of the Sistine Chapel were cleaned with a mixture of egg yolk, honey, and cleaning materials to remove the soot from the thousands of candles that had been burned in someone's memory. The frescoes that Michaelangelo had painted in 1508 were discovered to have retained the brilliant blues and reds after the ceiling had been cleaned and restored. The Italian dealer in Rome followed Fritz's advice, and they installed some air-conditioning machines in the area of the back side of the chapel walls. To preserve the purified air from all the soot-producing candles. The Vatican invited Fritz and me to come to Rome and go behind the wall near the ceiling, to walk along the catwalk they used, to service the air-conditioning equipment. Through slits in the wall, we were able to look right out on the ceiling at the same level as Michelangelo had lain on his back, painting.

I could have reached out and touched the hand of God.

Travel to the Nth Degree

With Fritz, the joy of travel was not the destination; it was the act of traveling. He never complained about having to get to the airport on international flights two hours ahead of time. He could have sat in the airport the whole time, absorbing the atmosphere of travel through osmosis. It was the drive to the airport, the checking in, the going through security, the boarding, and then the actual flight. He lived in the moment.

When we reached a destination, it was almost a letdown, and as soon as he had seen his relatives or friends and they had had a chance to see him, he was ready for the next place. It was the act of Going that gave him the adrenaline rush.

And Eurailpasses? Don't remind me! Fritz's idea of a successful trip was to buy a two-week Eurailpass, initiate it in Copenhagen, or Finland, and try to see how many stops he could make before it ran out at the southernmost tip of Spain. I have schlepped so many bags on and off of trains, it's a wonder I have any rotator cuffs left. Sometimes as we would be pulling into a station, Fritz would suddenly stand up, start grabbing the bags, and say to me, "This place looks interesting; let's get off here and stay overnight." Then I'd sit with the bags in the station while he would walk around the block, find a hotel, and come back for me. Bags with wheels became my favorite invention. We would spend the evening walking around the town.

Then, next morning, we'd hop on the first train leaving in the direction we were generally heading to, and off we would go. He thrived on the Going …

If the Shoe Fits, Cinderella

I had been this inexperienced nineteen-year-old naive girl who read so many Danielle Steele–like novels always with a Happy End; I believed in Happy Ends. The storybook meeting by chance, love-at-first-glance, happily-ever-after kind of love. He would be Prince Charming.

On a home leave visit to Auburn, my sister introduced me to a group of her friends, saying, "This is my Cinderella sister, Jan." I was startled but, smiling, asked "Cinderella?" Without hesitation she replied, "Well, you married Prince Charming, didn't you?" I reflected on my struggles to adjust to yet another foreign location, the loneliness I felt, the inability to communicate, how isolated I had become with only Fritz to talk to. But I ruefully perpetuated the fantasy. "Oh, right!" I realized that to someone stuck in Auburn, married to a telephone repairman, living abroad would seem like a glamorous life. People just did not rationalize that you still did laundry, cleaned house, and bought groceries. But you had to do it in a language you didn't speak, with an uncertainty that followed you everywhere. No security.

Haiku: On flying to a new residence in a foreign country

What fate awaits me
through this dark and starry night
bound by this gold band?

My memories took me back over the years. All the dreams I had had. The romantic speculation when Prince Charming had awakened me with a kiss. I worshiped him; put him on a pedestal. My wildest dreams had come true.

But over the years, little by little, the blocks of that pedestal had been chipped away, one little blow after another. And the god fell in the pile of rubble. My doubts of ever being able to meet his expectations grew. What happened then? Why did I go on? Was it a sense of duty by then? I've always felt that duty has no feeling of love in it, just sacrifice. I prefer to think of it as loyalty. Because the dreams never die, you live with hope. Every. Single. Day. The hope that love will conquer all.

On my fridge, held by two tiny magnets, is a quotation. The newspaper is yellowed now from age. It shows a sketch of a forest of bare birch trees and a double pair of footprints in the snow fading to one pair in the distance. It says, "I can't promise you that I will be here for the rest of your life. But I can promise that I will love you for the rest of mine."

My favorite television-watching is the Hallmark movie channel. Uh-huh: mushy, sentimental, but tender. And one minute before the end of every movie, they kiss. At one minute to nine, or one minute to eleven every night, you can set your watch. Happy End. But in real life I'm left standing, looking at my god-statue lying in the virtual rubble. Remembering, remembering, all the unfulfilled dreams. Another myth, dashed.

You have a lot to answer for, Hallmark.

6

Swiss-German Dialect

When our daughter graduated from high school in 1965 in Phoenix, Fritz transferred to the international department of Carrier Corporation (air-conditioning). He was assigned to the Zürich office. We moved the next day.

Joana was accepted at Stanford, so we knew she would be well taken care of during her university years, and would visit us in Switzerland each summer. I had no idea what awaited me, but I knew it would be difficult. More difficult for me than for Fritz, because he had been brought up speaking German as his mother tongue. Zürich is an international financial city, and its inhabitants are taught all three official languages (German, French, and Italian), and a fourth one—the Romanisch dialect—which is a combination of French and German, with a bit of Latin for good measure. English was unofficially the fifth language that all the Swiss spoke. What I didn't know at the time was that in the German-speaking provinces, high German was spoken while conducting business with foreigners, but amongst themselves, the Swiss spoke the dialect called Schwyzerdütsch, pronounced sort of like "Shveetzerdoootch." The dialect itself has been informally described as a bunch of people strangling each other. All the "ch"es sound like you are choking to death. And it is frightfully difficult to understand when spoken quickly. You feel like you should be augmenting the Heimlich aneuver.

Fritz was second man on the totem pole in the Zürich office, but since the manager was American and did not speak any foreign languages, Fritz had most of the contacts with the distributors and dealers. His territory included all of

Europe except for England, which had its own office. He enjoyed visiting the dealers and distributors because he spoke fluent German, Spanish, and French, and he could understand and communicate in Italian and Portuguese. Everywhere else, people spoke or understood English. Becoming essential to the Zürich office gave him a sense of self-esteem, so necessary to his character. He was held in high regard by all the dealers and distributorships, who felt Carrier had finally chosen a good man for the position.

I shopped weekly at Jelmoli, a large department store on the Bahnhofstrasse. It had a huge grocery department in the basement. I quickly learned the little things that you *didn't* do: You NEVER reached over the piles of tomatoes, apples, etcetera to select a few for your shopping basket. The forbidding frown you would get from the clerk and the stern "Kann Ich Ihnen helfen?" (Can I help you?) soon told me that the Swiss were so painfully honest that if you needed three tomatoes, you would simply tell her "Drei, bitte," and she would then ask you explicitly if you needed all three for "today." If the answer was no, she would then select one ripe one, one semi-ripe one, and one green one for you. Done. Perfect. Proudly chosen to be just right; I called it the Goldilocks Complex. As I began to pick up a little vocabulary (I always spoke in what they call high German), I made a vow to ask first in German. And they invariably answered me instantly in English. I would come home and complain bitterly to Fritz, "Darn it, I asked for such and such today, and I know I said it right, but the clerk still answered me in English." He would assure me that they were just showing their diversity. Then one day he came home from work to find me beaming with pride. I was just so happy that it was noticeable, so he asked what had happened that day that had me smiling so much. The words tumbled out of my mouth: "Today I was at Jelmoli and I asked the clerk for something in German, and you know what? She answered me in *French*! I must be saying something right!"

I enjoyed introducing the newly arrived Americans to all the cultural pleasures of the city, showing them how to ride the trams and passing on what I had learned from Fritz about reading the entertainment section of the paper. A lot of the wives had no interest in participating in anything; I felt sorry for them.

One curious little phrase the Swissies used as they air-kissed you goodnight after an evening out was "Schlaf gut, miteinand." It's the Swiss dialect for "mit ein ander" in high German and translates to "Sleep well with one another." Since the Swiss used it in greeting "Grüezi, miteinand!" I thought of it as "y'all."

In our second year there, the Women's Club asked me to be chair of the welcoming committee because I had earned the reputation of being enthusiastic about anything Swiss. I had learned enough German to speak a bit at the monthly meetings when we had Swiss professionals speaking on different subjects. One of our speakers was Charles Schultz, the originator of the *Peanuts* comic strip; he had retired to Switzerland. What, you didn't know that one of the most American comics was produced in Switzerland?

By our third year there, I decided that as head of the welcoming committee, I should do more for these ladies. I went to the second-largest department store, which gave lessons in Schwyzerdütsch to the foreign workers, and convinced the manager to teach high German to the rest of us foreigners. They were reluctant at first but finally agreed and gave a class once a week in the store. It quickly filled. In the meantime, I enjoyed the shopping Zürich offered, and I especially marveled at the jewelry in the stores on my Bahnhofstrasse meanderings. If only I could afford to buy some of the beautiful artisan jewelry!

I heard about the famous Migroschule, which was a night school and gave all kinds of classes in a large building in downtown Zürich, mainly to teach all the foreign workers (Italians, Spaniards, and Algerians) how to speak Schwyzerdütsch. Migros also maintained grocery stores all over Switzerland and was famous for having conducted an interesting experiment in running several on a trust basis. They allowed the customers to check out their own groceries and pay for them, but in the way of all flesh, it failed. They employed cashiers again. Migros also gave classes in arts and crafts. When I saw their program included a night class in Gold und Silberschmuck (gold and silversmithing), I deviously hatched a scheme. I told Fritz that if I took a class in silversmithing, I would be able to improve my German. Skeptical and doubtful, he finally said okay, but I would have to get downtown at night by tram. In good, clean, honest Switzerland I never gave it a second thought. I enrolled the next day with dreams of making my own jewelry dancing in my head.

On the first night of my course, I took my place in a room of several work-benches and six other eager prospective silversmiths.

And the teacher only spoke Schwyzerdütsch! As I despaired, holding the strip of copper helplessly in my hand, two guys on each side of me turned and, with hands moving straight up and down, grinned and said in perfect English, "He wants you to saw this way."

This language thing is a two-way street.

How to Avoid a War

I have been fortunate that in my long life, I have been successful in avoiding confrontations or unpleasant encounters. At least in person; with emails taking the place of "conversations," that is a different matter now. While we were living in Zürich we marveled at how the Swiss managed to avoid confrontations with other countries and maintained neutrality, in spite of the many cultures and religious differences. We often discussed it together but could never come up with the reason. Until one day …

August 1 is a national holiday in Switzerland, a lot like our July 4: a big parade, lots of bands, guilds marching in groups, all in colorful costumes. One group was actually a military band from an American base in southern Germany, the Stars and Stripes proudly fluttering in the breeze.

Neutrality. Where was the neutrality? How do you avoid fighting wars?

The answer came with the last group to march by. It was reservists (every Swiss man has to serve two years in service). Each man shouldered a rifle.

At the end of each muzzle was a flower poking out.

Swiss Christmas

Another Christmas, another country, another little custom that was curious and cute. In 1967 we were enjoying everything about life in Switzerland. We loved going down to Bürkli Platz in front of the Opernhaus on days when the tour buses were lined up, wandering down the rows of buses reading their destinations for the day, chatting with the drivers, and then deciding which sounded the most interesting. We soon discovered that several bore a strange title on the windshield: *Fahrt ins Blaue* (Trip into the Blue). When we asked where the Blue was, the driver laughed and said we would have to trust him, that it would be to a beautiful place, but it would be a secret until we actually arrived there. On those trips, we discovered Johanna Spyri's prototype village, high in the mountains, that she used for the Heidi books. Another was to an elegant spa-hotel in Baden-Baden for a wonderful Kurkonzert, with the Kur Orchester. But the most fun was the 5:00 p.m. departure of a bus simply titled *Besuch nach Samiclaus* (Visit to Santa Claus). We climbed aboard along with a lot of happy, chattering Swissies, wondering where we would end up. It was already dark out as the bus climbed out of Zürich and the city lights. Soon we were driving through isolated alpine villages, all gaily bedecked with Christmas lights everywhere. Driving off the main road and along a plowed-out side road, the driver pulled to a stop and asked us all to continue the trip without him. As we climbed down from the bus into the snowy landscape, we soon heard the merry jingle of sleigh bells. Two large wagons on runners, pulled by teams of horses, drew up, and we climbed aboard. They took us through the dark forest with the pristine, glistening snow, and when we rounded the next bend in the track we gasped. Right before our eyes was a log cabin all lit up with colored Christmas lights. There to greet us was, of course, Samiclaus in his red suit and white fur. He invited us into his house for dinner and singing and music. We all trooped in to see several long tables set up with festive decorations, a roaring fire, and a dance band in one corner. His elves began serving us dinner, and that was the comical part: all the Swissies there had obviously visited Samiclaus before and knew that he was very generous, so out of their purses and bags came plastic grocery bags, and when each one was served an entire half of a roasted chicken, with pommes frites and salad, they quickly stashed sections of the chicken in Saran Wrap and the plastic bags to take home for another day. Being Swissies, they generously offered us some plastic wrap and a bag to use. Samiclaus entertained with Swiss-dialect jokes and led the singing of Christmas carols. There were some costumed dancers and some dancing, and we all piled back into the wagons, and then through the Stille Nacht we made our way back to the buses and down the hills to Zürich. It brought back childhood memories of Santa and the mystery of his sleigh riding through the starry sky, and turned all of us into children of wonder for a few magical hours. Merry Christmas, ho, ho, ho!

Lest We Forget

. . . what Christmas is all about.

It's not about gifts and decorations. It's not about a tree with lights and silvery balls on it. It's not about office parties and drinks. It's not about Santa Claus, who originated as Saint Nikolaus in 280 AD. Reindeer and jingle bells are not Christmas. It's not about Black Friday or Green Monday. It's not about listening to traditional Christmas songs all day long from Thanksgiving until the day after Christmas. And email letters sent out at Christmas outlining every little trip you made during the past year is not about Christmas; it's about you.

What it is about is the birth of a child destined to change the hearts and minds of the entire world. One way or another. It's about the deeds of a man who taught his followers everything we need to know about how to treat one another. It's about a birth in a humble manger, not a mansion. The idea of giving gifts originated with the three kings who brought gifts of gold, frankincense, and myrrh to the baby Jesus.

Let us dwell for a moment on the real reason we are celebrating this season. And, in all humility, try to be better. This tree does not have lights or glitter. It has thirty-three live red roses, one for each year of Christ's life. Let us come together and celebrate.

7

Christmas in London

While living in England we would often take the train down to London, a mere thirty-five-minute ride, get off at King's Cross, hop on the "tube," and go to the studios at the BBC. They did many of their comedy series shows before a live audience, and it was lots of fun to see the famous actors come out ahead of the filming and chat with the audience. Then the "applause" cue guy would come out and encourage us to laugh and applaud when something "tickles your fancy." And all this fun for free!

London always went far out to decorate for Christmas. An afternoon on the train into London to attend the latest show that had opened, or picking up half-price tickets obtained at the little booth down Piccadilly for a show about to start in a couple of hours, then getting out in the dark to see all the decorations lit up was an incomparable freebie. The department stores outdid each other in competing for magnificent window displays with moving trains, carousels, exquisite Christmas decorations, and music piped out to the street. It sure put you in the Christmas spirit.

Leave No Scone Unturned

Back in the theaters in the 1970s, they still had the delightful courtesy of serving you high tea for an additional price. You ordered it from the usher when you took your seats upon entering, and then during intermission, the lady would pull the little shelf up out of your armrest and soon return with a tray of finger sandwiches (yes, indeed, paper-thin cucumber slices, with the crusts trimmed off) together with little cakes, or you might get lucky and land a scone with berries and double cream. A nice pot of tea, with china cups. So civilized.

One time my sister and family were visiting us in England, and to give them an interesting insight into English culture, we decided to take them to the Law Courts, which are completely open to visitors and could be audited. We looked at the signs outside of each set of closed double doors to see what was being heard and then, selecting one that sounded interesting, opened the door and walked silently in, creeping into a back row. We had only been seated a couple of minutes when my ten-year-old niece, Linda, spotted the white curled wigs on the heads of the solicitors trying the case, along with the judge, and in a delighted voice declared, "Look, Aunt Jan, it's just like on TV!"

Opera in Weimar

Fritz loved opera: attending performances and listening to recordings. Being able to speak German and French, he was able to understand them and follow what little plot they had. He would have gotten a kick out of a definition of opera one of my fellow writers gave me: "Dialogue by Dick and Jane, plot by *National Enquirer*, and music by God."

When he was studying engineering in Weimar, Germany (1932–1937), he had season tickets at the Opernhaus and attended all the performances on opening night. His seat was on the left side, which allowed him to watch what went on behind the curtains on the right side.

It also meant that he was directly opposite the State Box on the right side of the balcony, which was occupied by Hitler.

Hitler had been in power since 1933 and was held in high esteem by most of the country for his bombastic speeches, show of force, and extravagant rallies held in Nurenburg and Berlin, where he held the enormous audiences spellbound. He would start a speech in a normal voice, almost a whisper, then gradually raise his voice till he was shouting. Hitler was fascinated with the powerful music of

Wagner, so he was occasionally in attendance on the same opening night as Fritz. Fritz found Hitler specious, and was curious as to how the public could be so taken in by this self-designated leader. So, it was often a toss-up between watching the slow-moving opera unfolding on the stage and Hitler's reaction to the opera, turning around to say something to one of his companions.

Music

This morning, at a new doctor's office, the patient advisor asked me if I was retired. I hesitated, so she looked at me, questioning with her eyebrows. I said, "Yes, I guess I am, because I gave up my website. But I'm still giving lectures, teaching classes in jewelry-making, designing custom orders, writing manuals, and I'm busier than ever, so I didn't know how to answer you."

I think when your "work" is also your "creativity," your brain is always thinking of new pieces, how you would design around an amazing fossil, or what you are going to say to your next class of students in order to get their creative juices flowing. It's impossible to turn yourself off. And frankly, when you get note after note, card after card, and email after email that they love spending the day with you and that you are their inspiration, how can you not love what you do? It fills me with profound gratitude that I found my life's path to happiness early enough to follow it for over fifty years. The path was not always smooth; sometimes I had to take detours, some years I had to be patient, some years I was discouraged when things didn't go well, but when you are instilled with a passion, you rejoice at every little success, and build on it. Creativity is good but not necessary to begin with. Enthusiasm is far more important, and then comes Experience. A quotation I often tell my new students is, "Good jewelry-making does not depend on your knowing how to do fourteen hundred different things. It comes from doing one thing fourteen hundred times." And *with those*, Creativity begins to creep in. You can't wait to get to your workbench, and when you finish a design that really pleases you, you feel such satisfaction that you run for the camera. Last night I had the urge to dredge up some of the pitfalls I encountered over the years. Some are evidenced in the dozen prescription bottles filled with scraps of silver which melted from overusing the torch. Lesson learned: I learned to adjust the flame, give the piece time to heat, watch the solder begin to liquify, and with time, solder many bezels on silver backings to hold magnificent opals, fossils, lumpy pearls, and natural stones. I also tell my students that if a mistake occurs, in jewelry-making, you are lucky: almost every mistake can be turned into an advantage. You just think outside of the box, change a couple of things, and you end up with something grand. Oh, all those molten scraps of silver? I have learned to pour some into a crucible, melt them so the solution looks like silver mercury, and pour it rapidly over upright, wet whiskbroom bristles, and the sterling scrap hardens into very unique pendants of solid silver in irregular shapes. We call them Broomstick Pendants.

When I was a teenager, the only jewelry I owned was a necklace of graduated white pearls my mother gave me when I graduated from high school. When I was one year in college, and then working as a sales representative for the New York Telephone Company, I never wore jewelry with any of my clothes. I couldn't afford to look at the jewelry displays in department stores. And in the forties, craft shows were not so prolific as they became later on.

It wasn't until I married and we moved to Switzerland that my interest in jewelry took hold. There were many stores along the main shopping street in Zürich for gold and silver handmade jewelry, and I found myself pausing in front of their windows and admiring the workmanship. But, oh, the prices! Not for the American housewife who received a fifteen-dollars-a-week "allowance" to buy her clothes, shoes, cosmetics, and hobby supplies. Instead, I spent my time and spare pennies on learning to speak German. I decided that if I wanted to own some fantastic jewelry, I would have to learn to do it myself.

The passage on the Swiss-German dialect will tell you that I saw an ad in the Neue Züricher Zeitung about a gold- and silversmithing course, and I convinced my husband I could learn to speak German faster if I took a course on jewelry-making offered by a night school. He okayed it, and I signed up for a six-week course. Although the instructor spoke only Swiss dialect, the two fellows on either side of me spoke English and translated for me. I think they were impressed to think that a flighty American would have the perseverance to stick out the dialect in order to make her own jewelry. I only had five lessons of the six-week course because we were transferred by Carrier to Rio de Janeiro for Fritz to become the president of Carrier Brazil and open a plant in Santos, in northern Brazil. And out of the Carrier office in Rio, he would be handling all of southern South America, a dream come true for Fritz.

By that time, I had managed to learn how to saw metal (copper). (The practical Swiss would not allow you to start on sterling silver.) How to bend the strip into a circle, how to match the ends together, how to sand them, how to flux the joint, how to place a tiny piece of solder on a firing brick and place the seam on top of it, and how to handle a torch to heat the metal, melt the solder up the joint, how to hammer the ring round on a mandrel, and how to polish the ring on a polishing machine.

Can you imagine my thrill and the pride I felt in that simple copper ring that fitted my ring finger perfectly? I had learned a few words of Swiss dialect from my fellow students. I gazed at that little ring and knew I had become a jeweler.

And: lo and behold, there we were, in Brazil, the source of practically every natural stone in the world. But I didn't speak Portuguese …

Strangely enough, while he was in Weimar, Fritz discovered another type of music to love: Dixieland. Hitler denounced any kind of American music, calling jazz decadent, appealing to the lowest of the masses. He actually outlawed it in Germany. Of course, that made it all the more enticing. Fritz and his fellow students would sit behind closed doors in their rooming houses and listen to the Dixieland records that one of his friends managed to smuggle in past the customs. Earlier, when we were living in Dallas (1948–1952), he collected Dixieland music with a passion. Whenever his visits to dealers or distributors took him close to the Texas-Louisiana border, he would hop over to New Orleans and head for Preservation Hall, there to soak up the genuine thing in the smoky, noisy atmosphere of the lounge. Nirvana. I always thought it was such a strange choice for my serious, straitlaced European, but when I gifted him with a baton one Christmas, it was truly a sight to see Fritz vigorously waving the baton, conducting either Wagner's booming chords or Pete Fountain's bouncy *When the saints go marching in.* It mattered not to him; he was in charge!

Growing up in Auburn, New York, I only listened to opera on a Saturday afternoon on the radio as it was broadcast live from the Metropolitan in New York. But only because it was assigned as homework.

For us, the highlight of the week was the Lucky Strike Hit Parade on Saturday nights, and if we weren't out at a high school–sponsored dance, where we danced to the Stardusters orchestra playing mostly Glenn Miller, we were sitting glued to the radio to hear what popular songs of the previous week had moved up on the chart. Is it any wonder I can still sing all of the forties and fifties songs by heart?

The main thing was that we both loved good music, plays, musicals, and theater, and enjoyed discussing what we had seen on the way home from a performance. When Fritz and I moved to Zürich in 1965, I was introduced to a form of music that I grew to love: operettas. We obtained Abonnement tickets to the Züricher Opernhaus, season tickets on opening night of each new production; our seats were in the sixth row, center, numbers three and four. Opening night required evening gowns and tuxes, and champagne during intermission. It was very festive. The opera house featured mostly opera, but each season they gave two or three operettas.

While I was bored with the slow-moving operas, their theme of tragedy, the sung dialogue, and the rather dreary music, I was carried away by the joyful, happy tunes of operettas, perky acting, and fast-spoken dialogue with a lot of comedy. Operettas were lively. They were meant to entertain. The costumes were lavish. They represented happier times. You can see the happy-go-lucky tone in the titles: *The Merry Widow, The Student Prince, The Bird Seller, The Gypsy Baron, The Bat,* and *The Land of Smiles*; the list could go on but you get the idea. After I started learning German, I would buy tapes of any operetta we had just seen and play them over and over, learning the lyrics and melodies by heart. I remember so well the first operetta I saw: *Die Lustige Witwe* (the Merry Widow). After listening to the melodious overture, which was a medley of all the songs to come, the curtains opened on a ballroom scene with couples whirling around the stage, waltzing. The women were all in white gowns, the men in tuxedos, swirls of black and white. Then suddenly the Widow appears at the top of the curving staircase, dressed in brilliant red, and dramatically descends. The dancing slows as each couple gains sight of her until all the dancers are gathered at the foot of the stairs looking up at her. Leaving no room for doubt as to who was starring in *this* operetta! What a dramatic beginning to a story of love and merriment, with "Dinner at Maxim's" and other fast-moving songs. I was hooked. Fritz and I were in a good mood after such a beautiful evening. We were holding hands as we walked back to our pension along a canal bank, with the gaslights on the path reflected in the water. I was merrily singing the song that Peter Alexander had just sung, and I hopscotched a few steps forward, then came back to Fritz, grabbing his hand again. ♫ "Ich liebe Dich, und Du liebst Mich, und da liegt Alles drin!" ♫ (I love you, and you love me, and that is all that counts!) For a brief moment in time, a window opened, and Fritz saw that his little lump of clay from Auburn, New York, had turned into Cinderella, dancing in glass slippers. And it wasn't yet midnight.

Freddie Quinn

Each time we traveled to Germany we went to Neustadt north of Hamburg to visit Fritz's aunt. I'm sure she never realized it, but Fritz was usually ready to go on to the next place on our itinerary after ten minutes of listening to Aunt Lotte's health problems, and it was only because of my intervention that we stopped for at least a day there.

What made it more worthwhile in his opinion was the opportunity to spend two or three days in Hamburg for a visit with his good friend Jochen Rehm. Jochen had inherited a major coffee-importing company from his father, importing beans from Costa Rica, roasting them in Hamburg, and shipping them to restaurants and grocery stores all over Europe. Jochen and Fritz had spent two years in POW camps in Texas and Oklahoma in queer twists of fate that brought them to the attention of American authorities in 1941 as possible German spies, a story which has already been told in a previous chapter.

While in Hamburg, we always got tickets to a musical or play in St. Pauli, the Broadway of Hamburg. I particularly enjoyed hearing my favorite German singer, Freddie Quinn, onstage in whatever concert or musical he was performing in at the time. His real name was Manfred Petsch, his father Austrian and his mother Irish. When he became famous, he used his mother's maiden name for his stage name.

He had started out as a seaman, sailing on freighters as a crew member. To while away the hours at sea, he taught himself to play the guitar, and he would sing sea chanties to entertain his fellow sailors. When they would berth back in Hamburg, his home, he would head to the Washington Bar, his favorite hangout.

One night, a music producer heard him singing and offered him a contract, and the rest, as we all love to say, is history. He made a fortune on records, movies, and appearances on weekly musical TV shows. He was at his peak in the mid-sixties with his live tours, with the famous James Last band backing him up.

After seeing him every week on his TV show while living in Zürich, we admired him and went to see him live on stage at the Congresshalle during a tour across Europe. We were so impressed with his excellent voice and his humility onstage that the next day I bought my first record of his concerts.

By the time we were transferred to Rio de Janeiro, I owned all of his records. He had also made about a dozen movies by then.

When Fritz traveled for two weeks at a time to the different distributors throughout South America, I would sit in the dark of the apartment in Rio with tears streaming down my face, looking up at the Christ statue, and listen to Freddie singing "Heimweh" (Homesick), remembering Zürich. I don't think I ever felt more alone than I did in Rio.

Freddie spoke seven languages fluently and sang in many of them. He made a record in Nashville, singing country songs with such a twang you would have sworn he had been born and raised there. He was one of those rare performers for whom the word "genuine" described him perfectly

Heimweh

I loved Zürich. The people were so honest. So industrious. So correct. Had so much integrity. Everything was so clean.

If a Zürich hausfrau hadn't polished her brass doorknob by seven in the morning, she felt like she had wasted her entire day. If you left some coins in change on the counter from a purchase you made, the clerk would follow you down the street to return them. If a Zürich woman was wearing a mink coat walking down the Bahnhofstrasse, you knew it was freezing cold out, not her showing off her husband's wealth.

So, when we were told after three years in beautiful Switzerland that we were being transferred to Rio de Janeiro in Brazil, I was devastated. Fritz was happy that I had taken so easily to Swiss life. I was beginning to speak German well, I had been held in high esteem by the American Women's Club of Zürich, which had asked me to be their president, I had done well as head of the welcoming committee to teach newcomers from the States how to get around and cope, and I loved everything about our life there. Loved the TV with good musical shows, loved the shopping, loved our little trips by train or bus every weekend, and wished I had a franc for every "Schoen!" (Beautiful!) I heard. I loved the elegance of attending the Zürich Opera House for the premiere of each opera or operetta. We had tickets in the fourth row and wore tux and evening gown while sipping champagne during intermission.

I wept when I begged Fritz to think of resigning from Carrier and getting a job with a Swiss company so that we could stay in Zürich. He loved Zürich too, and since Portuguese was of course the *only* language he didn't speak (that's the way Carrier executives make decisions), he only thought for a moment before he agreed. He started at the top: took the train to Wilderswil and was interviewed by Braun Boveri, the largest engineering company in Switzerland. They offered him a position.

But when he returned home, his face was green. He couldn't do it. His father had worked twenty-six years for Carrier, and Fritz had been with them for thirty-five. His loyalty to his company was too strong. The blood coursing through his veins was Carrier blue.

In July 1968, we left for Rio. When we were on the Swissair plane, the manager of the Swissair Business Club, which Fritz was a member of, came to our seats with a bottle of champagne and also upgraded us to business class. Once we got to Rio and Fritz had to fly to all the other countries in his territory, rather than flying Varig, he would wait for the once-a-week incoming flight of Swissair and fly on with them to Argentina or Uruguay. I always reaped a little box of Swiss chocolates from those flights.

Rio was another learning experience for me to get used to. We were fingerprinted at the customs arrivals at the airport. I found a lovely apartment, newly built, right next to a favela (slum or shantytown) on the same hillside. TV programs in the evening featured telenovelas (soap operas) or a ridiculous clown hosting an amateur hour. Poor homeless people slept in burlap lying on the sidewalks, and beggars were on every street. I couldn't understand anything being said when I went out to buy groceries. I was required to have a cook and cleaning people as a way of life. The cook "lived in"; a room and bath were provided for servants in every apartment. We had no social life except on the Ipanema beach with friends from Spain whom Fritz knew. I joined the Woman's Club of Rio in order to use their library. Fritz got along fine at the office, where his staff spoke English, and he hired an Argentinian chauffeur. (I negotiated the Rio traffic in our Karmann Ghia.) There was no driving test, and when I saw drivers speed up for red lights, I understood why traffic was so suicidal.

The funniest incident happened when Fritz and I flew to Brasília to see the entire modern city built by Oscar Niemeier. Brasília had become the capital of Brazil. There was no provision for housing within the city for all the workers, so slums sprang up like dandelions all around the city.

We exchanged some traveler's checks at a bank. When we got outside, we discovered that the teller had made a mistake and had given us three thousand cruzeiros too much. We turned around and went back in, up to the teller, and told him the mistake. When he realized that we were giving him back three thousand cruzeiros, the look on his face was like Mastercard: priceless! He had never had that happen before.

I decided to teach English to some Brazilian wives of judges, and I had a university student exchange Portuguese-English classes with me. I exchanged guitar lessons with a brazileira, but I learned more sambas than she learned English.

Through all my attempts to meld and learn the culture, I spent a lot of time alone in our beautiful apartment, overlooking the Lagoa. Fritz traveled extensively, supposedly setting up Carrier's dealers and distributors, but frankly, because the rest of his territory was Uruguay, Paraguay, Argentina, Chile, and Bolivia, all Spanish-speaking, he was in his element. He was gone two weeks at a time. We had no phone in the apartment, so he would call a couple of times via satellite to the concierge's office in the lobby, and I would hear a staticky voice asking, "Are you okay?" I assured him I was, and that was it. End of call.

In reality, I never suffered so much loneliness in my life. A letter to Stanford to our daughter took a month, and phone calls were out of the question because of the expense, so I never heard my family's voices in Auburn except once a year for a few days while on home leave. There was no such thing as internet or Skype. What a difference that would have made! The American women in Rio were mostly diplomatic wives and kept to their own embassy parties. Joana came for two weeks in the summer when classes were over at Stanford. While she was in Rio, we spent the time on the beach, no traveling. The time flew, and then I was alone again.

The tears ran down my cheeks as I ached to be once more in Zürich with someone to talk to.

8

Brazil

I quickly realized that not speaking a word of Portuguese was worse than knowing some German and being able to apply it to Schwyzerdütsch. I wasn't going to be able to find a class in jewelry-making in Rio, to continue my newfound passion. I did find the American Woman's Club in Rio but quickly ascertained that it was very much a social club for all the embassy wives, none of whom had any particular wish to learn Portuguese.

During all these discoveries, I found the two most famous jewelry stores in all of Rio: H. Stern & Co. and Maximilian. Of course, the staff spoke English to sell the jewelry to the tourists who came by cruise ship and for Carnival. During my frequent visits to the stores, I met a few of the echelon staff and became friendly with Maximilian himself. When he found out I had studied goldsmithing in Zürich, he would go to the back and bring out some stone that was a spectacular specimen of that particular line and then explain all the characteristics of the various types of that stone, pointing out the good ones as well as the bad.

Gradually, during my two years in Rio, I learned what to look for in quality of all the various gems mined in Brazil. Fritz and I even took a few days off and visited Minas Gerais, the town in the center of the mining area. I bought some cabochons and faceted tourmalines at very reasonable prices to be set when I was able to further my studies. My time in Rio was well spent, learning all I could about every gem. And to widen my creative side? I bought oil paints and began painting scenes from my growing stash of art books. I propped the canvases on the washing machine, and after my maid left, I stored the painting supplies in her room.

Oh, yes, I also invited three ladies to learn basic English from me: They were wives of judges and friends of an Argentinian lady who lived above me on the third floor. I could speak Spanish with her, and I enjoyed the socializing with the Brazilian women. I gave them jokes in English, and the next week they had to tell me what they meant in Portuguese.

I also learned to play the guitar, exchanging guitar lessons for English lessons with Lydia Maria. I could play all the winning sambas from carnival to carnival. I loved playing the guitar; I'm sorry that I gave it to a Waldorf teacher some years later in Canada. I miss it. Lydia Maria loved teaching me to sing the sambas and folk songs and wrote me a lovely note when I left Brazil.

Compassion

We were on a cruise up the west coast of Africa on our beloved *Crystal Symphony* and had been overnighting in some famous and exotic islands off the coast. Saint Helena, belonging to England, was the first, and we were now approaching a tiny island with large, tall blackish rocks reaching into the sky at one end of the island, waning down to a green meadow and sandy beach at the opposite end. We could see three small rowboats pulled up on the sand, turned upside down. Behind them was a red building. It was strange to see some evidence of habitation.

We were finishing breakfast in *Crystal's* dining room when the captain came on the loudspeaker and announced that the *Symphony* would be making a detour on their route because the island to be seen off the port side of the ship was in dire need of help, and the ship was offering aid. Our ship stopped its engines and remained in place while two lifeboats were being prepared to be lowered.

As the lifeboats were filled with provisions, the passengers assembled at the railings to watch. The captain filled in some details: The island was called Sao Pedro e Sao Paulo and belonged to Brazil. It was manned by twelve Brazilian sailor-scientists, who lived in the red bunkhouse. A supply ship came only every three months with fresh food and supplies. They used generators for electricity. Their main purpose was to maintain the satellite dishes on top of the tall rock formation at the northern end of the island. The island was a short distance north of the equator.

As I look back now during Covid-19, I compare the isolation as an extreme form of social distancing.

I ran to the cabin and got some stationery and a pencil and rushed back to Fritz's side at the railing. I began sketching the island in its entirety. Since I didn't have any colored pencils with me, I wrote in "green" at the meadow, and "blackish-gray" on the stone pillars. Blue and white for the water and waves crashing on the shore.

We watched excitedly as the ship's doctor and nurse boarded one of the lifeboats with medical bags and supplies, as well as food. The second lifeboat was manned by two of the crew and filled with fresh veggies and fruits, frozen food in plastic-wrapped boxes, cartons of eggs, and fresh baguettes protruding out of wrappings. The lifeboats were cranked down and landed with a splash, heading to the sandy shoreline.

The *Symphony* started her engines again as the captain informed us we were going to have the rare privilege of touring around the island, coming back in a few hours to pick up the lifeboats. It was exciting to see the other side of the island, in its virginal state. At four in the afternoon, we passed the large rock outcropping at the southernmost end and slowed to a stop again near where the lifeboats were waiting for us. They were now completely empty of supplies, and only the crew members were on board. They were slowly cranked up, and the doctor and nurse said they had examined the men and administered vaccinations and bandages, etcetera, so the navy scientists were all in good shape. The two crew members had tucked a volleyball net, posts, and ball in amongst the food and had installed it on the sandy beach. The sailors were astonished at the generosity of the *Symphony* to have given them a happy diversion to their solitary life there. When I got back home, I had a lot of pleasure and reflective thinking as I painted a larger watercolor version of this experience.

Is it any wonder that I have named this painting *Compassion*?

Living by the Rules

After living in a hotel in Copacabana for three months while Fritz opened the new Carrier office in Rio, we finally ended our apartment search when we found a newly constructed three-story apartment building at the top of a hill in the area called Lagoa (Lagoon). It was on Rua Generalissimo Guillermo, a short street off the Rua Fonte da Saudade (Fountain of Homesickness Street)—a name which turned out to be more descriptive than I had imagined. We ordered our furniture, which had arrived from Switzerland and been in storage all that time, to be delivered to the new apartment. Since the elevators were not large enough for the entertainment unit we had bought in Switzerland, we watched with palpitating hearts as they put ropes around it and hauled it up the outside wall two stories. It was about nine feet long by six feet high and contained a drop-down bar for wine glasses and bottles of liquor, a cabinet for the TV, another for the radio and record player (this was 1968), and shelves for books, art, and sculptures, with drawers making up the bottom section. The movers removed the windows, which encompassed the entire front of the apartment, then shoved the wall unit through the window space by turning it on its side so the six-foot height went through sideways. A heart-stopping display of Brazilian ingenuity. All of our Swiss and American modern furniture looked wonderful in the Brazilian apartment. It had jacaranda wood floors, sort of a dark mahogany, and the dark wall unit looked good against one entire wall. Once the glass was replaced, the wall of windows across the front gave us a good view of the lagoon, and of the mountain where the Corcovado statue hovered, illuminated at night and appearing and disappearing with each passing cloud. Christ's outstretched arms embraced the poor mortals beneath. Being Rio, it quickly became known to me that I was expected to have servants. Not speaking Portuguese yet (eventually I did), I gratefully accepted Maria's offer to hire them. Maria was the lovely, petite wife of Carlos, a friend of Fritz's from Barcelona. His father had been the business partner of Fritz's father, so Fritz had grown up with Carlos and his brother. Carlos had become the president of the huge chemical firm Bayer in Brazil, which made much more than aspirins. He had married Maria, who was Colombian, and they were now living in Rio de Janeiro, expecting their second child. This was very nice for Fritz, because we spent every weekend on the beaches of Copacabana or Ipanema with Carlos, Maria, and their best friends, all speaking Spanish instead of Portuguese. Very relaxing. The guys, being guys, would nudge each other every time a gorgeous mulatta (mixed-race woman) would walk by in a very minimal tanga (string bikini).

When I brought up the subject of maids, it was Maria and the other wife who convinced me that I could not *possibly* do the housework myself and would need a cook, cleaning lady, laundress, and male floor polisher. They were totally shocked that I even considered doing the work myself. After all, this was Brazil. This was the way you helped the poor uneducated masses.

I had never had maids and did not care for the idea that servants were beneath you, just because you were rich Americans and could afford to have several.

As I had joined the American Women's Club by this time, I was hearing the same thing from all the American wives, but they all thought it was fantastic to have servants at their beck and call, whereas I considered it a nonissue, and what was I going to do with all that free time? Besides, how could I tell them what to do if I couldn't speak Portuguese? Didn't matter. You had to have servants; this was Brazil. Fritz concurred. That settled it.

So, enter Maria, my sweet little coconspirator. She asked her servants (she not only had the requisite four but also a nanny) for names of their relatives, and promised me that she would find *one* who would clean, cook, and do laundry, and I would have the man come in once a month to wax the floors and sit on the window ledges, outside, to wash the windows. That way I wouldn't have to have two extra people around me all the time.

Maria interviewed several of the ones recommended and told me I now had Francesca (pronounced Fran-chess-ka). Francesca turned out to be a doppelgänger for Aunt Jemima of the pancake mix fame. As we say tactfully now: heavy. With a white turban on her head, and a white apron stretched around her ample figure. But friendly and kind and wanting to be helpful, she proudly informed us that she could read. Being literate was actually a major achievement; most servants weren't. With Maria translating, and me speaking Spanish with both hands, Francesca indicated that she could understand me well enough. Hired.

Then Maria told me I would have to provide her with two uniforms: one for casual work around the house, blue with a white apron, and the formal one for when she served dinner at night, black with a smaller, fancier apron and a white cap. As I recall, I had to purchase the largest size available. I bought two sets of each version. Francesca moved into the maid's quarters behind the laundry room and kitchen, and began teaching me what she would be doing. She had one day off per week and usually spent it visiting her friends. She was from Bahia, in northern Brazil, so had no close family in Rio. She was paid $30 per week (the going rate) and had room and board.

I had to accept that my life was going to be less quiet from now on and that a stranger would be in my kitchen singing Fados all day long while washing dishes or cooking. I secretly lamented my loss of privacy. But Francesca also turned out to be meticulously clean, taking a shower every day, before starting our breakfast, wrapping a clean white cloth around her head. She did a good job cleaning. After doing the laundry, she would then iron. She even ironed the strings in Fritz's undershorts.

I was getting used to it, and began taking Portuguese lessons from a university student, and guitar lessons from Lydia Maria, who taught me to sing Brazilian folk songs and sambas. To fill my free time, I started painting, propping the canvases up on the washing machine in the laundry room, and painting landscapes from my art books. Francesca was impressed with "a senhora" (the lady, ah-sane-your-ah.)

The clatter of dishes in the all-tile kitchen, the singing, and the constant awareness that I needed to give her another chore to do was distracting to say the least, but it seemed to be working out, even though I complained nightly to Fritz about how I longed for peace and quiet.

Maria came over to visit occasionally to find out if Francesca was satisfactory. Two months after I had bought all of her uniforms, she informed Maria that she was going to quit. That surprised both of us. No problem with a senhora, but her relative had told her she could make more money if she sold candy on the street, like so many of the Bahian women did. They sat on the street corners, in their colorful dress, with a large tray around their necks and sold brown-sugar toffee. The relative would supply her with the candy. Maria, who spoke fluent Portuguese, tried to talk her out of it, but could not convince her to stay. She was going to give up her little suite with us, live with the relative, and be on her own.

Adieu, Francesca; who needs large-sized uniforms?

But at last peace and quiet reigned. It was beautiful, it was fantastic. I cooked food that did not contain rice and beans, and left out half the garlic. Fritz and I enjoyed a Campari with soda before dinner, and I made American casseroles and interesting food items that I found in the Feria (fresh-air market) each week.

Whistle While You Work

My friends at the Women's Club were astonished that I wasn't rushing to interview another maid. Fritz kept nagging me. Then our daughter arrived for the summer vacation of Stanford, and she tried to talk me into getting another servant. I was adamant that I could get by with just the man who did the floors and windows. They argued some more. It was a stalemate.

Then one night, after Joana had gone back to California, and we had had dinner, I was in the kitchen drying the dishes. Fritz came and leaned against the door, watching. Then suddenly he said, "Okay, you win."

I stopped, looked up, and asked, "I win what?"

He said, "You don't have to get another maid. This is the first time I've heard you whistling since we left Switzerland."

We stayed in Rio de Janeiro for two years. I was the only American woman in the Club who did not have a servant. I taught English as a second language to three Brazilian ladies once a week, who invariably breathed a sigh of relief and pleasure as they arrived and commented, "It's so nice and quiet here, Janisse." And then I would tell them a joke. In English. They sat back and relaxed.

In Rio, we held an open house the second Christmas we were there (1969). I had sent out written invitations which said in Portuguese that we would be holding a *Bate Papo*, (pronounced *bahtchee papo*). According to my guitar teacher, Lydia Maria, this was slang for "bat your beak" (like a parrot), meaning to chat freely as you come and go during the hours of the open house. She and I exchanged hourlong lessons for the guitar and English, but I got the best of that bargain, mainly because she was not as adept at learning English as I was at learning to play and sing sambas. Anyway, our interpretation of the openness of an open house got sorely tried as the people came, never left, and the room filled ominously with more and more people, batting their papos. Suddenly, Lydia Maria took over and told me to get my guitar and they would all sing. I played and sang some solos, and then she garnered my guitar, and the party took off. Fritz looked as if he could strangle me, but he just didn't realize that this was the Brazilians' way of having a good time, singing. They finally all left several hours later, saying what a wonderful party it had been and how amazing that I could sing all their famous sambas

The Perils of Brazilian Life

My husband was made president of Carrier Air Conditioning, Brazil, and his task was to oversee the rebuilding of a factory in Bahia and run the office in Rio, as well as supervise the already-established dealers and distributors throughout Brazil, Argentina, Uruguay, Paraguay, Bolivia, and Chile. His job would require a lot of traveling, and since I would be left on my own, without speaking Portuguese, I would need a well-located apartment, which would not require much driving to reach ferias (outdoor markets) and shopping areas. We found a lovely apartment in a three-story building that was still under some construction in the Lagoa area, the lagoon where many of the swimming and rowing events were held in August at the 2016 Summer Olympics. Rio's Lagoa was faulted for its fecal pollution and the effects it might have on the swimmers, but in 1968 it was fairly clean. We lived just off a main street on the Lagoon called Rua Fonte da Saudade; in English: Fountain of Homesickness Street. We bought a car, a little Karmann Ghia, manufactured in Brazil. The first day my husband decided to drive to downtown Rio to his office, he found himself driving the wrong way on a one-way street, which was so traumatic that from the office he arranged for a chauffeur. José was from Argentina; he lived in a favela, had his own Volkswagen Beetle, arrived promptly every morning in a spotless white shirt, drove Fritz to his office, and at 5:00 p.m. picked him up and drove him back home. Since Fritz spoke fluent Spanish but no Portuguese, he enjoyed his morning and evening trips with José. From then on, Fritz only drove us to Copacabana and Ipanema beaches on the weekends while I, on the other hand, ended up driving the Ghia myself for all my errands, shopping, etcetera. We'll pause here for some serious contemplation of Men are from Mars, Women from Venus. We adapted. Well, he enjoyed, I adapted. He had an entire office force at his beck and call. And the chauffeur. I put an ad in the English-language newspaper offering to exchange English lessons for Portuguese and soon was entertaining three judges' wives once a week in our apartment, taking a weekly lesson in Portuguese from a young university student so he could improve his English, one hour each; also, a lady who played the guitar wanted to barter an hour of guitar lessons with an hour of English with me weekly. That was interesting, and I can still do a mean version of "The Girl from Ipanema" in Portuguese. Fritz and I spent weekends on the beaches with friends of my husband, whom he had grown up with in Barcelona. Our Danish-modern and Swiss furniture looked nice in the apartment and we were very comfortable.

Our apartment looked down on the Lagoa and up at Corcovado, the Christ statue on top of the Corcovado mountain, with his arms outstretched, blessing the population. The statue was illuminated at night and as clouds drifted over and around the figure, it disappeared and reappeared as if truly in the sky. Every time she passed a living-room window, Francesca would look up and cross herself.

But this idyllic life soon developed a different and ominous tone. We began reading about a menacing problem: Executives of large American companies were being kidnapped and held for ransom, and on at least one occasion the CEO was killed because his company did not shell out $200,000 to $300,000 for his release. Fritz received warnings from the American Embassy to be careful. In the English-language paper, they mentioned that death squads existed: The

Esquadrão da Morte was a paramilitary organization that emerged in the late 1960s; its actions resembled traditional vigilantism, as most executions were not exclusively politically related. In talking to others, we found out that the purpose of the original "death squad" was, with the consent of the military government, to persecute, torture, and kill suspected criminals (marginais) but then they discovered it was more lucrative to kidnap foreigners. In general, its members were politicians, members of the judiciary, and police officials.

In 1970, in this era of peril to foreigners living in Brazil, we were informed we would be transferred to Puerto Rico for Fritz to start managing the office there. That meant that we would have to make arrangements to sell our car and all the furniture. Since we would be going to a "state" of the United States, we decided to purchase all new American furniture and an American car when we reached San Juan. We advertised the Ghia and the furniture in the English-language newspaper classifieds. Fritz and I had a serious talk about the danger of having strangers coming to the apartment, and we devised a plan to ensure his safety. It would require that I remain calm and organized even though the fear of his being kidnapped was always with us. Back in 1968 to 1970, there was basic telephone service only in business offices, not so many in private homes or apartments, so naturally we had no telephone service to make appointments for people to come see the offerings. There was one phone in the concierge's office in the lobby of our apartment building for all the residents to use or to receive calls, which the concierge would then deliver. Right after the ad appeared, the concierge knocked on our door one evening to say that there were two men who wanted to see the car, and they were waiting in the lobby. Fritz went down in the elevator to take them to the parking garage, and as prearranged, I hastily grabbed a clipboard and dashed down the servants' stairs to the garage and hid behind a column, peeking out at Fritz and the two men as they examined the car. I wrote a detailed description of the men, in case they kidnapped Fritz, which I could give to the police. It was only later that we discovered that it was indeed the police who were the death squad perpetrators, and my descriptions would have been of little use. Fortunately, they bought the car on the spot and paid cash, and he came upstairs safely.

Then my husband decided to leave on a final trip throughout the territory, to say goodbye to the dealers, leaving me alone to sell the furniture. One evening after Fritz had left, the concierge came up to the apartment to say he had a phone call from a man who wanted to come by in a half hour with a friend to see the furniture. I panicked. What to do? I quickly ran up to the third floor and knocked on Olga's door: She was one of the judges' wives who were learning English from me. Could she come down and be with me while these men looked at the furniture? Yes, of course; she would be right down! A few minutes later she arrived carrying a large purse and made herself comfortable on the couch. She could see that I was very nervous and frightened, so, to calm me, she opened her purse, and I saw a gun inside! I squealed in fear and Olga said, "Nao te preocupes, Janisse; nao tem bolas!" Had she really just said, "Don't worry, Janice; it doesn't have any bullets"?

Shortly afterward, the concierge arrived with two men and with a flourish ushered them into the apartment. One was an older man, casually dressed, and the other younger, dressed in a business suit. They both spoke good English. They spent a half hour looking around and decided to buy the Danish teak dining set of a table and six chairs, some appliances, and knickknacks. The older man was making the decisions, but it was the younger man who wrote out a check and promised to send a truck around the next day to pick up their purchases. I breathed a sigh of relief and, with a hug, sent Olga back upstairs with her empty gun.

A few days later I was attending the monthly American Women's Club luncheon when a stranger approached and said, "I heard you sold your dining room suite." I thought, My goodness, word sure gets around fast. Then, when she saw I was a little bewildered, she smiled and asked, "Don't you know who bought it?" I replied that I didn't, and she told me, "That was the Italian Ambassador and his chargé d'affaires."

I wonder to this day if the Italian Ambassador ever knew how close he came to being shot by two ladies with a gun that "didn't have any bullets."

9

Learning Spanish ... the Hard Way

Fritz was always encouraging me to increase my language skills (possibly so that he would not be seen as having a dumb wife during all our fêtes when he was managing different foreign offices for Carrier). I was feeling a bit more confident with the language and, strangely enough for a shy person, I didn't hesitate to try to take part in any conversation. I actually didn't mind making grammatical mistakes because I felt that all our friends could take the noun and the verb and figure out what the rest was. Of course, along the way, I did make a few remarkable mistakes: One time we were vacationing in Mazatlán, Mexico, and I saw a very interesting swimsuit in the window of a shop. Fritz told me if I spoke in Spanish I could go in and buy it. Boldly, I marched in and, confusing "nadar" (to swim) with "nacer" (to be born) I politely asked to try on the "trajé de nacer" (birthday suit) in the window, and yes, it has the same second meaning in Spanish that it has in English. When the clerk and Fritz stopped laughing, I walked out with the suit. I had to disregard my total discomfort in having to bargain. In my mind, haggling is degrading, but Fritz was brought up in a country well-versed in bargaining, and he kept trying to explain to me that it was a game they all played. You ask how much; they double what they want; you offer half of that. They smile. "De acuerdo." (Agreed.) And afterward everyone walks away happy that each side has "won."

One time in the fifties, in Mazatlán, I admired the beautiful handwoven palm-leaf hats the beach vendors peddled. They were very "in" in Phoenix, where we

103

lived at the time, and I coveted one. They were made from fresh palm leaves and green, but after you bought one, you took it home and stored it in the freezer for a week, and it turned a gorgeous milk-chocolatey brown. It looked awesome when a pretty scarf was tied around it. Fritz refused to acquiesce to my pleas and said if I wanted one, I would have to bargain with the guy. Well, I tried all the usual compliments on how pretty it was and how much I wanted one, but couldn't pay so much, and after all the banter I got him down a couple of dollars, paid him, and returned to our spot on the sand with my trophy, quite satisfied. Then Fritz said in his fluent Spanish to the vendor, "Hombre, how much would it be if I bought one?" The vendor smiled at his fluency and answered "La mitad." (Half.)

In Spanish, one little letter can make a big difference. On one occasion while visiting Mexico City, at a large cocktail party given for us by Fritz's distributor and dealers, the ladies were on one side of the room and the men congregated on the other side. The women spoke so fast that I had difficulty following the conversation, but when they paused for a moment, I decided to jump in. I smiled at our hostess, pointed to the embroidered pillows that were on the couch I was sitting on, and said, loud and clear: "Que bellos cojones tiene!" The women exploded in laughter, the men looked askance, and one of the wives told them what I had said. My husband looked horrified, and I thought he was going to melt right through the tile floor. Just one little letter. Pillows is "cojines"; "cojones" is vernacular for testicles or balls. Eventually I improved, increased my vocabulary, and even knew when to switch to the subjunctive.

Puerto Rico

In 1970 we were transferred from Rio de Janeiro to San Juan, Puerto Rico, and rented a two-bedroom apartment in the Condado section of San Juan. It was on the top floor of a six-story apartment house, had terrazzo marble floors and a small kitchen, and was a short block to the beach. We joined the Sheraton Hotel Beach Club and spent our Sundays lolling around the pool, reading the *New York Times*, and then going for a walk along the fine, sandy beach.

We enjoyed buying new furniture and appliances, having sold all our modern

American and Swiss pieces to the Caraqueños before we left Rio. We bought a lot of red-, green-, and pink-leafed tropical plants in pots for the balcony, which we lit up from underneath at night. Because we had to buy all new appliances and gadgets, I had a lot of interesting-shaped Styrofoam blocks, so I picked the larger ones with curves and forms that had fitted around a TV, waffle iron, and coffee-pot, glued them together, and made a large sculpture, which I named *Affluence*. It sat in the corner of the balcony with the colorful plants in front of it. Looked like a large white tombstone.

We purchased local—which meant curved—arched rattan furniture made on the island, upholstered in velvet, in a white and black grillwork design. It looked good against the white marble floors. It had a very Spanish-y look to it, which would come in handy when we later moved to Spain.

We also went to Woolworth's and bought a bird. Do you remember when the five and dimes used to have animal departments? He was a little blue parakeet, and I looked forward to teaching him to say "Gimme a kiss, gimme a kiss!" We bought a black wrought-iron cage and enough miniature toys for three birds. We named him Zuli, diminutive for Azulito, Little Blue One.

But Zuli was not a talker, he was a doer. After a dozen times of repeating phrases over and over and over again, I learned that some parakeets are little tricksters instead of talkers. Zuli had the run (flight?) of the apartment, and I would often find him comfortably perched on the top of the drapes in the living room or one of the bedrooms. If I went around calling, "Zuli, where are you now?" I would hear some chirps.

If I put some of his toys on the dining-room table, he would happily push the miniature baby carriage with his beak all across the table at breakneck speed. If it beat him and ran right off the table, he would then swoop down to the floor and continue pushing it all across the floor, a much wider playground.

But his absolute favorite playtime was in the shower. When he saw me walk into the bathroom carrying his little red ladder, he knew the fun would begin. I set the ladder in the sink leaning up against the faucet to anchor it and turned the water to a warm trickle, and Zuli would hop down the ladder, backwards, one step at a time, hop over to the falling water, and stand under it, getting all nice and wet. He was such a bedraggled little scrawny thing! I had to laugh, to see him lift first one wing, let the water run under it, then turn around and lift the other wing and finish his shower by playing in the little puddle of water in the bottom of the sink. I began to wonder if there was such a thing as underarm deodorant for birds. When he finished, he would climb up the ladder and sit on the edge of the sink while I picked him up and dried off his feathers with a soft cloth. Zuli became our entertainment factor whenever we had guests.

I have to tell you about the earthquake that struck Puerto Rico in early 1971. Fritz had already left for the office. I was sitting in my soft rattan armchair after breakfast, having coffee and reading the morning English paper, looking out the glass doors to the balcony, when without any warning, my chair started to slide across the floor. Funniest damned feeling ever! I felt nauseous, and then I noticed that the balcony railings were going up and down like a seesaw. First I saw the railings, and then they went below the horizon. The couch started to slide, but not as fast as my chair, which was by now in the middle of the room. Dishes started to clink, and my alert mind accurately predicted: *Good Lord, this is an earthquake! I'm in an earthquake! What do I do? What do they tell you to do in the case of an earthquake? Get in the middle; that would be the stairwell. I'm on the sixth floor: Am I supposed to run down all the flights or stay put?* I knew I shouldn't get on the elevator. *Is it better to stay up here and fall six flights with all the cement, or run down and maybe get buried under tons of cement? Why is this happening?* I never thought Puerto Rico was on a fault. As I sat there, shocked into unmoving nothingness, the balcony got more active, like on a ship in a bad storm, and I felt really seasick.

Suddenly the motion stopped and everything was back to normal. The phone rang; it was Fritz asking me, "Did you feel the earthquake? Are you OK?" His office was on the ground floor, and it had not been as noticeable, so I regaled him with all kinds of exaggerated movements on the sixth floor.

Zuli sat it out, swinging on his little trapeze. Aren't birds supposed to feel the ions changing or something, so they can warn you?

I joined the Welcome Wagon group when I first arrived—first to get all the goodies they gave newcomers, and then later to enjoy the monthly meetings with interesting speakers and to learn more about Puerto Rico. I'd made friends with a charming lady named Resi Birk, who had arrived at the same time as we. Resi was married to Udo Birk, who was the manager of IBM.

We had a lot in common; they were both the same ages as we, and they were both Germans, so Fritz got to talk to them in German, which he loved, and Udo and Fritz were managing large companies in San Juan.

We had dinner or lunches with them frequently, and they both had a sense of humor, especially Resi, whose dry wit was so unexpected that it tickled me. Udo was a huge guy, built like a football player, and typically German in appearance: light hair, tall, big, not particularly handsome, just solid, sturdy, like the Mercedes he always drove.

One day Resi and I attended the monthly meeting of the Newcomers Club, which was going to be well attended as the guest speaker was José Ferrer, the famous actor who was married to Rosemary Clooney. He was a native Puerto Rican who had made a number of films, appeared on TV series, and had a number of directing roles. I later found out that he had been married five times, three to different women and twice to Rosemary Clooney, having a short divorce in between having five children with her, one each year. She probably needed the rest.

Resi and I took a small table for two along the side of the room, with me facing the stage and Resi with her back to it. There was a hush, and then the president introduced José Ferrer, and he entered from offstage. He wasn't particularly good-looking but had a certain charm to his smile, so I told Resi, "He's onstage, turn around." She turned her chair, looked at him long and seriously, then turned back and said to me, "I tink I shtick mit Udo."

We celebrated any occasion in the hotel's dining room or lounge, especially when someone famous was performing there. In the early seventies, a lot of singers and movie stars would go to the elegant hotels and resorts in San Juan, much like they performed in Las Vegas.

So, there we were one night, sitting at a table for two next to the dance floor, and enjoying a show with Eddie Fisher, who was in the news at the time. He had recently had a rather scandalous divorce from sweet Debbie Reynolds and had married Elizabeth Taylor. In the middle of the show, Eddie decided to "play the floor" and was walking from table to table while singing some love song. As he approached our little table, he stopped and continued singing just to me. He took my hand, and then as the song ended, he kissed it and walked back to the orchestra.

Well, Fritz was apoplectic. He acted as if I had invited Fisher to sing to me. He didn't speak to me all the way home. Then I had a brilliant idea. I turned to him, and with a wicked smile, I said, "You do realize he's married to Elizabeth Taylor, don't you?"

Fritz began getting bored with Puerto Rico and decided suddenly one day that it was time for him to think of retiring. The love of traveling was clearly part of the reason. He kept talking about retiring in Spain because we had bought two hectares of land on the Costa del Sol in the sixties from his school friend Hans Hofmann. Hans had purchased a huge plantation (finca) and divided it up in parcels bordered with oleander hedges. He provided each parcel with pure water from the mountain spring above the property, pumped into the finca's reservoir. The idea was appealing and would allow us to travel whenever and wherever we wished. On the next home leave, we stopped in Syracuse, and he completed the details of the decision. And what that meant was: I was completely ready to take over the construction of our villa while Fritz went up to London to take over the London office for a major expansion to manufacture room air conditioners for Europe on the Isle of Wight.

At least that's what he said. What happened to the idea of retirement?

I had just read the book about Charles Lindbergh, which, while fiction by the author Melanie Benjamin, was based on all the details of the Lindberghs' marriage, which so coincided with Fritz and mine. One of the blurbs on the back cover of *The Aviator's Wife* was by Stephanie Cowell: "This soaring novel of a woman's journey through a difficult marriage to self-discovery is sure to be a book-club favorite."

I made many quotations from the book:

"In practicality, he needed me to remain weak …"

"---most angry at myself, for following Charles whenever he snapped his fingers …"

"I'll never forget what he taught me."

"I began to build a life for myself …"

"… finally I was strong, I was able …"

"… to strike out on my own, at my age …"

So many similarities.

England and Spain

From Rio we were transferred to San Juan, Puerto Rico. Since Puerto Rico didn't offer anything in jewelry-making, I stuck with more guitar lessons and learned to sing "En Mi Viejo San Juan" while studying Spanish. We were only there a year and a half when Fritz abruptly decided to retire. Since we had purchased a large parcel of land on the Costa del Sol in Spain when we lived in Zürich, we decided to move there and build our Forever Home. While starting construction on the villa, Fritz was called back to Carrier as a consultant, operating out of the London office. It was supposed to be a six-week assignment, so I was the delegated construction manager while he whiled away his time in a lovely little studio apartment right on Hyde Park Square. The six-week assignment expanded to a year and a half, the house in Spain got finished, and more changes took place. By that time, we had become hooked on British TV and couldn't bear to give up all the entertainment joys we had there, so we found a cheaper apartment in Hitchin, Hertfordshire, and for eight more years divided our time between the apartment in Hitchin, the villa in Spain, and, the rest of the time, beginning our many trips to the farthest places Fritz could find on our world map.

I loved the little apartment in Hitchin because finally, after all these years of postponement, I was able to turn to jewelry-making again. What a joy it was! What an opportunity it was! Fritz was so happy to be able to take the train into London and visit his Carrier colleagues in the London office that he had no objection to my taking night jewelry classes at the community college in Hitchin. They offered silversmithing, taught by a professional goldsmith who was a member of the Goldsmiths' Guild in London. He took the thirty-five-minute train ride to

Hitchin once a week, and he had a completely outfitted lab filled with every kind of machine. I was in seventh heaven again. The first project I made was a pair of French cuff links for Fritz. I sketched out triangular shapes, made a frame around them, and, since I was having some bridges made on my teeth, I had the dentist give me the scrap gold, cut off pieces of it, and melted the gold into balls, which I soldered in the center of the silver cuff links. I learned how to solder the folding bar on the back, which went through the cuff holes, and then to oxidize the silver backing, turning it black under the gold balls. Fritz actually liked wearing them with his tux on cruises. Later, when French cuffs went out of fashion, I took the cuff links, sawed off the bar on the back of them, and turned them into a pair of earrings for me. I still have them.

At those classes at the community college, I immersed myself in all the techniques of jewelry design and fabrication because the school had all the machines, from stonecutting to soldering all sorts of metals, and I learned through experience that if you made a mistake, you started over; maybe the most important lesson of all. Having a professional for a teacher was so impressive. It was also possible to get books from the Hitchin Library on gems and minerals and how-to books on enameling and other techniques.

During this period, I also took up other crafts while we spent two to three months at a time at the finca in Spain. Still painting, I took up silk-screening, calligraphy, needlepoint, embroidery, and gardening. Eventually, the jewelry instructor tired of the trip to Hitchin each week, and the lessons discontinued. But by that time, I had begun to acquire my stash of tools and supplies, which I'd purchased, frugally, at the gem show in Tucson. I began attending the gem show during our annual trip to visit Joana and her husband, Stan, during the winter months. With the gem show, and our next move, began an earnest effort to turn my jewelry-making hobby into something more relevant.

Spain

Franco had died in 1974, and it wasn't long before we began marking changes. Franco was seen as a dictator and had acted so back in 1936, during the civil war in Spain. By 1974, King Juan Carlos and Queen Sophia were actively reinstated, and the country rejoiced in the normalcy of life once more. Franco had run the country, but all was calm and well organized. We had had four years of relative tranquility and a peaceful life, where our American dollars of a pension and Social Security went a very long way. Building the house had cost slightly less than $100,000 USD even with the size of it and the marble floors, cork wallpaper, latest appliances, and all of the accouterments. Food was purchased at the mercado in Estepona, with fresh seafood caught that night. Our gardener planted a vegetable garden in part of the free land below the house. Wine was fifty cents a bottle. Restaurants were inexpensive. Cultural benefits were nonexistent, but as we were able to do those to our hearts' content in England, Spain was mostly R & R for us, a place to enjoy the simple life and relax.

Free elections came after Franco died. All along the coast, the small villages elected communist mayors and city councils in defiance of all the years under Franco. Gradually, over the next few years, prices and taxes began to rise. But only for the "extranjeros" who had received their "residencias" (permit to live in Spain permanently), not the Spanish residents. Every year the property tax rose significantly.

Strangely enough, it was not the property tax which became the straw that broke the camel's back. No, it was the garbage fee! In 1977, the fee for the monthly garbage pail collection suddenly jumped from four hundred pesos per month to four thousand pesos. Fritz had a hissy fit. The exchange rate in 1977 was eighty-one pesos to the American dollar, thus $49. Never mind, it was the principle of the thing.

Especially when Fritz discovered that the residents in the *Pueblo* Cancelada were still paying four hundred, while all the foreigners in the *Finca* la Cancelada were being charged four thousand. That did it. He went to a realtor and put our house on the market. We decided we would finally move back to the States, even though we weren't entirely happy about the growing problem with the materialism we found so evident there every time we went back on our annual home leave.

Quite frankly, I think Fritz was getting bored with Spain. He did not make friends with any of the finca residents, except for one English couple. All the rest came and went, sometimes when we were there, mostly when we were enjoying the English apartment. I would have been content to stay there, but then, I had my hobbies of silk-screening, painting, gardening, sewing, and knitting. And, of course, the seventies were when we began adding all those pins to our world map. But I didn't mind a bit moving back to the United States: We would be able to see Joana and her family in Tucson and my family in Auburn more frequently, and of course Fritz would be able to maintain contact with all his Carrier workmates.

But the question remained. Where?

Speaking Perfectly

One time we were returning by train from a vacation through various countries in Europe and entered Spain at the border town of Puigcerdá between France and Spain. The passengers had to disembark from the train to go through aduana (customs) to change to the Spanish train with narrower rails. As we walked the long platform to the small office, Fritz took out our two American passports and had them ready in his hand. I went through first, then Fritz, and the official asked him where we had been and where we were going. Fritz explained in Spanish that we lived on the Costa del Sol and were headed home after a vacation. The official looked at the passport again, then said, "Usted habla Español muy bien, Señor." (You speak Spanish very well, sir.) Fritz smiled and replied, "Usted, también!" (You, too!)

Why Youth Is Wasted on the Young

Ho hum, another day, another cliché.

But clichés become insignificant just because they are so universally used.

What if we stood the cliché on its head? What if we gave all the wisdom that comes with old age and experience to youths? Would they even know what to do with it?

Youth is all about having fun. Isn't it? That is why young kids ride their skateboard up a slanted wall, jump off into open air, and land back on the wall to descend. Sometimes they don't land right and break a leg, arm, ankle, or shoulder when they crash. Is it considered serious, a "lesson learned"? Nah, after a quick, noisy trip to the hospital with sirens blaring (what FUN!), they're back at it, bungee jumping.

Kids don't appreciate good health like old people do. Physical strength is a given. And then you don't have it any more. And boy, do you bitch. But for a youth, it's just another way of having fun.

Old age reflects. Youth reacts. Wouldn't it be nice if the two met somewhere in the middle?

But it's not ALL fun and games. Sometimes youths contract devastating illnesses, incurable illnesses, traumatic illnesses that leave their parents sick with worry and sometimes grief. And then they want the compassion that only Old Age understands. And these older people spend their days and nights, weekends, too, sometimes YEARS, thinking up cures, developing medicines to treat these diseases so that no parent has to suffer their beloved child's death.

Youth rides motorcycles. Old Age travels in motorhomes. The youths ride fast, speeding past scenery, the goggles of their helmet allowing sight only of the road ahead. They are dressed for safety, with leather clothing, gloves, kneepads, and heavy boots. Old people look at the mountains, the waterfalls, the hawks circling, stop to cast a line in that creek right next to the highway, pull into a camp for a night under the stars and to meet some friendly strangers.

Old people know how to do things, because wisdom comes with old age. The brain is always available for another crease to be made in it. If we could purchase a brain of a scientist, or a professor, or a philosopher, and implant it in the head of a sixteen-year-old, I wonder what he might be capable of accomplishing.

I've given this a lot of thought, and I reached a stunning conclusion. Instead of lamenting that Youth is wasted on the young because all they want to do is have fun, why not turn it on its head—again. Why not make Old Age the time to have fun and make Youth the Learning Experience? Pay more for good teachers, who will teach our young people to think for themselves, to make wise decisions, to figure things out. (Why doesn't the earth fall down?)

And let us Old Folks have some fun. I'm having more fun at the rental house by myself than I had in my entire life. Give us knees that can run, stomachs that can eat anything, and passionate love affairs. And let us bungee jump naked if we feel like it. I think I'll take that last sentence back; sounds like a kid.

Reflections on Becoming a Grandmother

It tends to sneak up on you. Just when you feel you have finally gotten the parenting thing down, you wake up one morning to hear that your daughter is going to be a mother. You suddenly age twenty years. How dare she? Grandmothers are mostly old people.

But some are surprisingly youthful, full of energy and enthusiasm. After the initial shock, you think, "Hey, I can handle this. It might actually be fun!" The waiting period begins. I have to tell you, this is not a thirty-day trial period to get used to the idea. No, this is a Forever Commitment.

The first time you are handed that tiny bundle in a blue or pink flannel blanket, you get such a squiggly feeling in your stomach that you feel sick. They call it instant bonding, but bonding doesn't even begin to convey what you feel at that moment. You control yourself as you gently touch those tiny fingers and make one of those inane remarks like, "She has Grandfather's eyes, or Grandmother's chin." As if that matters.

You think about this little miracle you're holding, marveling that those tiny molecules will grow up correctly and become an energetic two-year-old, a curious ten-year-old, a monstrous athlete at fourteen who will eat you out of house and home, and an obnoxious teenager who at sixteen knows everything. And you automatically project, "OMG, he is going to *drive!*" And thus, the responsibility of becoming a grandparent begins: You are there to worry.

But before the worrying begins, you get to enjoy. Seeing that first smile, enjoy. Holding your breath with the first step, enjoy. Realizing she knows the meaning of "NO!" and delights in tormenting you with it. Enjoy.

I assure you that the consensus among experienced grandparents is, when this little human has a tantrum or stamps her little foot, she *did* come with a return clause. She can be handed back to the parents while you pour yourself a glass of wine.

The single most delightful moment is when your precious little grandchild is cuddling next to you on the couch as you read *Goodnight Moon* for the gazillionth time and when you turn a page, she says the next word before you do. Miracle of miracles, this genius can read at two! Smartest kid in the world. Then the deflation sets in as your best friend who became a grandmother two years ago and now considers herself an authority tells you, "That's just memorizing." Well, you think, with a memory like that, this child could become a superior actor. And you finish *Goodnight Moon* for the gazillion-and-first time.

Then your friend pulls out two photos from her wallet and asks, "Did I show you these new pictures of Eli?" You admire them and retaliate with three photos drawn from *your* wallet.

And that is when you become a grandma. For the rest of your life.

The Grandkids

I was surprised at how completely Fritz took to being a grandfather. He had not been an active father. I was amused to see how his imagination kicked in. When our grandson was around five, the two of them would take a sheet out of a closet and drape it over the couch, and it became a "mountain." The pillows became hills and valleys under the sheet. Out came all the play cars with police car, fire engine, ambulance, helicopter, and Bill and John. They were Lego people who were very real. First, Fritz's voice would come on like a police monitor: "Calling all cars, calling all cars. Private plane has crashed on top of A Mountain." A few siren sounds—waaaawaaa—and the police car with its flashing lights would be driven by Andrew up the bumpy mountain. "This is Car 63. We need a Medivac helicopter on A Mountain."

A helicopter would be flown by Fritz high above the mountain and circle to find a suitable landing spot. Sometimes the crash occurred at night, and then they would turn off the lights in the living room and attach a pocket flashlight to the bottom of the plane with a rubber band, and it lit up the ground as it circled. The medics, Bill and John, would find the injured (other unnamed Lego people), load them on a stretcher, into the helicopter, and with much noise, the helicopter would take off. "Attention, TMC landing pad. This is Medivac number one, arriving in two minutes. Have surgery prepared. Four injured." And the helicopter would land on top of the coffee table. All lives were saved. This game could be played over and over again, the "sirens" getting louder with each rerun. Our grandson now goes through the whole thing with Don and Cameron, his own six- and three-year-olds. Bill and John are still the medics. They don't get to be retired.

When Andrew was five or six, he learned magic tricks from his barber. He would walk up to us, holding a pack of cards in his hand, and say, "Pick a card, any card." But he would forget to build up the story first. The disappointed look on his face was so funny when the trick didn't solve itself. Fortunately, he never did learn how to saw a lady in half.

Fritz always picked the kids up at school in the afternoon and drove them to their busy after-school activities: gym, soccer practice, acting class, Shakespeare, and piano lessons. Andrew loved to tease. I have to admit I was an excellent target. I believed everything he told me with a straight face. One day they arrived home and Andrew wore a guilty look as he entered the kitchen from the garage. He was thirteen or fourteen at the time. I immediately inquired what had happened. In a low voice, he confessed that the class had received their report cards that day and his was not good. He didn't want to show it to his parents. I was shocked because Andrew always had outstanding report cards. I anxiously asked him what had happened, and he confessed that he didn't really know but that he had some Cs. My face probably reflected my astonishment, but I hastened to assure him, "Don't worry, hon, Papa and I will help in any way we can to smooth things over with Mom and Dad."

Maybe it was Fritz's ill-concealed smile, but my suspicions set in. I asked him, "Are you sure that it's that bad?" At which point he couldn't keep up the charade, broke into an infectious grin, and gave me the report card. All As. He and Fritz had cooked up the story on the way home.

Andrew was a strong, sturdy guy. He loved picking up his mom or me and giving us bear hugs. Joana could handle him, but with me, the hugs usually came at the kitchen sink where he'd grab me around the waist and lift me high off my feet. I was sure I was going to topple over. I would kick helplessly and pound his back, screaming, "Andrew, you nut, put me down!" After a few wild turns and whirls, he would set me back down, satisfied.

One day when Andrew was in his sophomore or junior year in high school, I asked curiously what he wanted to be when he grew up, thinking he would say a doctor, like his dad. He considered it quite seriously and then said with confidence, "Well, first I'm going to be a judge, then the governor of Arizona, and after that I'm going to be the first Jewish president of the United States." Our daughter had converted when she married Stan, and the children were raised Jewish. I was caught off guard at that one and inwardly laughed at his high ambitions. I facetiously asked, "Do you mean to tell me that we will have our first honest politician?" He backed out of the kitchen and reached the doorway. Then he grinned infectiously and said, "I wouldn't count on it, Grandma."

He attended Boys State, a mock government program in high school where they introduce laws and pass them. He graduated from Stanford and Yale Law School, and joined the Truman National Security Project. He is still an active member, attending the annual meeting in Washington, DC. He was an intern at the White House during the Clinton administration and, no, he did not meet Monica, but he did meet the president. He is married to Karin, also a lawyer, and they have two boys. He prosecutes drug and occasional fraud suits, and is mentioned in the newspapers when he wins one of those cases. I figure he can skip the governorship. I'm looking forward to the elections in a few years and working on his presidential campaign.

Going back years before, in 1981, Fritz and I were visiting Israel. On February 9 we were in Bethlehem. We got back to our hotel room late at night, and as we unlocked the door, we heard the phone ringing. I answered and heard this excited little three-year-old voice on the line: "I've got a baby sister, Grandma!" Then Stan came on and said both mother and daughter were doing fine, and she would be named Adriana. The next day our itinerary took us to the church that they say is the spot where Christ was born, and with great joy we told the rest of our English tour group that we had received a call the night before that our granddaughter had been born. After the smiles and congratulations, our group burst into a spontaneous rendition of "For unto Us, a Child is Born." It was an unforgettable moment. That afternoon we left a little folded paper in a crack in the Wailing Wall, wishing her a life of good health and happiness.

When Adriana was two, she loved being read to and easily memorized all of the books after hearing them a couple of times. One day I was reading a story about the discovery of popcorn in the New World as early as 3600 BC. It was about the archeologists who discovered it in Mexico. While I was reading the book to her (again), as she cuddled up next to me, I turned the page and stopped to take a breath. She immediately looked up and said, "That word is ark-ee-olo-jist, Grandma."

"How do you know that big word, honey?"

Her answer came easily: "I know it's the first word when you turn that page." After that I often asked her to read to me. She would pick out any book and start "reading," turning the pages to exactly where the words divided. We were a little afraid that she would follow in her brother's shadow, he won so many awards and competitions, but that fear was put to rest when she was fourteen and tried out for a Shakespeare competition in high school that led to the state finals. She had memorized a lot of Shakespeare and was as prepared as she could ever be when she was called to the stage to recite a long verse selected by the judges. She froze. The seconds dragged on as she tried desperately to remember how it started. Nothing. She apologized to the judges and left the stage, numb.

Sitting huddled in the first row of the audience, suddenly she was able to recall all of it. After the presenter who had followed her finished, she stood up and addressed the judges. "Please give me another chance."

They acquiesced. She walked confidently back on stage, started speaking, and received a huge round of applause at the end. That is my gutsy granddaughter!

She turned out to be a natural gymnast, and we loved watching her turn somersaults from one corner of the mat over to the opposite corner. She walked along the balance bar, one foot in front of the other, never losing her balance, and perfected somersaulting off of it and landing perfectly straight and still, never a forward jerk, before holding both arms up over her head in triumph.

Adriana loves the outdoors and belongs to a bicycling group. One year her group went en masse to Iowa for a week's pedaling from one end of the state to the other. They camped out some nights or were invited to stay overnight with some of the friendly folk along the route. She claimed she had never eaten so many blueberry pies in her life, and it was good that she pedaled the calories off the next day. She also belongs to a curling team, and I kid her about it being a Canadian sport. I offered to sweep the broom down the lane for her. Our granddaughter also attended Girls State for a week, learning how the government worked (back when it actually did). She was part of the legal team in mock trials, and when she was sixteen, she spent a summer in Montevideo with a student exchange program. She has a knack for languages and went to Argentina for nine months before entering Stanford. She speaks Spanish fluently, and occasionally we'll use a word or two in our emails to make a joke.

Any special accomplishment was always celebrated at a Dairy Queen. We basically kept the franchise in business.

One thing Andrew and Adrianna loved to do when we were visiting them was to go rock crushing with Fritz. They would arm themselves with a couple of hammers from Stan's arsenal (he probably wondered how his hammers got so dinged up), put on their swimming goggles, and hiked up the street till they came to a vacant lot. Then the search for pretty stones would begin. Sometimes they found little geodes which, when bashed open, displayed sparkly crystals inside. Mostly the finds were white quartz with flashes of mica in them, or stones streaked with colored lines. When you are three and six, anything that you can bang apart looks beautiful.

While we visited Tucson, they entertained us every morning with that day's "weather report." They would come into the living room where we cuddled in the sofa bed which was hidden behind a three-section folding screen. Our grandson was the newscaster, and Adriana was the weather girl. They had the words down pat, just like they heard it on TV. Pointing to the birds and flowers on the folding screen as if they were various cities, Adriana would give a detailed report. "There is a big storm coming up from the Gulf of Mexico, gaining in strength, and will turn into hurricanes by Sunday. And China has been hit by a 7.8 earthquake." There was always a major disaster somewhere. Their "pointer" was a baton that our daughter had given Stan so he could conduct while listening to music on his earphones. The baton lent a certain authenticity to the news. Andrew would hand the baton over to Adriana, whose job it was to mention that there was a cold front coming down from Canada. That part knocked us out, laughing. Grandma and Grandpa came from a brrrr-y cold place!

On long drives from Tucson over to Del Mar, California, to visit Stan's parents, we cooked up another way to keep the children entertained. We were in a van, with our grandchildren on the fold-down seats in the middle, and Fritz and I became airplane passengers in the back seat. Andrew was pilot, of course (we still had no gender equality back in the eighties), so Adriana was stewardess. Around about Gila Bend we heard this deep masculine voice saying, "This is your captain speaking. This is flight 208 to Los Angeles. We have clear weather and don't expect any delay. Welcome aboard." Then Adriana would take up whatever she could find that looked like a microphone and continue.

"Ladies and gennelmun, please pay attention while I demonstrate the seat belt to you. Even though we don't expect any tur-ba-lunce, we ask that you keep your seat belt fastened during the flight. As soon as we reach cruising altitude, we will begin beverage service and lunch." (Those *were* the good ol' days!) If Fritz pointed out to me somewhere around Yuma the railroad ties that formed the basis of the Pony Express tracks, a few minutes later we would hear, "This is your captain speaking. If you look out the left window you will see the famous Pony Express tracks going across the desert." The old Pony Express was a part of western history. Because the horses and coaches got mired in the sand, they had laid railroad ties next to the railroad tracks. The ties were laid touching one another and made a smooth trail for the horses and wheels to roll smoothly. Over time, and sandstorms, they have become a jumble but are still visible to history buffs.

Of course, Fritz could never leave it at that. Oh, no, the next thing was that he looked out the window, then called to the stewardess. Emergency! Smoke was pouring out of the left engine! Adriana was unfazed. She reported it to the captain and then came back on the microphone.

"Ladies and gennelmun, life jackets are under your seats in case we have to make an emergency landing on water." In the middle of the desert? Never mind. The captain always managed to bring the plane in on a wing and a prayer. They loved that game.

One summer they came up to Kelowna for a visit, to escape the heat of Tucson. It was on July 1, when Kelowna celebrates Canada Day, a national holiday like our July 4. There was to be a parade through the downtown streets, and the Waldorf School (which Fritz and I had helped found) had a float in it. The theme was Fairy Tales. I asked one of the parents if we could borrow a costume. It looked like a brown furry bear and fitted Andrew perfectly. Adriana was all dolled up in a pink satin bathing suit with a pink net tutu, a crown of flowers from the garden in her hair, and a magic wand (the ubiquitous baton—Fritz had one, too) with streamers. We hung a large sign around Andrew's neck, and our grandchildren were transformed into Beauty and the Beast. They loved walking alongside the Waldorf float, waving regally to the audience lining the curb. What hams! They got a lot of applause as they walked by and won a little prize from the judges.

Adriana graduated from Stanford and received her MA at Berkeley doing two majors at the same time, public service and public health, which pretty much means that she can take her pick of any job in the medical sector that the government dreams up. She now lives in Colorado and is into skiing.

I like to think that her facility in public speaking links back to her courage during the Shakespeare experience. She also listens patiently to my raves about the marvelous Canadian medical system.

So, friends and potential voters, when Andrew becomes president, he can appoint his sister secretary of health. (With nepotism running rampant as I write, why not?) Then we'll have a country we can be proud to live in again. Trust me.

Knowing Barry Goldwater

We lived in Phoenix from 1952 to 1965, enjoying our beautiful Beadle homes while Joana went through grade school and middle school, then graduated from Camelback High School as salutatorian in 1965.

Our second Beadle house was at 6001 N. Palo Christi Drive, and from the backyard we could see Barry Goldwater's antenna against the skyline. He was an avid ham radio operator. We had been keenly interested in anything Goldwater, after his Senate office in Washington had sent us the telegram saying that Fritz's difficulties with getting a passport had been resolved with Barry's intervention so we could take our first trip to Europe in 1954, renewing Fritz's love for travel.

When Goldwater entered the race for president in 1964, Fritz and our daughter took papers around our neighborhood extolling his accomplishments. Goldwater's house was on a hillock and a wash behind our house and was in our homeowners association, although he was never in Phoenix at the time of a meeting.

However, on Election Day, he had to vote (for himself) in his home precinct. The polling place was in the Country Day School, two houses down from our first house, on Stanford Drive. This was before computers, so national media in the form of ABC, NBC, and CBS were there in force and were following his every move as he entered the school and voted. Margaret and Barry Jr. were also there to vote. After Barry had voted, the various news anchors were interviewing him outside. Fritz and I had gotten there early and had already voted, so we stood near and listened to the questions put to the senator. Barry Jr. then approached his dad and said, "I'm going in to vote now, Dad."

Barry replied, "Oh, good!"

This was when you either pulled the single lever for the Republican or Democratic party and voted for everyone on it, or you had to mark your ballot for individuals of each party, whomever you thought was best qualified. Barry Jr. was gone for a long time, and when he rejoined the entourage around the senator,

Barry looked at him and growled, "What the hell took you so long?" The press loved it.

Kissing the Blarney Stone

The other day during a jewelry class I was giving, I told a story about one of the places I had lived in abroad, adding a few funny embellishments, and as the class was laughing, one of the students said, "Oh, Janice, you have the gift of the gab. You must have kissed the Blarney Stone"! I stopped and said, "Well, you caught me, because I *have* kissed the Blarney Stone. Would you like to hear what it's like?" They nodded, because they knew another story was coming whether they agreed or not.

While staying in our apartment in England, Fritz and I had gone to Wales for a week: he to do gliding, and I to do a painting course. We would be staying in a manor house, which had been turned into an education center. The week got off to a great start because the manager-host greeted us with the question, "Are you vegans or carnivores?" The gliding course had been of keen interest to Fritz, who had gotten his glider pilot's license years before in Elmira, New York, at the famous Harris Hill Soaring Association. At the Wales site, it was more of a challenge because they towed the glider plane and pilot up to the top of a high hill by truck, they attached a bungee cord to its nose, and the other end of the rubber band was fastened to the back of a truck down on the runway. The truck would race down the runway, tightening the cord and pulling the glider off the hilltop so that it caught a thermal draft under its long, delicate wings and was free to soar. When the glider pilot felt he had reached enough altitude and the thermal was substantial, he pushed a button in the cockpit to release the cord, which fell back to earth and was rewound on the bed of the tow truck. The pilot gained control of the glider and began a series of circles, going from thermal to thermal, and could float for hours in the magnificent silence. In the States, the method to reach altitude was to have a small plane tow the glider up into airspace, and when the pilot was satisfied that he was high enough, he released the connecting cord, which was hauled back into the towplane. Fritz found the idea of plunging off a hill more exciting.

My painting course had also been somewhat of a challenge. It was supposed to be a beginner's course on watercolor painting, given by an instructor who was an expert on Dylan Thomas's poetry. He opened by reading a poem by Dylan Thomas and then said, "Now paint what comes to mind." (?) Well, since I had never heard of Dylan Thomas and had not understood one word of meaning in the poem, I was at a dead end. I had expected a lecture on which brushes to use or how to mix colors, which would have been geared to a beginner. My thought was, "And I paid £160 for this?"

I noticed the man next to me had already painted two flesh-colored breasts, and wondered how he had come up with that interpretation. I dug through my large handbag, hoping for ideas, found a brochure from the Spanish Tourist Bureau, flicked through the pages, selected a little two-inch photo of the white pueblos of Andalucia, and decided to go for it. I drew graph lines to divide the little picture into equal spaces and did an enlarged version of the graph lines with a soft pencil on the twelve-by-eighteen-inch heavy watercolor paper. Then I sketched in each building as it fitted into each little square. Thus began my very first attempt at watercolors: the finished painting has pride of place in my bedroom. Though deciding how to paint all the different shadows in all the different houses was a challenge, it beat figuring out the enigma of a Dylan Thomas poem. Even the teacher agreed it was a good painting.

At the end of the week, which we had both enjoyed tremendously, we decided to do a little sightseeing before taking the Green Line bus back to England and our apartment in Hitchin. We booked a bus tour across St. George's Channel, ending up at Blarney Castle, six miles from Cork, Ireland. I took the obligatory photo of Fritz holding his hands and arms out in front of him so that the camera saw him propping up the wall of the castle. It tilts like the Tower of Pisa. We also have a photo of Fritz keeping Pisa from falling over. Europe would collapse if it weren't for Fritz holding everything up.

The Blarney Stone is in the wall of a stone tower on the grounds of Blarney Castle. We followed the crowd of tourists to the tower and climbed the stone steps to the roof. The guide explained the history of the Blarney Stone, which is a block of Carboniferous limestone built into the battlements of Blarney Castle. This is the third structure of Blarney Castle. The original Blarney Castle was built out of wood in the tenth century. Around 1210 AD it was replaced by a stone structure, and the Blarney Stone was set in the tower of the third structure in 1446 by its architect Cormac McCarthy. According to legend, kissing the stone endows the kisser with the gift of the gab. Irish politician John O'Connor Power defined it as more than false flattery. It is flattery sweetened by humor and flavored by wit. For over two hundred years, world statesmen, literary giants, and legends of the silver screen have joined the millions of pilgrims climbing the steps to kiss the Blarney Stone and gain the gift of eloquence. Its powers are unquestioned but its story still creates debate. How did it get its reputation? A number of stories attempt to explain the origin of the stone and surrounding legend. An early story involves the goddess Cliodhna, the goddess of love and beauty. She presided over the Celtic Otherworld, which was a happy place for feasting and hunting, without death or aging. It was also a place full of beauty, and Cliodhna herself is supposed to have been extremely beautiful. Cormac McCarthy, the builder of Blarney Castle, being involved in a lawsuit in the fifteenth century, appealed to Cliodhna for her assistance. She told McCarthy to kiss the first stone he found in the morning on his way to court, and he did so, with the result that he pleaded his case with great eloquence and won. Thus, the Blarney Stone is said to impart "the ability to deceive without offending." McCarthy then incorporated it into the parapet of the castle. The proprietors of Blarney Castle list several other explanations of the origins of the stone on their website. One legend suggests that Queen Elizabeth I requested that Cormac McCarthy, the Lord of Blarney, be deprived of his traditional land rights. Cormac travelled to see the queen but was certain he would not be able to persuade her to change her mind as he wasn't an effective speaker. He met an old woman on the way who told him that anyone who kissed a particular stone in Blarney Castle would be given the gift of eloquent speech. Cormac persuaded the queen that he should not be deprived of his land. Take your pick.

Once upon a time, visitors had to be held by the ankles and lowered headfirst over the battlements. One man was dropped and died. Today, the owners are more cautious for the safety of their visitors. The tower is separate from the buildings of the castle. The outcrops which form the parapet walk around the tower jut out from the wall and look down upon the grassy area outside of the tower. The Stone itself is still set in the wall below the battlements, on the outside of the wall. To kiss it, you have to lie down on the walkway, with your feet toward the outside and your head looking back at the wall, and lean backward holding on to two bars. Fritz took one look at the gullible tourists hanging upside down and decided to pass; it was undignified. I, on the other hand, figured I'd never have another chance like this to become eloquent, and it beat Toastmasters all to pieces. I lay down on my back on the hard slab and grabbed hold of the iron bars, and the assistant slid me forward so my head was hanging down, over the open space. He urged me on: "More! More"! Then my back was over it. He kept calling, "Bend your head back more." I did as told, until my face was looking down at the grass twenty feet below, allowing my lips to quickly touch the stone. I was hauled back up, and the assistant shouted, "Next!" The prize is a real one as once kissed, the stone bestows the gift of eloquence. So, did I experience a profound change in my psyche? No. Did I find a new and exciting way to flirt? Afraid not. Was it worth all those germs? Did I develop an eloquent manner in speaking from that moment on? I must let this book stand or fall as testament to that. Because as I was dangling there, I confess the only thought passing through my mind was, "Don't blink! Don't blink! Oh, God, please don't let my contacts fall out!"

A Place in the Sun

On a trip to northern Germany in the 1980s, we stopped as usual in Hamburg to say hello to my husband's good friend Jochen Rehm. Jochen and Fritz had met when they were both arrested in the forties for being suspected of spying for Germany at the start of the war. Jochen had been arrested in Costa Rica on a coffee-bean buying trip for his father's company, and Fritz had been arrested as he returned to Colombia after he had been contracted by his air-conditioning employer to report on the security measures for the Panama Canal. They were both sent to an internment camp in Texas where they met, and later to another one in Oklahoma. They were held for two years and formed a friendship that was a strong bond. Both were eventually cleared and freed. Jochen had inherited his father's coffee-importing business, and Fritz had retired from Carrier Corp in 1972. Jochen owned a beautiful house on the Alster River in Hamburg, as well as a large house on the Isle of Sylt on the North Sea coast. He had reconfigured the Sylt house to four luxury apartments which he rented out to tourists during the high season in summer. In today's travel lingo, Sylt would be known as a destination vacation. Sylt was famous for its seventeen-mile-long sandy beach on the North Sea. The beach was known as the "Textilienstrand." The so-called Textile Beach was a misnomer if ever there was one. Why? Because the Textilienstrand was renowned for being a perfectly legal authorized nudist beach which was immensely popular with fresh-air fiends all over Europe. At the time of our visit, we were not aware of this. While in Hamburg, Jochen had invited us to stay in one of his apartments on Sylt while he did some business there, refurbishing one of the apartments. The three of us took the train from Hamburg to the northwest corner of the border between Germany and Denmark and changed to the train which traveled over the isthmus to Sylt, the tracks just skimming the surface of the North Sea. It was a strange sensation to be sitting on the train, looking out of the windows on both sides, and seeing only water beneath me. The next day over breakfast, Jochen and Fritz had their heads together as they discussed the plans for the day. I was rather surprised at the alacrity with which Fritz agreed to a day at the beach for us while Jochen bought some china in town. It's not like we hadn't enjoyed beaches when we lived in Brazil, Puerto Rico, and, for ten years, on the Costa del Sol in Spain. What made a beach in Germany so interesting?

It was agreed that Jochen would drop us off in his car and then come back at four to pick us up. Oh, well, I figured I would catch up on some reading.

You can imagine my astonishment as Jochen sped off and I looked down from the bluff—and saw hundreds of naked people cavorting below: old people, young people, fat people, wrinkly people, people who should *never* be seen without clothes on, and carefree little children gaily running in and out of the crashing surf. To clarify this further, this was not just a topless beach; it was also a bottomless beach. In my entire life I had never seen anything like it. Keep in mind, this was long before waxing became de rigueur, and European women didn't even shave under their arms. It was strictly au naturel.

This beach had another peculiarity: You rented beach chairs and a little building similar in size to a porta potty, where you changed your clothes. The ludicrousness of changing out of your clothes inside the closet and then stepping outside nude did not elude me.

Then you arranged the two chairs in the center of your space and further defined it by scuffing up a sand berm with your feet in a circle around your area. You could see all of these little "crop circles" up and down the beach as the families enjoyed their property for a day of wholesome fun in the sun.

My motto wherever we moved, no matter which country, was to "grow where you are planted," so I plucked up my courage, shed my clothes, and joined Fritz in our little berm. I was beginning to laugh at how those two had outwitted me with their scheme and decided I would enjoy this escapade if it killed me. Fritz sat down in his Adirondack wooden chair, took up the newspaper and modestly left the rest of it strategically in his lap.

Shortly afterward, a single man arrived next to us and built his own little berm around his chair. When I got up to retrieve a magazine from our closet, he walked casually over to our berm and, looking directly at me, holding a cigarette in his fingers, asked me, "Entshuldigung. Haben Sie Feuer?" (Excuse me, do you have a match?)

I was so startled with the question, and the novelty of the situation, that I could only look at him, bewildered, shrug, turn my hands up, and say, "Wo?" (Where?) Meaning "Wo würde ich das?" (Where on earth would I have one?)

He laughed, excused himself, and walked back to his chair. I went back to my chair and sat down, and I have to confess that I wondered just for a moment how I had looked compared to all the others he could have asked for a match.

We passed the day leisurely, enjoying the snacks Jochen had furnished, but mostly people-watching. It amazed me how nonchalant everyone was, being totally nude in the midst of all the others. And frankly, I was aware that as "no two snowflakes are alike," the saying could also apply to all the naked bodies on that beach. But no one was gawking lewdly. They just liked the feel of the salt water, the sun, and the breeze on their bodies, and the freedom it induced. Late in the afternoon I glanced up from my reading, to the top of the bluff, and there, silhouetted against the afternoon sky, was a man who had obviously been aroused by something. Or someone. Yes. Very clearly aroused and silhouetted. Wow.

At four o'clock we re-dressed and climbed up the hill to find Jochen parked, waiting for us. He mischievously inquired, "Did you enjoy yourself, Janice?" I told him primly I thought it had been very interesting. Fritz got a kick out of telling him about the man asking me for a match, with me innocently replying, "Where?" Made their day.

Addendum

In August of 2017, I submitted the above article to the writers competition by the Society of Southwestern Authors and recently received their comments.

Entry: A Place in the Sun
Comment:
Amusing story. A humorous description of discovering the vacation home the author and her husband rented overlooked a nude beach and being good sports, joining in. The voice is reflective and the story is told without many details. If it could be expanded a bit, it could be even better.

Left me shaking my head and wondering where I would draw a line in the sand (excuse the terrible pun) between humorous details versus pornographic expansion. Seemed to me I had already come dangerously close.

10

The Cold War (Moscow Diary)

In 1967 we were just past the midterm of our three-year sojourn in Switzerland. It was during the height of the Cold War, and Russia was isolated from the rest of the Western world. No airlines flew into Russia, and Aeroflot only flew within the Soviet Union. In June of 1967, President Lyndon Johnson and Premier Kosygin met in Glassboro, New Jersey, for a three-day summit, presumably to alleviate the high tensions that existed between the two countries. Less than three weeks prior to the summit, Israel had won the Six-Day War in which the United States had supported Israel and the Soviets had supported the Arabs. The talks were supposed to continue during a Johnson visit to the Soviet Union in 1968, but a brutal Russian intervention that crushed a revolution in Czechoslovakia led to a cancellation of the trip. It was therefore quite unusual to read in the *Neue Züricher Zeitung*, in August 1967, an interesting advertisement about an "Artistic Tour to the Russian Winter Festival" in Moscow which would take place between December 27, 1967, and January 3, 1968. Because Switzerland was a neutral country, Swissair was granted permission to be the first European airline to exchange flights with Aeroflot, both airlines flying between Moscow and Zürich.

It sounded like a good opportunity to see what a Russian winter was really like and to take in some excellent entertainment at a very reasonable price. Of course, Fritz was intrigued with the idea of being on such a historic inaugural flight.

I'm sure the reader must be asking why we would choose to go to such a possibly dangerous place. Fritz tended to choose risky adventures; that is why we went into East Germany before the Berlin wall came down. And why we went to China on the first foreign flight into that country, which required us to use military planes on some of the interior flights. And why we took our first trip to Europe in 1952, after the war, flying in a DC4 to Iceland and on to Copenhagen instead of one of the American airlines direct to Frankfurt. He got his kicks from a certain element of danger. But in this case, with a reassurance from our travel agent, I think the idea of traveling with a planeload of Swiss people meant that two Americans would be lost in the crowd. We were advised not to wear or take blue jeans, which young Russian men would kill for, and definitely NO BALL-POINT PENS, a novelty for them. The disquieting concern of the few friends we told did not deter us from our plans, while acknowledging the fact that the Russians had recently arrested and put on trial two young American university students who had dealt in black market rubles on the street and, as a prank, had stolen a bronze bear from a hotel lobby as a souvenir of their trip. They were sentenced to three years in a labor camp and fined. We armed ourselves with traveler's checks and promised our friends we would only *buy* souvenirs. We met our fellow travelers, 185 in all, at the Zürich airport. A young man from Boston and we two were the only Americans; all the rest were Swiss and a few French. We learned that because of bad weather in Moscow, our two planes had been delayed. Since Russia had no regular service to Switzerland, in this case they were allowed to fly in empty, refuel, board their inaugural passengers, and then take off for the return flight to Moscow. We had to wait until 4:00 p.m. before being allowed to take off in the first plane, a Tupolev jet. The second plane took off directly behind us and was an Ilyushin. Our plane had old-fashioned upholstery and lamps. Instead of the usual leather, our seats were fabric in a paisley design. The lamps hung on the side walls and were similar to what you would see on a train. And the plane had no loudspeaker system; the stewardess stood at the front of the plane, she made the announcement without a microphone that we would be landing in Budapest, and that was it. The stewardesses never checked the seat belts or described what to do in the case of an emergency. Curiously looking around the plane, we checked the pockets in the seats ahead of us and found our first sign of communism: the hammer and sickle neatly printed on the airsick bags! The plane had no fresh-air vents and no oxygen mask compartments. The reading lamp was concealed in the seat ahead. Our compartment (there was of course no first class) contained an altimeter on the wall leading to the cockpit which showed that we were cruising at thirty thousand feet. Hardly any pressurization, so my ears hurt and popped often. I deliberately tried yawning frequently in order to pop my ears open and relieve the pressure. The captain or copilot never came on to make any announcements.

Landing in Budapest, we spent an hour in the very modern and well-built airport while they refueled. In the duty-free shop we bought some little cloth bags of Hungarian paprika, anticipating some authentic goulash when we got back home. All prices were quoted in dollars. Reboarding the aircraft, we were served a dinner of cold cuts and caviar with vodka. When we landed in Moscow it was almost midnight and, as we stepped out of the airplane, we got our first taste of the "Russian winter": 11 degrees below 0 degrees Celsius and a bitter wind. We had to fill out declaration forms while the Swiss guides told everyone which hotels they would be in.

We met our Intourist guide on the bus that took us into Moscow. Her name was Frau Liudya, but speaking in German, she immediately explained that in Russia they do not distinguish between Mrs. and Miss and that we must just call her Liudya. She was one of the four Intourist guides (two French-speaking, two German). It was so cold the snow squeaked underfoot. At the Hotel Metropol we had to surrender our passports to our guide, never to see them again until the day we left, making us very uneasy.

The biggest shock to us was the dirt: All the sandy, snowy slush from the street was tracked into the lobby to mix with the sawdust on the floor and then continued up the carpeted stairs. The sawdust was occasionally swept up and fresh sawdust laid on the carpet.

Our hotel room (which, with the Hotel National where the rest of the group stayed, were considered the two best hotels) was simple, with poor construction. Mostly unfinished wood (the door to the bathroom was pressed plywood with no finishing varnish or paint) and plain furniture. The ceiling was twenty feet high, but actual floor space in the bathroom was four by five feet including the tub. The toilet was partly squeezed under the sink.

We were wondering what we had gotten ourselves into. After breakfast, we had a city tour with Liudya. We saw the outside of the Kremlin, Saint Basil's Cathedral, and Moscow University. Liudya said that it would take seven years to just go in and out of each room of the university because it serves thirty thousand students, and they are all housed on campus. I don't know who was recruited to figure that out, but I've always wished it would come up as a question in a trivia game. So far, no luck.

Streets were wide enough for six or seven lanes, but there wasn't much traffic except for buses and trucks. Buildings were tremendous compared to buildings in other European cities, but they were proportionately correct for the wide boulevards. The buildings, offices, and stores all looked alike: huge cement boxes, one after another. There were no trees to speak of; at least we did not see any: just buildings, sidewalks, and wide boulevards. We saw old women everywhere, constantly shoveling snow off the streets. The women were very evident, never any men, doing the most menial work. They wore felt boots which were more impervious to the cold than leather would have been. The first strong impression you received were the sidewalks crowded with shuffling hordes of people. When you were on the street amongst them, eventually this overwhelmed you. They were like lemmings on their determined march to the sea. You got the curious feeling that if you should stumble and fall, this horde would plod right over you. The people were well-dressed, and many wore fur coats.

Liudya took us shopping to the souvenir stores in the afternoon. The touristy souvenir shops had cheaper prices than the government-run department stores where the Russian people purchased their needs. (They weren't allowed to shop in the souvenir shops.) Most of us bought fur hats; I bought a black mink for around $20. Prices were quoted in dollars. We noticed that Christmas trees and decorations were being put up, also on the streets. While denying the Christian holiday, the Russians had not given up the festivities—they simply changed the name and date. They celebrated it as "New Year's" but gave gifts, decorated trees, and even kept Santa Claus, complete with red suit and white beard, while calling him "Father Frost." On every floor of the hotel, there was an older woman sitting at a desk just in front of the elevator. With a stern visage, she demanded your key each time you left and handed it back when you returned.

At midnight the second night, we were shocked awake by the phone ringing. Fritz answered, and the voice rattled off something in Russian. Fritz said in English, "What do you want?" The man answered in German "Auf wiedersehen." This frightened us, and we tried to figure out what it was about. When we decided that perhaps it was only someone who had rung the wrong room by mistake, we tried to go back to sleep, but were unnerved all over again by a second phone call twenty minutes later. No one spoke, but we could hear a beeping sound. We spent the rest of the night sleepless and anxious.

The next day we visited the Kremlin. In spite of the scare during the night, we were determined not to let it mar our learning about Russia. We saw the tsar's robes, crowns, dishes, even horses' bridles all covered with precious jewels. I was especially interested in seeing the jewel-encrusted Fabergé eggs, which impressed me so much because of the incredible workmanship. The Lenin Mausoleum in Red Square was open, and we joined the long line of patient Russians. The mausoleum closed capriciously for "repairs," so one never knew exactly when it would be open for viewing. When Liudya came and arbitrarily jumped us to the head of the queue, ahead of all the compliant Russians, we didn't protest because we were freezing. Neither did the line of people; they must have been accustomed to foreigners moving to the front of the line. We trudged down a flight of stairs. The body of Lenin is encased in glass with a pinkish light shining on it and guarded by four soldiers. It did not seem gruesome at all, for the simple reason that it did not look real. We concurred with the suspicion that what is on display is a wax model, thus the frequent closure for repairs.

We had read so much about the massive GUM department store that we walked to it one afternoon. It was huge and packed with shoving people. Everybody was eating ice cream, so we bought some too. We found this so ludicrous with the weather so cold, but for them it must have been considered a treat. The cones were tiny, with just a little ball of ice cream and—of course, what could you expect?—only vanilla. The Intourist Service Bureau at the hotel got us tickets for the circus that evening. The circus was an excellent show: They had trained their big black bears to perform the way we train lions and elephants. The star was a magician who really had some good tricks involving disappearing from the stage and reappearing at once in the highest balcony. In retrospect, probably twins.

By this time, we had become acquainted with a very nice Swiss couple named Steiner who invited us to join them for dinner. We were somewhat relieved from our nervousness when they told us they were very good friends with an attaché at the Swiss Embassy.

In subtle ways we were beginning to see that much of what we were interested in was either ignored or glossed over. You would have had to be very dense not to see through it. After lunch at the hotel, Liudya offered to hold a discussion period at which we could ask her questions. This was set up by the other American, and it soon became obvious that he was a communist. He led the questioning with comments flattering to communism. That evening we went to Tschaikowski Konzertsaal and heard a performance of the Pjatnizski Choir singing folk songs. Also performing were excellent folk dancers with colorful costumes and lots of ribbons flying as they twirled in their full skirts and their knee-high red leather boots. Walking on the streets was a different matter: Several times we were asked in English by young men if we wanted a good price on rubles for some dollars (we could only change our traveler's checks at the hotel; we never saw any banks). When we said no very forcefully, they then wanted to know if they could buy jeans, or if we had any ballpoint pens. We ignored them, feeling it was much safer not to say anything. They followed us quite a way.

Walking along Gorky Street gave a much better impression. There were a lot of food stores along Gorky, well stocked, but people stood in long lines waiting to buy things. They had a very inefficient method of purchasing: You had to go first to a counter to find out the price of an item you wanted, then go to a cashier and pay for it, then back to the counter to pick up the item. Even if it was only a cup of coffee and a roll. We were astonished to see that all the cashiers used an abacus instead of a cash register.

Stores closed early because of New Year's Eve. The festive New Year's Eve party, which was part of the tour, started at 11:00 p.m. The tables were lavishly filled with platters of salmon, caviar, etcetera. A little gift of an astronaut souvenir was at each seat. Vodka, white wine, champagne, ginger ale, and mineral water were offered. First came a fish dish. We toasted in the New Year at midnight with champagne; everyone at our table was nice and friendly. At 3:00 a.m. the meat course came: chicken breast with an egg crust on Chinese noodles. St. Nicholas (Father Frost) came around and toasted everyone. There was a good orchestra and entertainment; the ballroom was all decorated. We finally had ice cream and cakes at 4:00 a.m. and left, although the party continued until breakfast. When we reached our floor, the ubiquitous Key Lady handed us our key and said, "Happy New You." She had a rather forbidding demeanor usually, so the mispronounced greeting had us laughing. Or maybe it was all that champagne. We noticed again the thoroughness that the Russians showed in changing every detail to conform to their theories. Where every other country shows their paintings dated, for example, "500 BC," the Russians put on their descriptive plaques "500 years before our era." We found that sort of neurotic.

Next, we decided to ride the Moscow Metro, another example of Fritz's perverse fascination with danger. We made stops at various stations to get off and admire the beautiful mosaics, fancy chandeliers, and lit-up glass murals. This was rather risky because the signs were only in Cyrillic, and we had to keep consulting our Moscow map showing the names in Cyrillic so that we could tell where our hotel was located. When we got off at some of the stops, we rode the escalator up to the street, stepped out, looked around to get the feel of the area, and went back down again, taking the train to the next stop going in the same direction. The Metro had four levels; we took a fast three-minute escalator ride down very deep. Our last stop brought us out at the Hotel Metropol; it was so cold that just walking across the street brought sinus pains to my forehead. We found out later it was −19 degrees Celsius (−4 degrees Fahrenheit). Getting back to the hotel, we made a hurried shopping trip to GUM to buy some teapots to go with the samovars we and the Steiners had purchased. And a balalaika (Russian guitar) for Joana; the crowds at GUM were absolutely claustrophobic.

That night we walked to the Kremlin—so cold!—to the Palace of Congresses. The Bolshoi was performing for us in the main hall where the Soviet government met. We saw a performance of *Swan Lake*. The ballerina was excellent: fluid arm movements. The stage settings were nothing special, but the costumes were good. The Bolshoi Theater was later found to be crumbling and deteriorating so badly that it was closed and under renovation while they completely restored it to its former glory. It took three thousand workers and specialists six years, and millions of dollars. Using scarlet satin, and gold leaf, they cleaned the intricate carvings with vodka and brushed the gold leaf with squirrel tails. A ticket for a single performance now commands $358. It reopened in 2011.

The main attraction for us was the building that night: It seats six thousand! Very plush, immense. Each seat had a hidden earphone, desk, and loudspeaker so the delegates could hear the political speeches. There were three balconies, with lighting all across the wide ceiling. There was a large self-service restaurant on the third floor; we had good wine with cherries in it. We bought a Russian calendar for some friends back in Phoenix. Russians poured down the aisles at the end of the second act to applaud the dancers but left, rushing, before the curtain came down at the end of the third. (With six thousand coats to hand out, they could have a long wait.) We decided to go to the evening meal at 10:30 even though we weren't hungry, because it was our final night. We were glad we did: Another champagne dinner, and Intourist gave each person a record of Tchaikovsky.

The promise in the original ad was for an "Artistic Tour to the Russian Winter Festival," and that promise had certainly been fulfilled; we saw many, many of Russia's cultural treasures. But it came at a price. The price of all the propaganda we were fed in daily doses which were not in homeopathic amounts. Mixed with a fear and tension that never really let you fully relax.

On January 3, the telephone woke us at 6:15, and we finished packing. In the lobby we were so relieved to be handed our passports again. The bus took us to the airport with lots of confusion while we filled out declaration forms. We had breakfast and did some final shopping, mostly tins of caviar, which were about $5 each. We were now carrying a balalaika, a samovar, a fur hat, and a shoulder bag loaded with caviar. It was snowing. We picked up some propaganda booklets in English. They announced a one-hour delay and we started to buy some stamps, but before we could get to the line with the abacus cashier, they announced the departure and we had to dash to the gate.

Our plane was Swissair, with Swiss pilots. We landed again in Budapest for refueling. Soon the captain came on the loudspeaker to tell us that we had just crossed the border of Switzerland, and the entire plane erupted into applause. And a resounding chorus of heartfelt sighs and smiles to our neighbors. Immediately after crossing the border, and with the beautiful sight of the snow-covered Alps underneath us, one of the Swiss guides walked down the aisle and told each one of us privately that a member of the tour had died of a heart attack on the second day of the tour. The man, a professor, was the only Russian on board and was returning to his homeland to see his family for the first time in many years. Fritz and I had spoken briefly to him the first day. The Swiss Embassy friends of the Steiners had told the Steiners but sworn them to secrecy; they did not want to alarm people more than necessary. When we questioned the guide about how odd it was that the Russian professor had died suddenly when he appeared so healthy and happy to be seeing his family again, they just looked at us steadily and didn't comment. The planeload of Swiss was quiet, perhaps reflecting on how lucky they were.

We flew in from the south, over the Adriatic, up to Lugano, and over the Swiss Alps. They had never looked so beautiful; we even saw the Matterhorn, pink and gold in the late afternoon sun. When the plane landed in Zürich, we were so grateful to be "home" again. Safe once more. Safe to reflect on what freedom means.

11

Impressions of China

In April of 1984, Fritz and I were invited to join our Swiss friends and fellow travelers on a tour to China. It was shortly after China had opened its borders to foreign visitors. The tour had been organized by our friend Rüdi Visini and his wife, Marlis, our travel agent friends from Zürich, with whom we had taken several unusual trips: The first permitted flight to Russia in 1967 from Zürich in the middle of the Cold War. A trip to Mongolia. A trip to Mexico loaded with disasters—people losing passports—in which Fritz played a huge role in serving as the translator for Rüdi to officials. And a lot of bus trips to Italy and around Switzerland. We knew we could count on it being interesting and well organized.

The plan was to fly in from Canada and meet up in Beijing with the thirty-one Swiss tourists who would fly with Swissair from Zürich. With Chinese visas in our passports but no advance hotel assignment upon our arrival from Hong Kong, we were very relieved when our Chinese guide, Chen, spotted us with our identifying Swiss shopping bag in the Beijing Air Terminal after clearing the rather rigid customs and immigration formalities. Chen had a taxi waiting for us which took us on a long ride to the Friendship Hotel on the outskirts of the nine-million-inhabitant metropolis. Chen started teaching us on the drive to the hotel. We learned that anything with the name Friendship in it was strictly for foreign tourists: Friendship Hotels and Friendship Stores were run by the government. Only foreigners could shop there and buy Chinese goods with US dollars, at very reduced prices.

Our first surprise was the many wide avenues which were clean and devoid of cars. They were clogged with bicycle riders everywhere. No pollution, but the noise level was high because the bike riders jingled their bells at the pedestrians, and the buses constantly honked at the bicyclists.

Chen pointed out that advertising posters had replaced the old poster wall of the Red Guards, but several red slogans were still to be seen on major intersections, Red Square, and many government buildings. We were shown the huge Parliament, the Mao Mausoleum, and the ostentatious Radio Peking building (shortwave radio station), the way the people got the news.

Arriving at the hotel, we were welcomed by our Swiss companions who had just arrived from Zürich. At least a dozen of them had traveled on other tours with us, so lots of hugs and "gruezis" were exchanged. It's nice to be greeted so warmly. The hotel with our three-room suite was adequate but very old-fashioned and worn. Fortunately, the central heating and plumbing worked okay, which was not always the case. Chinese meals were fun and palatable once you learned to use chopsticks or could ask for a fork. One of the Swissies, a well-known artist and sculptor, made a practice of asking for a fork as soon as we were seated and presenting it to me with a flourish. At every meal. Fritz was not amused; he did not like it when a man paid attention to me. I don't know why the guy did it; he probably thought it was funny. Many courses were placed on a large rotating Lazy Susan in the middle of an eight-seat table. You could spin it around, helping yourself from chicken, beef, or duck dishes and vegetable side dishes, with sticky rice, good beer, and green tea on every menu.

Communication in China was a major problem. Even in large hotels you could seldom find a Chinese person with whom you could converse in English or any other language. Of the many guides we had, only a few were fluent in the languages they were supposed to interpret. The poverty and hard life were evident by the number of people used to do the jobs of machines in more advanced countries. Anywhere there was construction taking place, you would see hundreds of people using hand shovels and wheelbarrows instead of bulldozers. People power was cheaper. Our first visit was to the Great Wall, and we climbed the steps to stand on the top of it. It is said that the Great Wall is so huge that the astronauts could identify it from outer space. The primary purpose of the wall was always to protect the Chinese Empire from the Mongolians and other invaders. Some parts of the wall date back two thousand years. Most of the current Great Wall we see today was built during the Ming Dynasty (1368–1644), when the various walls were joined together, and it's approximately six thousand kilometers long.

We visited the Forbidden City, the Summer Palace, the Ming Tombs, and the Peking Opera (where we found the voices sounded so artificial, very squeaky and irritating). We tried the Peking duck, from webbed feet to the head—and all the parts in between. The feet were ghastly. Our flight to Xi'an took place in a Russian-built Ilyushin jet with a characteristic high-speed rattling landing. Xi'an has 2.4 million inhabitants and eight hundred thousand bicycles. It is hard to picture a "small" city, but that's what Xi'an is compared to Shanghai and Canton, with nine and five million inhabitants.

From an archaeological point of view, Xi'an was the highlight of our tour. In 1974, workers digging a well outside the city of Xi'an struck upon one of the greatest discoveries in the world: a life-sized clay soldier poised for battle. The government sent archeologists to the site. They found not one, but thousands of clay soldiers, each with unique facial expressions and positioned according to rank. The terra-cotta army, as it is known, is part of a mausoleum created to accompany the first emperor of China into the afterlife. He had taken the throne in 246 BC. At the age of thirteen, he took the name of Qin. During his rule, Qin standardized coins, weights, and measures and is credited for building the first version of the Great Wall. Qin ordered the mausoleum's construction shortly after taking the throne. More than seven hundred thousand laborers worked on the mausoleum for twenty-seven years. Only four of the pits have been partially excavated, and Qin's tomb itself has yet to be uncovered, but it may never be. The pits have a very high concentration of mercury, giving credence to the rumor of rivers of mercury flowing through the hills of bronze to the sea. The pits that have been excavated have uncovered over six thousand clay figures and many rows of four horses, also full-sized, as well as weapons. While at the museum for this tourist attraction, I decided to use a "ladies' room." It was in a long building next to the museum, and was a twenty-five-foot trench in the ground, six inches wide. You had to squat over each side, and there was no toilet paper. Fortunately, I had been forewarned and brought my own roll from the hotel. Millions of people come to see this army of clay soldiers; wouldn't you think …?

On the way back, the bus pulled off the road to where craftspeople were selling eight-inch versions of the clay soldiers, and we bought souvenirs. At the time of our visit, the curiosity of the Chinese about foreigners was great, but could also be daunting, as Fritz discovered. One afternoon when I had gone to one of the Friendship Stores, he decided to get a shoeshine when he saw a Chinese man looking for customers on a street corner. In no time, he was surrounded by some thirty onlookers as if he were a strange animal. When he pulled up his pants, revealing white socks, he heard a sudden surprised gasp from the audience. They had never seen white socks before. He was glad when the ordeal was over, as he later told me: "I'm not used to being a curiosity on a street corner in a strange city!"

The flight from Xi'an to Nanking took place in a military jet as a charter flight. China had no domestic airlines then, only military planes. We had good service on board with gifts of silk scarves and souvenir candy boxes. The hotel in Nanking, the Jinling, was as plush and up-to-date as any latest Sheraton or Hilton in the United States. It was built by a Chinese American as part of a chain for future tourism. The local population formed a long line as they paid to tour the hotel facilities in groups of thirty to forty at a time. They stared in awe at the luxury of the lobby, the chandeliers, the furniture. The revolving door was a confusing experience for them as they had never seen one before, let alone gotten tangled up in one. They didn't know how to step out when they reached the inside of the lobby. A guard was placed there to grab the arm of the person going around and pull him out.

We were surprised that none of the guides had given us any political propaganda whatsoever. When we had been in Moscow, we had to listen to the Intourist versions of history every day. Yet the Chinese guides pointed out the free markets which one could see here and there. These markets gave the Chinese their first experience in free enterprise. The peasants on the communes were now better off than their city brothers because they could sell their extra produce in the free markets and afford to buy TVs and appliances.

The guides also talked freely of the one-child-per-family quota. With all the millions of people we met in every shrine and temple, we saw only one pregnant woman on the entire trip. The garden city of Suzhou, with five hundred thousand inhabitants, is also known as the Venice of China because of its picturesque canals and waterways. This visit was unforgettable, because our excellent guide, Liu, not only spoke German and English but had a sense of humor that was outstanding. A great guy and guide, we'll long remember his wide, friendly smile. He took us on a boat ride along the Grand Canal known originally as the Imperial Roadway, built by an emperor as a whim to enjoy boat rides and now used as the main commercial waterway between Peking and Shanghai. Some of the barges are made of cement because of the wood shortage in China. (When you make an airtight box of cement, it floats instead of sinking.) In Suzhou we visited a silk factory, and I was stunned to watch the production from cocoon to thread. One cocoon yields *four thousand meters* of thread! The worms are fed mulberry leaves. As the white cocoon becomes about one inch in diameter, they stop the silkworm from producing more of the cocoon. After soaking the cocoons in warm, soapy water to remove the sericin which binds the fibers together, they place the end of the thread on a reel which spins the infinitesimal thread on the reel without breaking it. The silk thread extruded by the worm is incredibly strong. I was amazed that it never broke. We went to a fan factory where we watched the artists sawing out the delicate sandalwood and ivory slats, others sewing the slats together, and other artists painting fans of silk. For someone who considered herself a "craft" person, it was crafter's paradise. Reluctantly, I tore myself away.

While we were in China we heard our guides discussing President Reagan's visit to China. He and Nancy had arrived a week before our tour group in order to clarify points President Nixon had made in their agreement drawn up in 1972, but still rankled the Chinese with Taiwan. Reagan's visit was considered a failure.

Another hour's train ride brought us to Shanghai, a harbor city with six million inhabitants: overcrowded, tropical, not as clean as the rest of the cities we visited, and busy as only the world's third largest city can be. We saw the same temple and six-foot Jade Buddha that Nancy Reagan had visited. We toured a beautiful water garden set in the city center's old streets. It was terribly sad to see old women who had had their feet bound as children hobbling along the streets with great difficulty and pain. They sometimes had to be supported. They had to bind their feet as young as six or seven in order to marry. That is the theory, but history finds now that it was an economical practice. It was thought that women would be more productive in weaving and other work if it was too painful for them to walk. The practice was banned after 1934.

It was raining when we arrived in Guilin, with its 680,000 inhabitants, so we visited a recently discovered grotto in this two-thousand-year-old city. The rain gave us a typical picture of the many rice fields in that region, filled with the little green sprouts of the plants all standing about two inches apart. These water-filled terraces climbed the hills. We couldn't help noticing how many of the people walked stooped over from years of planting and harvesting rice. In the afternoon we visited a kindergarten, which gave us the opportunity to compare their method of teaching with the Waldorf school system, which we endorsed in Kelowna. We were positively impressed with the sweetness and self-confidence of the children. All the activities were group-oriented. In one of the classes, Fritz was chosen to direct the class in a familiar singing exercise. He chose "Jingle Bells," which all the children knew. Their little bows and smiles at the end were so typical of what we had seen, and the sweet voices were so charming, that you didn't notice at first that all sang, bowed, and smiled in unison. They had been drilled to perfection. We also visited a large commune and heard the production figures from their leader, who gave a thorough description of the communal way of life. Sounded like we were back in Russia. The five-hour boat trip down the Li River to Yangzhou surpassed the beauties of a Rhine cruise in many ways. Every turn in the river gave a new view of the misty mountains with their rounded tops. It looked as if they had cloned the Sugarloaf in Rio de Janeiro hundreds of times.

A rather bumpy flight on a modern 737 jet into Canton, with its five million inhabitants, prepared us for the exit from Red China. Its many taxis, neon lights, tourist shops, and restaurants announced the West's influence.

I asked our guide to write in Chinese "Ming Dynasty porcelain shards," and Fritz and I set off to find an antique store near the hotel. Showing the proprietor the paper, with me demonstrating by seemingly throwing a porcelain dish on the floor, he finally understood and opened a drawer to show me broken shards of Ming Dynasty porcelain. The Ming Dynasty (1368–1644) was renowned for its excellent porcelain and was becoming a popular jewelry trend. I knew I could sand off the rough edges and make some spectacular jewelry out of the blue and white antique pieces. I bought some of the shards and eagerly looked forward to getting back to Kelowna. There, I would set them in silver and make pendants. The owner was left wondering why a tourist would want a broken dish.

After a short train ride through the barbed-wire border, we arrived in Hong Kong. The two days at the luxurious Furama Hotel provided us with an immersion in extravagance, especially with the lush buffet breakfasts and the farewell banquet at the rotating rooftop restaurant. All the lights of Hong Kong at your feet! A compromise between the life of Xi'an, Shanghai, and Hong Kong may well be the answer for the future China, and it looked to us as if this was apt to happen before the end of the century. Boy, we sure missed the call on that one!

May You Live in Interesting Times

I used to say that to friends, thinking I was wishing them well. Then one day someone said, "You know that is actually a Chinese curse, don't you?" I googled it and discovered that despite being widely attributed as a Chinese curse, there is no known equivalent expression in Chinese. While this may sound like a blessing or a warm wish, it is always used ironically, to indicate a period of chaos or disorder. It was first used in 1936 by the British ambassador to China. Last week in my writers group, we each had to go through the box of cards giving suggestions for a social conversation and select one we liked or thought we could write about. I drew "What is the strangest place you have ever been?" One of the members commented, "Well, that should be easy! You've been to so many places." I nodded agreement, thinking I had an easy-peasy task.

To prepare for the article, I stood in front of the wall-sized map I had purchased as a gift for Fritz many years ago. I had it mounted on one-quarter inch Styrofoam. The idea behind the gift was that once he saw all the pins stuck in every continent, he would be content to stay home for a while and we could explore Canada. That backfired when he would gaze at the map until he found a bare space, then go the next day to our travel agent to book a trip there.

As I gazed at the map, large pins where we had lived, smaller pins where we had visited, it brought so many memories rushing back that I had to make some notes on a piece of scrap paper. I had been all over and had so many interesting stories bottled up in me that I puzzled over which to use as the strangest. I began compiling incidents as I went down the list. Kathmandu? It was a mystery, high on that mountain in Nepal: the people dressed so differently, the fragile houses built on stilts, the strange figures written for the language, the eleven-year-old little girl who was the reigning Living Goddess, who gave our group an audience. The bungie-like takeoff of our jumbo jet as we hurtled down the runway straight at Mount Everest, banking sharply at the last minute and gaining altitude so we wouldn't collide with the Himalayas. Holding our breaths as we filmed the mountains up close from the cockpit. What about climbing up all those steps to reach the top of the Great Wall in China, so immense that it can be seen by the astronauts in their spaceship. Or the pyramids in Egypt, wondering how the laboring slaves dragged and pushed each huge stone block into place. Going around the furthermost point in South America and having our pictures taken under the large curved arch, welcoming us to the End of the World. What a disappointment when the fog prevented us from flying on our booked excursion from Ushuaia to the research station in the Antarctica to visit with the brave souls deployed there. What about coping with the strange religion in India, where we observed the people in the street walking respectfully around a sacred cow stopping traffic while stepping over the figure of a man huddled in a burlap sack sleeping in the middle of the sidewalk, holding his leprosied hands out for coins. Trying to understand the caste system. Staying overnight in the

Treetops Hotel in deep Kenya, the rooms raised on stilts so you could spend the night awake looking down from the observation deck at the elephants, and wild animals coming up under you to drink at the lagoon. Remembering that this was where Princess Elizabeth learned she was now queen. Our ship detouring up the western coast of South Africa out to the tiny island of Saint Helena, where Napoleon was exiled and died in 1821. We scrambled down the rough path to the tomb, picked up a little stone from the ground, and reflected on the humble end to a man who reveled in power and control. How the mighty fall. The exciting visit to the Sistine Chapel when we were invited by the Vatican to tour behind the scenes of Michaelangelo's frescoed ceiling, which had been cleaned and was now protected by Carrier air-conditioning, which Fritz had organized from Zürich. We were taken on the narrow railinged observation walkway around the edge of the ceiling. I could have reached through the slits and touched the hand of God. And how could I leave out the strange departure from Brazil? We had lived for two years under the threat of the death squads, with the fear that diplomats and CEOs of foreign companies would be kidnapped and held for ransom. And when we were transferred to run the office in Puerto Rico, we decided to sell our car and furniture. The night when Fritz was traveling to say goodbye to his dealers and distributors and I was left at the apartment to handle the sale. When two men showed up to look at the furniture, I arranged to have my neighbor sit with me, and she assured me that we were safe while showing me the pistol in her bag. She then assured me it had no bullets. It was a stroke of comedy a week later when I found out that our dangerous buyers had actually been the Italian ambassador and his assistant.

So many strange things, places, people. Events tumbling over each other in their eagerness to be mentioned. But what about the good times? The interesting learning experiences? I have often compared moving to a strange country, learning the language, learning the culture, and learning to survive to a piece of raw iron in a blacksmith's shop. You're put in the furnace fire and heated fiery red. Then they bang the hell out of you and shape you into something beautiful. The little picture that went everywhere when we faced a new assignment: a flower with deep roots which said, "Grow where you are planted." The fear of starting over, the insecurity, the desire to succeed, to make something of myself, to prove I was worthy. Whether sixteen or seventy, there exists in the heart of every person who loves life the thrill of a new challenge, the insatiable appetite for what is coming next. You are as young as your faith and as old as your doubts.

I pondered: WHAT was the strangest place of all? And then, suddenly I knew. It had been right there all the time.

Interesting times, chaos and disorder? Happiness? Weird? Disgusting? Depressing? Discouraging? STRANGE? Yes, right here, right now. 2024.

12

Life on Las Ramblas

Fritz finally managed to get back to Barcelona in 1952, the first trip we took to Europe after World War II ended. His mother and father had passed away, and his brother was living in Venezuela, married to a Caracas lady. Fritz loved walking the streets of Barcelona with me, showing me the amazing Sagrada Familia church, Parque Guell with its mosaic sculptures by Gaudí, the unusual curving houses of the architect Antonio Gaudí, the harbor, the boulevards. He pointed out the blocks that had the corners cut off in order to soften the boxiness of the buildings.

We visited the museums of Dalí, Gaudí, and Picasso, the little side streets which led intriguingly to small cafés where they made hot chocolate so thick you could stand a spoon in it. We would indulge in dipping our churros in the chocolate. We went to two of the houses Fritz had lived in, which had been turned into apartment buildings. We visited his mother's grave and arranged to have a new marble slab to replace the cracked one. We had get-togethers with his student friends; they were mostly women, so we called them Fritz's Harem. We ate in the Quatre Gats (Four Cats), where Picasso, Hemingway, and other famous people had dined back in the twenties, their photos on the walls. One of our favorite restaurants was called Las Caracoles (the Snails), where Fritz would enjoy the peasant food: garbanzos with sausages. We always snagged a seat near the open kitchen so that we could hear the cooks shouting as they slapped a plate down on the counter. "Marcha!" The signal to the waiter that the meal was hot and ready and he had better "march" it to the diner. Just about every year we would manage another trip back to "Barna," as it is affectionately called by the Catalans. we would visit some of the old, familiar places. But mostly we would spend our time on the Ramblas. The heart and soul of Barcelona.

Las Ramblas. How do you describe them? You may as well try to describe life to a Barcelonan. The street started out as a dry, sandy river bed, with houses built in the early eighteenth century, and the street appearing in the late eighteenth century. It became a wide pedestrian promenade, flanked by roadways on either side of its Raval and Gothic quarters. It is a tree-lined pedestrian mall, starting at Port Vell near the cruise port terminal at the southernmost end, running 1.2 kilometers long, to Plaça Catalunya at the northernmost end. The center of the promenade is filled with tourists in August, smiling, relaxing, renting a chair from the watchman and ordering an espresso from a waiter who would appear from one of the cafés on the street side, cross the traffic to the Rambla, and take your order. Read the international paper, catch up on a book, listen to a classical guitarist, and people-watch, quietly enjoying life on the Ramblas. In Fritz's time, it was also a way for a young girl (with her chaperone, of course) to walk up and down on one side, while the young men would walk on the other side and make polite, discrete contact. Many a romance got its start on the Ramblas.

The Ramblas were divided into about six sections, each section the equivalent of a city block. The pedestrian center remained an oasis of tall shade trees, with benches and tables to sit at. But the part that brings Barcelona alive, that sets it apart from other cities, is that each section of the Ramblas has a "character" to it. The first block below the Plaça Catalunya is called Rambla de les Flors. (I'm using the Catalan names.) The Hotel Montecarlo, where we always stayed when in Barcelona, was on the Rambla of flowers; we stepped out of the hotel entrance, crossed the narrow street, and were immediately surrounded by all the tents and stalls on each side of the pedestrian walkway filled with the most beautiful flowers and arrangements you could ever see. Plants for your garden, bouquets for celebrations, bunches and bunches of flowers, all in large buckets of water. So colorful with the perfume in the air you breathed.

The next section was La Rambla de los Pajaros, and I have to confess it was my favorite. Cages and cages of parakeets, cockatiels, parrots, and canaries, singing their little hearts out, the cages stacked one on top of the other or hung from wires strung across the roofs of the tents. I could spend hours wandering from one merchant to another, listening to them extol the virtues of this or that bird, and the little children begging their mother, "Oh, Mami, podemos comprar este? O aquello?" ("Can we buy this one? Or that one?") I remember my grandkids, the first time they saw the Rambla de los Pajaros, enchanted to see all those birds for sale. I could visualize their single birdcage in Tucson expanding into an aviary.

Then came La Rambla del Arte, where painters sat hunched in front of their easels, painting every kind of still life, landscape, abstract, portrait or caricature, and even a few Picasso wannabes. The artists chatted with all the tourists in their mother tongues, lending a casual quality and intimacy to their art.

And lastly was the block of "Sculptures." Rambla dels Caputxins. They were actually live people who had painted their face and body with white grease paint, draped sheets or materials over themselves, and stood on a pedestal, without moving, for long, long minutes at a time, replicating a well-known sculpture in the Louvre or the Prado. Our grandson, who was about ten the first time he saw the statues, walked around and around the statue. When we gave him a few coins to put in the cup on the sidewalk, the statue said, "Muchas gracias." Our grandson jumped a mile. We then laughingly pointed out to him that it was a living person, dressed as a statue. He decided that was pretty cool. This was also the block for acrobats, mimes, and flamenco dancers, all very talented.

Then on your right was La Boqueria, the huge public market, where you could buy anything from a pinch of saffron (dried crocus stamen, to color paella) to the eyes, tongue, and other parts of a cow you would rather not contemplate. The educated stomach of Barcelonans.

How many times Fritz and I walked the length of the Ramblas, from the port with the statue of Christopher Columbus pointing forever to America, to the opposite end at the Plaza Cataluña, rambling along slowly hand in hand, savoring life in Barcelona and recalling his past.

I seldom turn the television on during the daytime, too busy to bother. But for some reason I turned it on today at 1:00 p.m., and the first picture that appeared on CNN was something I thought I recognized. I said, "Hmmm, that looks like the Ramblas!" I watched, horrified, the unfolding of the carnage happening in Barcelona; it grabbed me and shook me by the shoulders, and I couldn't stop crying. Memories kept flooding back as I felt the tears wetting my cheeks. On August 17, 2017, a madman rented a van, zigzagging it at high speed all the way down the center of the Ramblas, killing fourteen people and injuring over one hundred. With this evil act, he sucked the life out of Barcelona. It lay gasping for breath in the midst of all the bloody carnage. Its voice, forever stilled. They will attempt to recapture its spirit, but it will never be the same again. Its joie de vie dead. The strollers, walking more sedately, mourning, mourning. The birds will sing quietly, the flowers' scent less sweet.

Oh, Fritz, my dear, I am so grateful you did not live to witness the death of life in your beloved Barna.

This article was published in the *Tucson Daily Star* in October 2017.

13

Experiences in India

While living and doing so much traveling abroad gave me an appreciation for and a tolerance of the cultures in various countries, I have to confess (sadly and with much regret) that after three trips to various parts of India, I never could reconcile their Hindu religion and cultures in my mind or heart. It was the difference of class, with the wealthy at the top of the scale with their mansions and many servants, down to what were called the "Untouchables," who were ignored and scorned, simply because of their birth. And then there were the lepers; what a tragedy. They were so poor that they had to keep their disease rather than treating it because they could earn more money by holding their hands up to the windows of tour buses, begging, in order to feed their families. I was horrified to suddenly see a hand with just stumps for fingers pressed against the window as we waited somewhere on a tour. On our first trip to India, as we were walking near the Hilton Hotel, we had to step around sacks of burlap on the sidewalk; but the "sacks" were poor people in burlap bags, sleeping on the streets. Then at the next street corner we had to wait while a cow (sacred to Hindus) walked by and traffic came to a standstill. I tried, I tried very hard, but in the end I just simply could not comprehend. Only the peace and tranquility I experienced at the tomb and park of Mahatma Ghandi gave me any solace.

14

The Top the Top of the World—ATW III

My husband, Fritz, and I took our first Around the World Cruise with Air Canada in 1987. It came about as we were sitting in the living room of our townhouse in Kelowna, British Columbia, Canada, and Fritz began his usual rationalization about having to go visit his aunts in Germany, thus lending credence to his desire to visit Europe again. My reaction was Been There, Done That—umpteen times. I happened to see at that moment a small ad in the local newspaper describing a new travel adventure:

Around the world in 23 days, on board a chartered 747, all drinks, meals, sightseeing, and entertainment included. Visiting Hawaii; Fiji; Perth, Australia; Bali; Kuala Lumpur, Malaysia; Kathmandu, Nepal; the Seychelles; Vienna. Air Canada $7,000/pp.

I tossed the paper to him, saying, "Now, this is interesting. Why can't we do something different for a change?" Fritz read the ad and sniffed, saying, "Just a bunch of snobs." The next day Fritz had to go to the bank, and when he came back a couple of hours later, he had this fishy expression on his face, almost guilty. At lunch, I saw two red envelopes on our plates. I assumed they were the usual Eurailpasses for Europe, but when I opened one, lo and behold, it was for an Around the World Voyage leaving Kelowna and Vancouver on November 7, 1987. I couldn't believe my eyes! Where would the money come from?

Oh, he had the answer to that.

The trip would be on a specially chartered 747; you would have the same seat and the same crew all the way. Normally a 747 carries 401 passengers; for this trip they anticipated a maximum of 230. (The final tally was half that, just 115.) There would be ten travel agency personnel plus twenty-four Air Canada people, seven more than are normal on a full 747. All sightseeing, meals, drinks, hotels, tours, and entertainment were included in the price, $10,875 per person. Gulp. At every stop our plane would be designated a private charter and the formalities of customs and immigration control waived or minimized. Well, when our travel agent explained all of this to Fritz, he realized that this was definitely different in the realm of our manner of traveling. No more schlepping luggage from the train and seeking out a cheap B&B. And … this rationalization ran riot. All during the seventies in England, the banks had begged for deposits, with interest rates spiking at 17 percent. When we sold our villa in Spain in 1981, we deposited the money in our English bank. It seemed as though our savings account earned another $2,000 every time we turned around. Fritz reasoned: What was the point of all that extra money languishing in the bank's hands instead of ours? I had to admire the way his brain could justify spending hard-earned money on travel, but niggle on anything else.

Since I was the one who had thrown that paper to him, asking why we couldn't do something different for a change, I suppose I had to share the blame on this one.

November 7–28, 1987

This Around the World trip didn't take eighty days, nor did it require a hot-air balloon. As one passenger commented, "I have always dreamed of taking off on a magic carpet, but I didn't know it would be in the guise of a 747." This fabulous experience could never be duplicated in today's world. You have to remove your shoes and belt to go through security, you have to be patted down, you cannot take a bottle of water on the plane, and everyone looks suspiciously at their fellow passengers. The potential for danger lurks in airports, metros, churches, and just plain markets. You are in danger if you try to buy some fruit. It's so easy to be in the wrong place at the wrong time. Back in 1987 the world was much more stable, and exotic sites were safe to visit. Not to mention how the costs of such a trip would have risen.

Compared to the service and care we received in a finer, more carefree time, I'm everlastingly grateful that we were able to take this unique trip.

Secretly, I thought it would be an amazing experience, seeing how the other half lives. I'm sure the thrill for Fritz was to feel that the 747 belonged to him: wielding his baton, take off now, land here, taxi there. He was a licensed pilot, after all. The unfolding description of the itinerary was something I read every day in awe. The flight from Vancouver to Fiji where we would "unlag" would be the longest. Each destination stop would last three days. No early-morning race to the airport. We would turn up around 9:30, be whisked straight on board with a Mimosa, and be pampered. I had never experienced being pampered, ever. I was sure it was something I could get accustomed to. But first came the packing. Oh, my goodness, what a surprise! We were allowed to take as many bags as we wished. After all, we had the huge underbelly of a 747 to fill. The only stipulation was that you had to pack a separate bag for Vienna, the last stop on the cruise. In Vienna we would be met with snow and cold temperatures after all the tropical places south of the equator. Also, the dress code for the gala final banquet in the Ferstel Palace (yes, a real palace) was evening gown and tux. This bag would be held in the hold until the last stop and then delivered to our hotel room. Fritz and I opted for one wheelie each for the rest of the flight plus the carry-on hand luggage. Checking and rechecking all the activities planned made it quite simple to determine what to pack. I had certainly gained enough experience by then! I had packing lists Scotch taped to the closet door for every possible destination, climate, medical issue, and souvenir possibility. After the first time when I forgot to pack cuff links for French cuffs on a cruise (you'd have thought the world was coming to an end!), I never made that mistake again. With mounting excitement, we talked of nothing else. Fritz was beside himself with happiness while still concerned that we would be encountering snobs. (Note: The only snobs aboard were the travel agency personnel, whose executives sat upstairs in the ultra-ultra first class.) The lady who had the seat behind us was a retired teacher whose kids had united to pay for her ticket as a retirement gift. As we got to know her, she was sweet and friendly. On November 7, 1987, we flew from Kelowna in a 737 to Vancouver and were joined by passengers who had flown in from Alberta and Saskatchewan along with other British Columbia guests. Air Canada personnel gathered us for a champagne reception, and we watched from the terminal windows as the Air Canada jumbo lazily floated in and landed, our blood tingling with excitement.

The plane had left Toronto at 9:00 a.m. with all the east-coast passengers and arrived in Vancouver for a fuel stop and to pick up all the west-coast passengers. There was a smattering of applause as the captain and copilot left the cockpit and, with some members of the crew, joined the party. We took the first of many photos of them standing under the departure board, with the notice *Air Canada Private Charter Fiji … 12:00 p.m.* up there between departures for Hawaii, Montreal, and Toronto. Captain Don Stinson and the entire crew were experienced personnel who were chosen for this trip as a reward for their good service. Captain Stinson was a thirty-year veteran pilot with Air Canada and had been in command on the first two charters. I remembered my favorite saying when flying (I was always a white-knuckle flier): "There are old pilots and bold pilots, but there are no old bold pilots." I checked: Don had white hair. Good.

We were led to our seats halfway down the economy section on the left side of the plane. Let me clarify: in deference to the cost of this trip, economy was now called "World Class." First class was called Executive Class and commanded an extra $5,000 charge for large reclining seats. We noticed at once that a lot of seats had been removed from the plane, especially in the area behind the Executive Class, making it very roomy. We laughed when we realized that with all the unused middle seats, we would be able to stretch out completely for a nap if we chose. No need for reclining seats. A large bar had been installed with bar stools, and an extra-large movie screen filled the wall behind the bar. The airline had changed the seat configuration on a normal 747 from three seats on each window side and five in the middle to two seats on each side, and they had removed lots of the rows of middle seats, making it very spacious. Our stewardess (back in

1987 they were still called that) introduced herself: Mary Dohey. She wore a ribbon pin on the pocket of her jacket. Later we were to find out why she had been chosen, but we had to weasel it out of her, little by little, as she leaned against the armrest of the middle seats.

Our Stewardess, Mary Dohey

Mary had been a Canadian flight attendant who was the first living person to receive the Cross of Valor award, Canada's highest award for bravery, for her conduct during the hijacking of a commercial DC-8 aircraft on November 12, 1971. Flight 812 had flown from Toronto to Vancouver and was on its way back to Calgary to refuel when a man, fueled by alcohol and wearing a mask, pulled out a shotgun and two bundles of twelve dynamite sticks from under his seat and demanded $1.5 million dollars or he would kill the crew and the 112 passengers. Mary Dohey was the flight attendant nearest him and was charged with holding the two bundles of dynamite without allowing the wires to touch. During the eight hours of terror, having the shotgun held to her head by this black-hooded man, she engaged him in talk, calling into play her years and training as a psychiatric nurse before joining Air Canada. She got him to agree to divert the plane to Great Falls, Montana, in order to pick up the ransom money. A briefcase was delivered to the plane, but Air Canada had only been able to round up $50,000 on such short notice. Mary negotiated with him to release the passengers and part of the crew. They would fly him wherever he wished with the rest of the crew as hostages. The plane was surrounded but no attack was made, to ensure the safety of the passengers and crew members as they walked across the runway. The hijacker offered to let Mary go, too, but she refused to leave her fellow crew members and went back up the stairs. He decided in his befogged state that the $50,000 was enough, and they took off.

When planning this hijacking, he thought it would be more profitable for him to leap from the plane with the money, to avoid capture. After demanding that one of the crew open one of the doors, when he started to untie his parachute, he could not get the knot untied. He demanded something sharp from the crew to cut the twine, and when he laid down the shotgun to take the fire ax offered by a crew member, another crew member kicked it out of his reach and grabbed him around the throat, and another one bashed him on the head, fracturing his skull. When the plane landed in Calgary, Paul Cini was arrested and sentenced to life in prison. He was paroled after serving ten years. Surprisingly, the same method was used only one month later when a man identified as D. B. Cooper hijacked a Boeing 727 out of Seattle and jumped with two parachutes and $200,000. He was never found, but $5,800 of the photographed bills were found on a riverbank in Washington years later. It is still considered an open case.

Queen Elizabeth awarded Mary Dohey the Cross of Valor in December 1975. Fritz was duly impressed.

Mary Dohey, heroine, would be our stewardess for the entire trip. What an honor.

The various parts of the trip have been shrunken and cut with surgical precision because my diary of each stop gave all the details of every spectacular meal, all the tours, every temple and cathedral, and every cocktail party, with every bit of entertainment and craft demonstrations. I've cut each stop into just the highlights that you might find interesting. The seven stops were Hawaii to refuel, and the captain flew our plane down low over the Arizona Memorial, the sunken ship for which we celebrate each December 7; the water was clear, and we could see the body of the ship resting on the ocean bottom.

We arrived in Fiji the next day. Crossed the international date line and the equator. They had a contest to guess the exact moment; I missed by two SEC-ONDS! In our hotel, flowers were stuck in everything: between towels, on the tub, in a gift basket, etcetera). The international date line added a day to our calendar. There were beautiful, big yachts in the harbor. The Fiji houses were huts, open. The inhabitants sit on reed mats to eat. We saw colored striped fish in the clear water. Fiji consists of over 330 islands. A Fijian drummer ran along the beach carrying a torch and lit all the gas torches, tikis, around the hotel grounds.

The next day was an eight-hour flight to Perth. It was Remembrance Day, and the captain made a short speech congratulating our stewardess for her courage during the hijacking; today was the anniversary of it in 1971. The fish course was lobster, shrimp, and crabs, and the entrée was chicken Kiev. We watched a travelogue to Australia. One opal store had an entire wall covered in rough opal with water flowing over it to show up the fire even more. The next day we took the bus into Perth. Perth was founded in 1859 by convicts sent from England. The America's Cup race was taking place at the time, and we could see all the sailboats which were taking part. Saw our first kangaroo and an emu bird. A troupe of Aborigine dancers performed.

The next day we flew to Bali. The heat and humidity were very high. Whenever the captain lands a plane in a new country, he raises the Canadian flag up through a hole in the plane's nose. There were musicians to greet us. The exchange rate was 1,600 rupiahs to the dollar, so our lunch of grilled lobster cost 37,000 rupiahs. Made you feel like a millionaire. Bali houses are also mostly huts, very primitive. We visited a batik factory and discovered how they make the layers of color using melted wax in cups. Hundreds of girls and women grab you and drag you to their batik stalls. We visited various craft stalls in Ubud, went to the jewelry village, and watched them gluing on teensy, tiny beads of gold and silver. I bought a pair of earrings. I also bought a bag of little red seeds that become the glue for the beads when you mush them up. The Bali dancers started performing their "opera" with various gods and goddesses. It was only three hours to Kuala Lumpur. Got through customs quickly and at the Shangri-La Hotel watched the customary greeting of drummers and girls dressed up in gold saris and gold headdresses, holding golden floral arrangements. We walked around the grounds and saw the funniest, fattest goldfish ever, in an aquarium. In Malaysia, there is a death penalty for drug trafficking. At 7:00 p.m. we went down to the captain's cocktail party, everyone dressed to the nines.

The entire trip up to Kuala Lumpur was amazing, with every luxury you could imagine: excellent food and entertainment at each stop, six-star hotels, unique sightseeing, and excellent service on board our private jumbo.

We were looking forward to the next stop: exotic Kathmandu, Nepal. The night before, at the captain's cocktail party, we'd been chatting with Captain Stinson, and I casually inquired if the crew had had to practice landing in all the destinations on a "test-drive." He replied that they had done it on flights to everyplace but Kathmandu. The following day would be their first visit to Nepal and the very first time a jumbo 747 had ever landed on a notoriously short runway, at the end of which lay the Himalayas. (That was not particularly reassuring to someone who white-knuckles a landing at Kennedy.) He went on to explain that the crew had laid out various templates of clear sheets of thick plastic, emulating all the heights and shapes of the various mountains, and had calculated exactly how many feet they had to come in on the landing. (We heard later in the Seychelles that the Air Canada crew had been discussing the takeoff in Kathmandu as the pilot muttered, "I hope this works.") As we neared Nepal, we could see the Himalayas from the right side of the plane. Beautiful! Then the plane began its descent, and we saw we were flying close over the lower green mountains. The captain came on the loudspeaker and recommended that we not buy too many souvenirs here, as he wanted to keep the plane light due to the short runway and the thinner air for the departure in three days. We could see hundreds of people looking up at our plane as the crowds pressed against the fence around the airport. Then we were down, and the whole plane burst into applause. The next day we were on the front page of the *Rising Nepal*, and TV cameras and photographers had recorded the first arrival of a jumbo, a big event for them.

The following day, we went back to the airport, where we saw a group of genuine trekkers preparing to start their climb of Everest, and reboarded our jet for a forty-five-minute flight over the Himalayas. Air Canada had provided each of us with a fold-out map showing what each mountain looked like so you could see when you came to Everest. They allowed two people at a time into the cockpit, giving us a view of the entire panorama from there and allowing us to shoot some spectacular close-up photos. During the three days in Kathmandu, we did a lot of touring, visiting villages, temples, and shrines, and we saw the little eleven-year-old girl who is the Living Goddess as she was carried to the window to look down at us in the patio below.

The Living Goddess

On the second day in Kathmandu, the guides on our tour excitedly informed us that our group had been granted an audience with the Kumari, the Living Goddess, a rarely given concession to foreigners, and that we should feel honored.

In Hindu religious traditions, the worship of the goddess in a young girl represents the worship of divine consciousness spread all over creation. Kumari, or Kumari Devi (Living Goddess), is the tradition of worshiping young prepubescent girls as manifestations of the divine female energy, or *devi*. The Kumari is revered and worshiped by some of the country's Hindus as well as the Nepali Buddhists, though not the Tibetan Buddhists. The word Kumari is derived from the Sanskrit meaning "princess," and the girls chosen are indeed given the royal treatment. Before entering the courtyard of the Kumari Ghar, the royal palace where she lived, the Nepalese guides gave us the history of the Living Goddess. I have condensed it greatly, leaving out many of the legends surrounding her raison d'être, but they all involved the kings in various dynasties. In one legend, more explicit than some of the others, a king was very promiscuous. He was also attracted to young girls. Unfortunately, during sex with a young girl, she died. This left the king completely distraught, guilt ridden, and bereft, and he repented the sin by concluding that the girl had returned to her goddess spiritual nature. He declared the creation of the *Kumari Devi* to perpetually remind the world of the sacred nature of young girls and virginity. Only a young girl is chosen over a mature woman because of her inherent purity and chastity.

Virgin worship has been around for a long time; there is evidence of it taking place in Nepal for more than 2,300 years. The Living Goddess belief is relatively new, having started in the seventeenth century. When the Kumari's first menstruation begins, it is believed that the goddess vacates her body. Serious illness or a loss of blood from an injury are also causes for loss of deity. The selection process is conducted by five senior Buddhist priests. The king and other religious leaders are kept informed that the search is underway. Eligible girls are from the Newar Shakya caste of silver and goldsmiths. (Forgive me for finding that significant; I'm a jewelry designer.) She must be of excellent health, never have lost blood, be without blemish, and not have yet lost any teeth. Those are the basics: After passing that scrutiny she must be further examined for thirty-two perfections of a goddess. Some of these are listed poetically as:

A neck like a conch shell

A body like a banyan tree

Eyelashes like a cow

Thighs like a deer

Chest like a lion

Voice soft and clear as a duck's

In addition to this, her hair and eyes should be very black, she should have dainty hands and feet, and she should have small and well-recessed sexual organs. As a final test she has to spend a night alone in a room among the heads of ritually slaughtered goats and buffaloes without showing fear. Can you imagine a four-year-old going through this?

Once she is chosen, she goes through several cleansing rituals, the spirit enters her, and she becomes the new Kumari. She is made up with paint on her face (a large eye on her forehead), and she walks across Durbar Square on a white cloth to the Kumari Ghar that will be her home for *the duration of her divinity.* That is the last moment her feet will ever touch the ground while she is a deity. From then on, she is either carried by her caretakers or transported on a golden palanquin. She will never wear shoes. She is bathed and dressed by her caretakers. Her family can only visit her on rare occasions. She speaks rarely. Her playmates are chosen from the children of her caretakers. If she wants a particular toy belonging to one of the playmates, they must surrender it to her. She will leave the palace only on ceremonial occasions.

The power of the Kumari is perceived to be so strong that even *a glimpse of her is believed to bring good fortune.* Crowds of people wait below the Kumari's window in the courtyard of the palace, hoping she will pass by the latticed windows on the third floor and glance down at them. Our guides had achieved a miracle: The courtyard was closed for just our group. The Living Goddess was carried by a man directly to the window, where she remained for less than a minute but looked out at us from that strangely painted emotionless face, raised her tiny hand, and was quickly taken away. The window was only twenty feet above us so we could see her clearly. It was such a short visual presentation that I felt no emotional experience, and I think that was the general impression for most of us. Perhaps our educated skepticism played a role in it. I can tell you definitely that good fortune did not follow me for the rest of my life.

We visited a Tibetan refugee camp where they carded wool and dyed it with natural dyes. Sitting cross-legged on the floor, children as young as twelve spent their days weaving the beautiful, renowned rugs with one thousand knots to the inch.

On November 22 we awoke to see that we were completely fogged in and wondered how we would ever get off at 10:00. But as we drove out to the airport, the sun broke through, and we could see the Himalayas and the blue sky encircling them again. At the start of the runway, we all held our breath as the captain gunned the engines to their highest power. When he released the brakes, the plane took off as if it were attached to a bungee cord, and we raced the full length of the runway. Just as the mountains came in view in front of us, the captain lifted off, then banked sharply to the left (I had the left window seat), and it seemed like the left wing tip was going to touch a hilltop. The crew told us afterward that the plane was only one hundred feet off the ground when they banked. When we reached cruising altitude, Captain Stinson came back on the loudspeaker and wryly said, "It is safe to say that we have approximately 155 flying carpets on board"—referring to all the carpets people had bought at the Tibetan refugee camp the day before. Maybe they helped with the lift-off!

Since then, I've often pondered about the lives of these little girls who do not live a normal life at all. Some are said to have had a very difficult time adjusting to life outside of the palace after they begin to menstruate and automatically *lose their deity*. They are returned to their family, which receives a small stipend for life. Since they have been tutored in the palace, they can't cope with normal school life, and developing friendships with classmates is subject to doubts. When your entire life up till then has been as a deity, and everyone including the king has had as their goal to kiss your feet, one can only question why they would not be confused. All of the Kumari in recent times have married, but despite exhaustive research, no mention was made of their having had children. It raises the question as to whether the husbands are intimidated to make love to a goddess. (I know several who would consider it their God-given right.) Most Kumari are between three and four when they are chosen. Just when they are beginning to understand the meaning of words, they are forced to learn how to reflect their divinity to adults who turn to them for wisdom and piety. At the time we were there, a little girl called Rashmila Shakya was the Living Goddess. She reigned from 1984 to 1991, seven years. The most any girl has reigned is eleven years, several only two or three years. Assuming puberty began at around twelve (some did not menstruate until sixteen) and doing the math, she would have been ten when she was brought to the window to give us her blessing, seven when she was chosen, and would be thirty-eight in 2017. I wonder what became of her: Did she accept reverting to a human, with all their peculiarities that she knew nothing of? Some of the girls had to learn to walk at twelve. Did she have any friends? Did she live life with her parents as a teenager? Did she have a boy-friend, get married? I hope she is happy.

This was one of the stranger lessons in Faith that we had ever come across in our travels and so we go on, learning as we go.

How do we define Faith? Is it simply being able to believe in something so strongly that you don't require scientific proof? Webster defines it as an unques-tioning belief in God, religion, a particular religion, or *anything believed*. Are we able to set aside any doubts when something bad happens, especially when a friend says righteously, "It's God's will," and you want to scream at them, "Is that the vengeful God you believe in?"

In 1981, a rabbi, Harold S. Kushner, wrote a book called *When Bad Things Hap-pen to Good People*, which attracted a lot of philosophical discussion about faith. He wrote it after the death of his son, who at fourteen had died from premature ag-ing disease (progeria). He wanted to help people who have been hurt by life find a faith that can aid in getting through their troubles rather than making things worse. Kushner attributed the *orderliness of the universe* to God, but held that the *ordering* of the universe is not complete: Some things are just circumstantial, and there is no point in looking for a reason for them. Some suffering is caused by the workings of *natural law*. There is no moral judgment involved—natural law is blind, and God does not intervene to save good people from earthquakes or disease, and does not send these misfortunes to punish the wicked. Kushner put great value on the orderliness of the universe's natural law and would not want God to routinely intervene for moral reasons.

Then why are we faced almost every day with acts of mass killings in which the perpetrator has invoked the name of Allah? Or the Christian and Jewish massacres conducted in the name of religion? Or natural disasters? It is a question to which there is no ready answer. Some cultures believe in gods or goddesses, relying on myths and ancient legends to define their religion. They are mystical, so we presume the incidents never really existed. Strange things that our educated minds tell us could never have really happened. We know these myths or fables have a purpose: to teach us how to live moral, ethical lives. So that we may enter Heaven unscathed? We have been told of many near-death experiences when the person saw the great Light, so we tend to accept the possibility of Heaven. But are there any stories of people who have miraculously returned from the portals of Hell? Is Hell merely called upon to keep us on the straight and narrow? (I wonder if there is a separate anteroom in hell for Little White Liars, those of us who write memoirs?)

I think of religion as a braid of hair. Little bundles of different religions or beliefs that are woven together to form a whole. And at the bottom of the braid, they are held together by the rubber band of faith. Then the hair fans out again to become a jumble of all the differences. But what can we be sure of? The Greatest Mystery of all will remain a mystery until our fascination with technology enables us to resolve evolution versus creation to the most skeptical among us. It will not happen in my lifetime. As the end of my life nears, I feel the need to believe in something, so faith makes a hesitant reappearance. The rubber band that holds it all together. Technology may eventually be able to isolate the one minuscule cell scientists believe life came from. But the eternal question remains, Where did that original cell come from? And if we evolved, why do we still have apes? If we were created, Who or What created the Creator? The braid fans out below the rubber band. Some of the hair is frayed. Rabbi Kushner asked at the end of his book, *What good, then, is religion?* Is there an answer? If we mean "Is there an answer which will make sense of it all," then probably not. But if an answer is a Response and we can forgive the world for not being perfect, forgive God for not making a better world, reach out to the people around us, and go on living *despite it all*, we may have our answer.

AWT III—6

With a touch of sadness, we prepared to fly to Mahe in the Seychelles as our Voyage No. 3 was coming to a close. But after all the excitement and strangeness of Kathmandu and the relief we felt to reach cruising altitude, a little R & R would be welcome. We left Kathmandu at 10:00 a.m. and arrived in Victoria, Mahe, seven hours later. We enjoyed a morning snack on board and then, later, lunch, which included hot savories, pâté en croute, roast beef en jus, bouquetière of vegetables, seasonal salade, and pineapple gateau.

The Seychelles are a group of ninety-two little islands, a thousand miles due east of Kenya, each as perfect as a grain of sand found on their beaches. The Seychelles are renowned for the varied bird life living there. The little island of Praslin, which we visited the following day, is the only site where the black parrot is found. I don't remember seeing one. We were housed in the Seychelles Sheraton Hotel and really appreciated the icy air-conditioning to get out of the hot, humid tropicality of the islands. In one of the travel brochures about the Voyage 3, they say the Seychelles are like the Caribbean thirty years ago. Quieter. Softer. Lazier. One of the passengers was quoted: "I found myself on a beach spending a lot of time considering the difference between my right big toe and my left big toe and finding that I enjoyed the mental exercise." In that vein, while we do a bit of navel-gazing, it gives me a chance to tell you some of the tremendous planning and organization that went into this extraordinary trip. All the details are greatly condensed, but those readers who are inclined to question "How?" or "Why?" will have some of their questions answered. First, Air Canada had to plan the route for Voyage 3, but since they had had tremendous success and acclimation with Voyages 1 and 2, the experience they had gained stood them in good stead. Although Google let me down for the first time, I can't find the itineraries for 1 and 2. At least 30 percent of the passengers from the first two voyages signed up for Voyage 3. It took dozens of people and countless hours of work to ensure that the globe-circling tour was a success from start to finish. The woman in charge of current operations checked the scheduling to ensure that a 747 was available. Then they had to decide: How many passengers did they plan to carry? What would be the seating configuration of the aircraft? What type of service would be offered? Once all these details were known, a costing was worked out. She had to obtain all government operating licenses and overfly permits and, at each stop, all necessary arrangements for passenger handling and customs and immigration clearance. There were representatives from various departments of Air Canada, including aeronautical services, flight dispatch, flight operations, in-flight service, maintenance, load planning, and petroleum administration. When the detailed flight routing was established, the man in charge of flight dispatch had to provide the flight crews with aeronautical navigation charts and be prepared to handle any last-minute routing changes.

For example, just twenty hours before the flight was to leave Kathmandu for the Seychelles, they were advised that the Indian government had changed the routing. Through flight dispatch, Captain Stinson was advised of the change. On each flight leg, block-to-block times were calculated, and alternate routings and airports were chosen in case weather or an unforeseen situation caused a diversion. All this data was put into the flight planning system, which was reviewed and fine-tuned by the flight crew prior to each departure. The manager of performance engineering had to study each airport from an aircraft-takeoff-performance point of view. How long was the runway and what was its slope? What obstacles (mountains? buildings?) surrounded the airport? I think the Himalayas qualified as an "obstacle." What were the instrument approach details? Once all this information was gathered and analyzed, it was stored in a computerized airport data bank and used to develop a table of maximum takeoff weight limits for each airport. The ultimate challenge came with planning the arrival and departure procedures from Kathmandu. Nepal's capital lies at 4,386 feet above sea level and is surrounded by ten-thousand-foot "hills." ("They don't call them mountains if they don't have snow on them," Captain Stinson said.)

Captain Stinson was at the controls as we descended into Kathmandu. After passing over the 10,500 ft. ridge south of the city, the pilots had to descend at 1,500 to 1,600 feet per minute—double the normal descent rate—to establish a normal glide slope of 3 percent. It left no room for error: Beyond the end of the runway, he looked down into a valley. The departure was equally exciting. They studied the Kathmandu airport and the surrounding topography with a fine-tooth comb and drew up templates to determine what degree of bank was required after takeoff to provide obstacle clearance. Almost immediately after getting airborne, Stinson banked the 747 at a twenty-degree angle and spiraled up and out of the valley. For maintaining the aircraft all along the route, the supply-support manager assembled an extensive supply of aircraft spares which were placed in two cargo containers. *They were required to have a spare part for repairing any function that could have grounded the aircraft.* Then there was the manager whose duty was servicing the interior of the plane and replenishing the galleys with commissary supplies carried below deck in six containers. This was the manager who determined that when leaving Kathmandu, the maximum takeoff weight couldn't exceed 627,000 pounds, including the weight of the aircraft, fuel, passengers, etcetera, and he calculated that only two thousand pounds of additional baggage could be uplifted. "Because of this, passengers were asked to limit their purchase of Tibetan carpets," he said. Although we were warned not to buy too many large, heavy items, which as the trip progressed, could have caused a weight and balance problem, one man just couldn't resist buying two seven-foot statues, one weighing eight hundred pounds! (That was Don, our farmer from Toronto.) The manager convinced him to ship one of the statues back to Canada.

Along with world-class service came sumptuous meals and choice wines and liquors. The manager of in-flight services started the planning early. She had to work with the routing department to have reliable flight kitchens at each station, requesting three sample menus to be drawn up. She and two members of her department had to taste all of these sample meals, and grimaced a few times while eliminating some of the choices. When choosing a menu, many things have to be considered, such as local dishes and availability, and the catering group had to set up the galleys with everything from skillets and pepper grinders down to stir sticks and doilies. The commissary catering manager had to make sure that every meal served to the passengers was appealing to both the eyes and the taste buds. They exceeded all expectations.

Well, resting in Mahe was very soothing, and our air-conditioned buses took us to visit potters, an art studio, and a fascinating studio making model boats, some as large as three feet long. They were complete in every detail, with little cords for the ropes on the sailing masts and miniatures down in the cabins. They showed us how they "aged" the sails by dipping the white linen in steeped tea. They also showed us how they built the little miniatures that were placed in wine bottles. Each sail was hinged to lay flat, with a thread attached, and the whole structure collapsed to be wiggled inside the *neck* of the bottle; then the threads were pulled simultaneously to raise the sails and parts of the boat before sealing the bottle with a cork. One of the interesting purchases we made on this tour was fresh cinnamon bark being processed and packaged in a factory in the jungle. That was a purchase Captain Stinson did not object to. After lazy days and languid nights, we were now ready for a contrast. Busy, exciting ornate Vienna, cold temperatures, opera, orchestras, a palace, the triumph of music, and a huge surprise that no one could have guessed was coming.

The flight to Vienna was nine hours, and we looked out over the dry and desolate deserts of Somalia and Ethiopia; then we were over Jaffe and Mecca in the distance. We could even distinguish the black building that was Mecca with the double highway going around the buildings to accommodate the thousands of pilgrims. We flew over Suez and saw the tankers lined up, waiting to go through the canal. Then we flew over the Nile Valley and saw the pyramids before landing. As we approached Vienna, we expected to see snow, but everything was green. They had been having Foehn winds, blowing warm up from the south. The bus driver said that normally they would have ten inches of snow by the end of November. We found a postcard from Joana waiting for us at the Intercontinental Hotel, which was nice. We took a walk and saw the ornate Opernhaus with its tiled roof. We called the family from the post office on the twenty-sixth and wished the family a happy Thanksgiving.

The next day was the twenty-seventh of November, the last day of the trip and the first day of horrible weather: raining, cold, and windy. At 6:30 p.m. we took the bus to the Ferstel Palace, dressed in our evening gown and tux. The palace was very elegant, with high ceilings, arches, and chandeliers. At the doors were men dressed in medieval costumes with long staffs, which they tapped on the floor as we entered the ballroom. The pages tapped and announced each course of a magnificent meal and each wine while an orchestra played. The page tapped the floor and announced the big surprise: twenty-six little boys all dressed in sailor suits marched out from behind the curtains: the Vienna Boys Choir, who were giving us an exclusive concert. Their high voices were enchanting as they sang songs in different languages, showing the exceptional education they received.

It was a gala evening to close out a fantastic trip.

But Air Canada wasn't through with their surprises yet.

At ten o'clock the next morning, on our way out to the airport, they announced that we were stopping at the Spanish Riding School because they had gotten the riders to let us attend a private practice show. Out came the superb white stallions with the riders, and they danced to music, leaped with all four legs off the ground, and performed in unison like the Radio City Rockettes, only on horses. What a terrific goodbye!

At the speeches the night before, the president of Air Canada had summed up the numbers for us:

We had flown sixty-three hours, but if we had booked our flights on scheduled flights, we'd have had to fly fourteen days. And it would have cost $25,000 per person.

They held a contest on the flight from Toronto to Vancouver, to win one of the pilots' route maps if you guessed how many watches had been bought by the passengers in Chinatown in Kuala Lumpur. The answer was 301; I had guessed 317. Because of strikes and delays we had to go standby with Wardair to Kelowna and only got back to Kelowna at midnight on the twenty-eighth. But we had each only had one cold on the entire trip, and it was an extraordinary experience. Even Fritz had to rave about it.

15

No Closeness

Fritz had a lot of trouble having close relationships with other people, which was the result of his mother's lack of intimacy with any members of the family. Her mother was the friend of Rudolf Steiner, the developer of the Anthroposophy movement, which you would have thought would make her empathetic and affectionate, but she was cold to Fritz's father, Reinhard, who had a sense of humor and was convivial with his comrades. Fritz had few personal friends; he only associated with his work colleagues. Speaking only of business with them, he never developed warm, enduring friendships, except with Rodolfo Planas (one of his school classmates in Barcelona) and Werner Schmidt, one of his classmates who attended the Engineer School in Weimar and smuggled the forbidden jazz records into their apartments. Later, he had a close friendship with Jochen Rehm (fellow POW inmate). In the forties, he formed a close relationship with a Carrier colleague from Syracuse, Art Rynearson, and his family. He convinced Art to be his service manager in the office in Bogotá, Colombia, and then through many years after we were married, we had numerous get-togethers with our two families. Even today, I am so grateful for his son- and daughter-in-law's frequent, loving phone calls. I think Fritz's inability to warmly embrace true friends was part of the desire to take an inexperienced young girl like me and mold me into the Perfect Wife, devoted only to her revered husband.

16

A Millennium New Year's

On December 31, 1899, Captain John Phillips was on the bridge of his passenger ship, the *Warrimoo*. She was sailing from Vancouver to Australia. His navigator had taken a star fix and told him they were only a few miles from the intersection of the equator and the international date line. Captain Phillips knew exactly what that meant and decided to play a prank on everyone. He had the opportunity of a lifetime:

He carefully adjusted engine speed so that he would strike it at just the right moment. The calm weather, the clear night, and the eager cooperation of his crew all worked successfully in his favor. At *exactly* midnight local time, the *Warrimoo* lay *exactly* on the equator at *exactly* the point where it crosses the international date line.

The consequences of the bizarre position were many. The bow of the ship was in the southern hemisphere, in winter. The date in the aft part of the ship was December 31, 1899. Forward, it was now January 1, 1900. The ship was, therefore, not only in two different days, two different months, two different seasons, and two different years, but in two different centuries … and all at the same time.

The people on board the *Warrimoo* were undoubtedly the very first to greet the new century, and Captain Phillips, speaking of the event many years later, said:

"I have never heard of it happening before, and I guess it won't happen again until the year 2000!"

As Y2K approached, all the talk was, "Where are you going to be on New Year's Eve, to celebrate the millennium?" The papers and TV were filled with hypotheses of all that could or might go wrong: Computers were going to crash, the stock market would be chaotic, the list of dire predictions grew with each passing day. There was a lot of hype around the possibility of taking a cruise ship to the international date line.

Normally we would be celebrating the New Year's arrival in our condo on the lakefront in Kelowna, British Columbia, Canada, with a glass of spiked eggnog, in front of the telly, avoiding parties and drunken drivers, and counting down the final minutes with Dick Clark. Watching the sparkling ball descend in Times Square, kissing each other with the wish that the New Year would be a good one. Then, practically, getting to bed ten minutes later, after calling the kids in Tucson to wish them a Happy New Year, too.

By now, you surely know Fritz and his penchant for doing the unusual, especially in the realm of Travel with a capital T. So, when we began getting emails from the Crystal Cruise Line (because we had taken several cruises with them already) excitedly extolling their plans to be on the international dateline for the millennium, Fritz began salivating like Pavlov's dogs. The only catch was that if you wanted to be there—at that propitious moment—they wanted you to combine it with their Christmas cruise. Which would definitely require some soul-searching with our banker.

For Fritz, it became a fait accompli. How could I possibly not want to have the trip of a lifetime? He booked it on May 10, 1999, cashing in quite a few of our carefully hoarded gold coins. The Christmas cruise would depart from Sydney, Australia, on December 17, and the Millennium cruise from Auckland, New Zealand, on December 28—seventeen days in all. We would have two New Year's Days because we would "gain" a day sitting on the international date line. I had a mental picture of a vertical line of cruise ships stacked on the dateline.

Booking the trip through our travel agent at Sears in Kelowna was a novel experience. When we told her what we intended to do, she nearly fainted: It was the largest travel commission she and Sears had ever made, and I'm sure she was named employee of the year. We would be sailing on our beloved *Crystal*

Symphony, so it would be like coming home. We already knew Captain Maalen and many of the crew members, and the president of Crystal Cruises would be on the ship as well; we looked forward to seeing Joe Watters again, he was very congenial. We knew that Crystal would pull out all the stops to make this an extraordinary experience, a memory to hold in our minds and hearts forever. We awoke on December 15 (the day we were to fly out) to the first snowstorm of the winter in Kelowna. It was almost a blizzard, and our hearts sank as we doubted we would be able to leave. They still wanted us out at the airport, and we were amazed when our flight stayed on the board, delayed a half hour, while many got canceled. We made it to Vancouver, on a very bumpy flight, and then with Alaska Air and United we were finally on our way to Australia in the most crowded 747 ever. Four inches of legroom, and very narrow seats.

As the title of this book indicates, most of my thinking time was done on flights: Fritz had the window seat, a grossly obese guy had the aisle and slept the entire way, and I huddled in the middle. Fourteen hours without moving, no going to the john, no sleep (I felt it was my responsibility to listen to the engines with the pilot), sheer agony. Panic set in when we landed in Sydney, and our bags didn't appear. They were the last ones off! Crystal people met us and took us to the docks where we finally boarded the ship midafternoon. I fulfilled my first task: I unpacked our Christmas decorations for the door of our stateroom, which impressed our nice Swedish stewardess, Jenny.

There were 750 passengers for the Christmas cruise, and the Millennium was full: 900. The entire ship was lavishly decorated, everywhere. The newsletter in the rooms told us the lecturers would be actress Patricia Neal, actor Alan Arkin, Bob Feller, and two political lecturers: one a Stanford professor, and the other the guy who did the television series of the great ocean liners of the past. President Watters held a reunion party the first night for those passengers who had been on previous President's cruises, and it was nice to renew old acquaintances. We had several visits with Joe Watters; he gave everybody a silver picture frame for Christmas. The slogan "the Crystal Family" became a warm, fuzzy feeling as we also received visits from Tania, one of our former stewardesses. Mario, the maître d' for the Prego restaurant, and one of our former waiters switched stations with each other so he could serve our table by the window for this cruise, which we appreciated; Fritz never enjoyed sitting at a table with other couples, so we always reserved a small table for two at a window. As we sailed along the coastline of Australia to Melbourne and beyond, we had our first class in the computer lab, and I began making interesting projects in the craft programs each afternoon we were at sea, instead of shore excursions on the days we docked. Fritz used my craft time for a siesta, which he always proclaimed to be the best part of every day.

The most exciting thing on the Christmas cruise was sailing into Milford Sound in New Zealand at 7 a.m. on December 24. It's incorrectly named because it's actually a fjord, not a sound. Because it had rained the previous few days, there were waterfalls galore coming down the high mountains. The pilot who came on board to aid the captain said on the loudspeaker that they had turned the waterfalls "on" just for us, as they had all been dry the last time the *Symphony* had sailed up the Sound. At the end of the Sound was the spectacular Sterling Falls, and Captain Maalen got permission to turn the ship sideways in the narrow Sound. The wall of the falls was sheer and went straight down in the water, which was extremely deep, so he was able to get right up under the falls with the big ship. He nudged the ship's bow under the falls so that the people standing on the front of the bow got all wet. That was exciting, and the captain and the pilot made a lot of jokes. The president said, "I should have known Captain Maalen was up to something when he asked me to bring a bar of soap!" We received a beautiful orchid and daisies arrangement from Sears, as well as a bottle of wine, which we selected at the Christmas Eve dinner.

The Christmas Eve show *Symphony Style* was the complete cast of entertainers, singers, and dancers in an Evening of Christmas Favorites.

On Christmas Day, Santa arrived in the Palm Court in his big sleigh, pulled by some of the waiters, for the sixty-five children on board. He gave out presents to all the kids by name (the LA office must have a terribly big organization staff). When we arrived in Auckland, we went up to the top of the Skytower, a very high space needle with various observation decks, each offering spectacular views of the city. The main one has an outdoor walkway all around the core of the building. The floor of this walkway contains heavy sections of plate glass (with the reassuring plaque stating that the glass is as strong as the cement floor). You can stand on it and look straight down to the ground. As a person with a fear of heights I was giddy, with nothing between me and several hundred feet. I squeamishly hugged the wall as I inched over the glass. The saying goes: You know you've been on the cruise too long when you start to check the luncheon and dinner menu as you leave the dining room after breakfast. We checked it so we would know whether to do the lido buffet or mosey up to the sandwich bar that day for a delicious grilled tuna melt. Or, when you go to the ice cream bar for a cup of ice cream and the guy now knows you well enough to say, "What, no cone today?" The ice cream bar let you make your own concoctions, with candy and cookie crumbles, various sauces and syrups, and liqueurs to splash on. Brandy Alexander, or coffee liqueur, yum. The menus were gourmet, like nothing we would ever order in a restaurant in Kelowna, even on a very special occasion. There were always two or three entrées, so we would each choose a different one and then share bites from the other's plate. One afternoon the chefs gave a presentation in the dining room to show us how to get those artistic garnishes on a plate by dropping colorful fruit sauces and yogurt in dots and drawing a toothpick through them to create hearts and flowers on the plates. *"On mange avec les yeux."* (One eats with the eyes.) I was fascinated and couldn't wait to try it at home.

One of the lecturers was Jack Weatherford, a renowned professor at Macalester College, author of many books on anthropology and political analyses, and a commentator on PBS, the *Today* show, Larry King, and others. His subject was the Millennium in the Pacific. He spoke without notes and was very humorous. At the start of one of his lectures he said, "I know now why Crystal schedules my talk at 1:30 p.m., just after we've all enjoyed that fabulous Asian buffet on the lido—it's for people who don't want to sleep alone." Another speaker was a professor at Stanford who lectured on SETI, the Society for Extra-Terrestrial Investigation, and whether somebody out there is trying to contact us. (He had to admit they haven't heard anything yet.)

On December 31 we would arrive at Nuku'alofa, Tonga. It is said that Tonga is the land where time begins. Long ago, cartographers curiously drew the international date line to zigzag five hundred miles east of Tonga, therefore east of the 180 meridian. And this mapmaker's whimsical detour afforded Tonga the honor, thusly, of being the first land in the entire world to "see the new day." Some 150 to 200 islands sprinkled across 575 miles of the Pacific Ocean belong to Tonga. Of these, only three dozen or so are home to year-round residents who till the soils, fish the seas, and educate their children, who boast a 93 percent literacy rate. At 8:00 a.m. on Friday, December 31, 1999, the *Crystal Symphony* anchored off Nuku'alofa, the nation's capital, and we went in by ship tenders. A shuttle bus operated from the pier to the central downtown post office every half hour so that the passengers could take all their postcards (which we spent hours writing the day before) to be stamped as being the place officially designated as where the sun first shone for the twenty-first century, a treasured franking for stamp collectors. A lot of grandchildren would be receiving these postcards in about a month; they would be franked and posted the following day, January 1, 2000.

That afternoon it was time to get ready for our first New Year's celebration; the second one would occur the next night. The first night was the official formal celebration and the theme was an elegant black and white ball. The men wore tuxedos or dark suits, and the ladies looked glamorous in their elegant ball gowns and glittering jewels. Even though Fritz professed to loathe having to wear a tuxedo, I think he actually enjoyed dressing up for this very special occasion. I wore a simple long silvery knit skirt with a slit up one side, a sleeveless silver knit top, and a black-on-black patterned satin jacket. I wore a unique piece of jewelry: Only 750 pieces were created, and each is numbered and certified. I felt it was the ideal occasion to wear the "oldest watch in the English-speaking world" (according to the *Times*, 1938). A Saxon pocket sundial—dated approximately 980 AD—made of gold and silver, was found during alterations to the Cloister Garth at Canterbury Cathedral. It was reproduced for the Ransom Gallery in London by the artist Alastair Melville, who first saw the sundial in the horological wonders at the Science Museum. Only 750 replicas were produced as a strictly limited edition. Fritz felt it would become a good investment over time, and I was thrilled to own such a beautiful piece of history. Being a jeweler,

I often choose to wear something that has a special meaning or significance for me, rather than just choosing something that matches the outfit.

The soup course blew me away with little flakes of 24K gold leaf floating on the top of bouillon, with julienned vegetables. I told Fritz that that should prevent my arthritis from developing, and he scooped out his flakes and added them to my bowl.

The menu contained the following wish:

As the moon sets on the silvery waves, history holds its breath in anticipation of the new millennium. May the golden moments of the past join together with the sparkling promise of the future for an evening of magic.

The entrée was served on a plate especially made for the cruise by Villeroy & Bosch, an iconic German bone china factory. It was cream-colored, with a black clock face with the hands pointing at 5 after 12. The next morning, they delivered the two plates to us as gifts, including a large stand to hold one on. It has pride of place in my China cabinet. The dinner was followed by dancing in the Galaxy Lounge until 11:45, but we left early to garner good seats for the countdown and champagne in the Crystal Cove, the main reception area. This space contained a large waterfall normally, but for this occasion they had installed sparkly black-and-white tall panels in front of the waterfall, with a clock built in and lots of black, white, clear, and silvery balloons. At 11:45 the captain and several of the officers came to the stage, the captain made a speech, telling us that we were anchored on the international date line, and then they counted down. Some cannons went off, with confetti. We were officially into the new century, one day before the rest of the world. In all our travels, I had the feeling that this was a truly momentous occasion and felt the thrill that Captain Phillips's passengers must have felt one hundred years earlier. Fritz's dream had come true.

The next day, the *Symphony*'s daily newsletter's headline read, "December 31 disappears!" But as our ship turned around and pointed its bow back across the dateline, it was December 31 again as we headed toward Apia, Samoa. But now we were celebrating the second New Year's Eve, the night when all the rest of the world celebrated it. The newsletter's headline that day read, "December 31, 1999, again!"

The second New Year's Eve was casual instead of formal, and it was based on an intergalactic theme where the passengers were dressed up like Darth Vader, including some of the crew members. They had gotten it all set up on the lido deck when the winds and rain started, so at 9:15 they started moving all the booths downstairs to the lobby. They had a lot of games you could play for points and win prizes. (Like E.T., Call Home where you had to throw cellphones through holes.) It was fun seeing our waiters and stewardess costumed up, having a great time. At midnight the guns shot off confetti and streamers again. (By breakfast time, the foyer was pristine.)

On Saturday, January 1, 2000, we docked at Apia, Samoa, probably most notable as the last home of Robert Louis Stevenson, who had escaped from Scotland's dampness seeking a climate which might aid in his fight against tuberculosis. In 1889 he set up his home in Vailima. Today, this home is the prime minister's residence, and the grounds are open to the public. Stevenson died four years later and is buried there. His famous poem "Requiem" contains the familiar lines "Under the wide and starry sky, / Dig the grave and let me lie … *Home is the sailor, home from the sea …*" In Stevenson's directions to Samoa, as quoted by Mark Twain's 1897 work "More Tramps Abroad": "You go to America, cross the continent to San Francisco, and then it's the second turning to the left."

We reached Fanning Island on January 4. Fanning Island is the Republic of Kiribati … and the great God Nareau picked flowers from the tree of the ancients and scattered them across the ocean north of Samoa … an ancient Kiribati legend explaining the origin of the islands. Fanning Island is a low-lying arid atoll in the shape of a footprint. As the ship approached, the island looked at first like a huge grove of coconut palms in the middle of the sea. As we came closer, we saw the shapes of small huts with thatched roofs. Because the climate is always warm but subject to cyclones, the hut walls are woven from coconut fronds. Each shelter is only a single room. Fanning Island houses usually consist of a set of huts, each one designated by function, such as sleeping room, dining area, or kitchen. The floors are bare earth covered with gravel, and sleeping bags are unrolled every night on them and rolled back up the next morning. There are no solid walls to obstruct sights or sounds, as the people prefer to be in touch with their environment. They practice ancestor worship: Living elders impart their wisdom only to those who are deemed worthy. (As I approach ninety-two, I find this an interesting concept.)

One day the newsletter quoted the Best Puns of the Millennium. My favorite was: Mahatma Ghandi never wore anything on his feet, and he ate so little that he developed delicate health and bad breath. The result was a super-callused fragile mystic plagued with halitosis. Another was, Better watch out, or my karma will run over your dogma.

The rest of the cruise was at sea most days with two ports of call, Honolulu and Kailua, so I had lots of time to indulge in arts and crafts. I made glasses cases in needlepoint, painted watercolors, folded origami; I was in my element, a different project every day. It was a friendly group of like-minded ladies who met in one of the lounges to watch the guest crafter or artist arrange the supplies for that afternoon's project. All the projects and materials were supplied by Crystal. And, of course, the wonderful entertainment every evening! Crystal ships have shows worthy of the finest Las Vegas productions, hiring singers and dancers from the States, England, and Europe. They also featured comedians, magicians, and classical musicians from Juilliard, as well as lecturers from the Smithsonian, authors, and entertainment personalities. On the last evening of every Crystal cruise, the lead male singer always sings the song made famous by Andrea Bocelli, "Con te partiró" (It's time to say goodbye). It is such a beautiful song and such a haunting melody that Fritz and I always felt very emotional as it was sung first in Italian and then in English, holding hands and thinking what a wonderful time we had had. At Fritz's memorial service five years later, I chose that duet of Andrea Bocelli and Sarah Brightman singing "Con te partiró." I think he would have liked it.

17

The Perfect Wife

When Fritz proposed and put the engagement ring on my finger, he mentioned that while small, it was a perfect stone. That comment should have rung a bell, if not actually set off an alarm. But when you are looking at the world through rose-colored glasses, who's listening to alarms? Fritz's preoccupation with perfection only became apparent slowly, over time. I worshiped the ground he walked on and wanted desperately to please him.

Just little things, at first: What would he like for breakfast? Lunch? Dinner? What section of the paper did he wish to read first? Was this outfit appropriate for dinner with the so-and-so's, his Carrier colleagues? Fritz didn't seem to care particularly one way or the other, and so I didn't worry; I just went on my blissful way. Then in the weeks and months that followed our wedding in September, 1946, I began hearing that I had said something foolish, or done something out of naïveté, and I began to get the feeling that I wasn't pleasing him. I attributed it to "the honeymoon is over" syndrome, and redoubled my efforts. I still reveled in the wonder that such a sophisticated, worldly man had seen something in me that he found attractive, something that he had not found in his previous girlfriends. He had told me about the carefree parties in Colombia, and the girls he had dated in Syracuse. I was amazed that he was still a bachelor at the age of thirty. When I asked him what the girls had been like (hoping to get a hint about what he admired), he would just indicate that it had always been a group of friends that did things together. It remained a mystery that he would

182

find anything attractive about a young girl who had never traveled, who knew nothing about other cultures, and whose only exposure to the world outside of Auburn came through avidly reading books. It was a puzzle that I recognized, but had no way of solving.

The answer came some thirty years later as I watched the film *My Fair Lady* on a flight from London to Johannesburg and heard the steward say that it came from George Bernard Shaw's *Pygmalion*. The story and plot fascinated me, and I read about it. Audrey Hepburn's role had such a familiar feel to it.

In Greek mythology, Pygmalion is most familiar from Ovid's narrative poem *Metamorphoses*. He was a sculptor on Cyprus. According to Ovid, after becoming disgusted by some local prostitutes, Pygmalion lost all interest in women and avoided their company completely. Pygmalion saw women as "flawed creatures" and vowed never to waste a moment of his life with them. He dedicated himself to his work and soon created Galatea, a beautiful statue of a woman, out of ivory. Perhaps he sought to correct in ivory the flaws he saw in women of flesh and blood. As he finished the statue's features, they became exquisitely lovely, and he found himself applying the strokes of hammer and chisel with increasing affection. When his chisel finally stopped ringing, there stood before him a woman of such perfection that Pygmalion fell deeply in love. He made offerings at the altar of Aphrodite, the goddess of love. Too scared to admit his desire, he quietly wished for a bride who would be "the living likeness of my ivory girl." When he returned home, he kissed his ivory statue and found that its lips felt warm. He kissed it again and found that the ivory had lost its hardness. Aphrodite had granted Pygmalion's wish.

In Shaw's play, the girl is brought to life by two men specializing in perfect speech—the challenge was to take a street urchin for six weeks, drill her relentlessly in how to speak, and for their masterpiece to then marry and become a duchess.

At last, I had the answer to "Why." Fritz had found me attractive because I was so unformed in my youthful inexperience and virginal purity that he felt he could take the lump of clay that I represented and carefully form and mold it into the perfect wife. Or perhaps a clearer analogy might be a chunk of marble that the sculptor slowly chipped away until (as Michelangelo described the process) a figure emerged. Falling in love with one's creation and then getting the desired object as wife was perhaps in Fritz's subconscious.

Unfortunately, the chipping away was a long painful process for me. Little hurts, little cuts, all designed to create something beautiful, but without the loving explanation of how or why it was being done. No teaching, no guidance along the path, just criticism, correction, and more criticism, with the result that I constantly felt like a failure. I was convinced that I could never reach that exalted plane, where I would be put on a pedestal and proclaimed Finished—a true Work of Art. Gradually, through all of our travels and living in foreign countries, and my vigorous attempts to adjust to every life-changing event, I think Fritz came to believe that my determination in the light of so much adversity was something he could admire. I once heard him say to someone that I had learned to speak German, Spanish, and Portuguese while actually living in those countries; that was not easy to pick up as an adult. (He spoke German and Spanish as his mother tongues.) He laughed as he explained, "Of course, she doesn't speak them *perfectly*, but she does speak them fluently, and she's not afraid to try." I remember feeling so grateful that I had at last succeeded in doing something right, winning his considered approval.

The ordeal of trying to achieve perfection finally resolved itself one day when I was in my seventies, wondering idly what did make The Perfect Wife, and I made a joke to myself: Fritz would be happy if he could combine Audrey Hepburn and Princess Grace. I realized instantly that that wasn't going to happen! From that moment of discovery, I began to relax, just did the best I could, became the best I could become, and let the rest go. Then I laughed as I remembered it had been Audrey Hepburn who had played Eliza Doolittle in My Fair Lady, the little Cockney who spoke with such a low-class dialect that Henry Higgins had taken his friend's bet and, with cold, determined doggedness, turned her into a Princess Grace, and later realized that in the process *had fallen in love with her.*

The First Check

Yesterday was a game-changer. It also happened to be Mother's Day. I won't ever forget it.

Yesterday morning I received an email with the subject Happy Mother's Day! It was from my friend Alison, who is the publisher of modernphoenix.net. I had written to ask her a few months ago if she knew the address of Nancy Beadle, the widow of the architect who designed and built our two glass houses in Phoenix in the fifties. I had written a chapter about the experience, and since Al went on to become internationally famous for his glass "Beadle Boxes" I wanted Nancy to read it and give her consent.

Alison wrote back that she would like to see it too, because she was in charge of Modern Phoenix Week in which they toured Beadle houses in the Phoenix area. She also told me about the complete Beadle Archives being stored in the Arts Library of the Arizona State University in Tempe, where visitors from all over the world could access them. I offered to donate all of the original floor plans, colored renderings Al had made of our houses, and the eight-by-ten-inch professional photographs that had been taken over the years for various magazines and newspapers. I told Allison she could pick it all up, and she drove down from Phoenix. She was thrilled to see my collection of Beadle memorabilia and to find out that the first house Al designed for us in 1952 had to be one of his very first client-ordered works, which had never been recorded. She also reported that Nancy was overjoyed to read the article, but had had a stroke and could no longer express her thoughts well. We had a fun visit, and I knew that I could trust her to do what was best for the collection. Alison wrote me that the article gave so much personal detail about Al's character that she wanted to publish it herself rather than have it chopped up and winnowed down to a smaller version in a *Homes* magazine, and offered to help critique it. We went to work on it, and she inserted all of the photos showing the construction and design details for which Al was so famous.

Today the revised version was in my inbox: it was perfect. Attached were a W-9 form, which I had to sign for tax purposes, and a contract: two full pages of fine print with more "whereases" and "wherefores" that only a roomful of lawyers could dream up. Alison was offering me $550 for the article! I had goose bumps. My first *paid* publication! When the check arrives, I shall photograph it and hang it on the wall over my computer, like the people who frame their first dollar.

I am so grateful to have found a safe place which will preserve Al's work and the collection I donated. I'm so glad that Nancy got to read my tribute to Al and to know how deeply he influenced the way I live. I'm happy that I lugged rolled-up floor plans and paintings all over the world each time we moved to a new location.

But last night something else occurred to me as I reflected on what a nice Mother's Day I had had. I poured a glass of wine and went out on the patio to think. I looked back on that night in the auditorium of the University of British Columbia in February of 2008, when my name was called to receive the bronze trophy for best designer of the year, and the pride I felt, that my decision to start a career at the age of seventy-eight had been so validated. As we were leaving the auditorium after the ceremony, the lady walking next to me remarked, "Your husband would have been so proud of you." I smiled and nodded, but I ruefully thought … Little do you know! If my husband had still been alive and had to sit in the audience while his wife was in the spotlight on the stage, he would have been inwardly seething at the slight to his importance. And that trophy would have found its place behind some books in the bookcase.

But this time it was different. First, I had mentioned Fritz's name prominent-ly throughout the article on Al. I had explained how each of them felt the need to be "right" and the compromises they worked out. I had written about how important Fritz's work had been to bring refrigerated air-conditioning to the des-ert. Fritz's life revolved around Carrier; he smiled when I told people the blood circulating in his veins was "Carrier blue." Alison had even dredged up an ad for Carrier room air conditioners from the fifties and inserted it in the article, which would have pleased Fritz to no end. His name would be preserved for years to come in the Beadle Archives in the Cultural and Arts Library of Arizona State University for the people researching midcentury modern architecture. And, lastly, my article was deemed worthy enough to receive payment. Cold, hard cash trumps a trophy anytime. He would have finally been proud of me. I suddenly felt a surge of relief flow over me as I realized that thirteen years after Fritz had died, I had become the Perfect Wife I had aspired to for fifty-nine years. I drained my glass and walked into the cool house.

Reflections

I recently finished a murder-mystery book called *The Cat Sitter's Pajamas*, by Blaise Clement, and I was very impressed with her profound thinking on a number of issues. In fact, I left the book on my kitchen table open to the page and kept reading her thoughts over and over again for several days. I realized that she had hit a nerve in my own beliefs and that I agreed with her concepts very strongly. Her main character was expressing her thoughts (following the theme of the book about fake designer clothes, with designer labels that were being marketed illegally with large profits realized in the sales). It was about the phoniness that pervades almost every aspect of life today—so much so that we tend to take it for granted. Not just phony political rhetoric ("fake news?"), but phony smiles and phony conversations by ordinary people in which nobody says what they really think. Photographs can have settings or people added or removed. Recordings of speeches or conversations may actually be random words spliced together. Athletes enhance their performances with muscles falsely created by steroids. Many people wear fake labels on their shoes, watches, jeans, and handbags to impress with what they think brings status. Does living in a phony world change the way our brains and cellular structures operate? I wonder. If we accept phoniness, will we do away with honesty and integrity altogether? The author questioned if we would make up new selves from day to day, with no obligation to mop up the messes the old selves had made. Most important of all, is it possible to be real in today's phony world? I find myself growing more concerned every day about the superficiality of today's lifestyle. A couple celebrating their wedding anniversary at an expensive restaurant, staring at their iPhones all during dinner. Is it any wonder that people are communicating constantly but saying less? They are so busy with life that Life is passing them by. Children are kept amused and entertained with games played on iPads, where the goal is to kill or damage something, but what is happening to their capacity to imagine, to think creatively and to spend quiet time reading good books that could stimulate their minds instead of their bodies? I worry.

I think back to my own childhood and the neighborhood we lived in. No computers, TV, internet, Skype, or Angry Birds. And the most Candy Crush we ever got was at Halloween, when we piled too much candy in our bags.

But when Dad put the revolving water sprinkler on out in the front yard after supper (we didn't do dinner back then), and the kids two doors down or the ones across the street heard us screaming and leaping over the sprinkler, it wasn't long before the whole neighborhood was in our front yard, with the parents enjoying a cool lemonade on the front porch. Some nights it would be out to the back garden where we would be handed a pint Mason jar from Mom's canning supplies. Dad had punched slits in the lid with a hammer and screwdriver, and we would run around in the dark catching fireflies and screwing the lid on fast to watch the growing collection blink on and off. All that running and leaping and catching wore us out enough that our parents usually read only one chapter of a book after we were in bed, before we fell contentedly to sleep. When kids are taught that their tees have to have a famous name on them and their jeans have to cost $75 and come with premade torn knees, it makes you wonder: Kids learning about status in kindergarten? This preoccupation with wealth and prestige; dear God, it has become an addiction worse than the computer. Why? Why do some people think that that sort of thing makes you more important, gives you more standing, *fulfills some kind of destiny*? It never used to be that way. Where did Americans go so wrong?

I was tempted to stop there and let everyone ponder the question. But then I knew that my writer friends would niggle me, "Tell us how you feel. What do you think is the answer?" I felt maybe I should make some attempt to figure out what had changed us so much.

If you were able to ask my husband Fritz, he would immediately tell you, "Blue jeans!" For him, blue jeans were the invention of the devil and the demise of civilization. You may laugh, but for someone who was brought up in Europe, where dressing for the occasion is an important part of the image you present to the world, casual blue jeans for the office or a party is anathema. An insult. And it wasn't a matter of a generation gap or prestige. Back then, jeans didn't sell for $250. They were Levis or, later, Wranglers, and in Fritz's opinion they represented sloppiness, and meant that the person did not care enough to respect his position. It was this *beginning of not caring* that was defined by blue jeans. He never owned a pair and always wore a business suit.

I, on the other hand, have often thought that Kennedy's assassination was the beginning of the end. When we sat in our living room in Phoenix on Friday, November 22, 1963, and saw Walter Cronkite look up into the camera and with a choked voice say, "The President has died," it seemed as if the world had come to a standstill. And when our hearts started beating again, it was a different world than what we had known. It had changed for the worse, with a long slide downhill.

In 1965 we moved to Switzerland for a career change, and for forty-four years we were away from the States, with only two- or three-week home leaves each year while Fritz was still working for Carrier. The first trips back home were from Zürich, where honesty and integrity are such a way of life; we became aware that our former neighbors were eager to tell us about their new cars, their larger television sets, their larger houses, their luxury vacations. On the way back to Switzerland in the airplane, we reflected on how they had become more preoccupied with money; it confused us. It didn't used to be that way. They used to join us for hamburgers on our patio of the house in Phoenix and talk about our kids, the parent-teacher meetings, their jobs, their volunteering for the United Way, and the funny antics of Lucille Ball or Milton Berle or Jackie Gleason on the newly evolving magic of television. These were the Eisenhower/Truman years when normal, decent guys ran the country, everyone had a stable job in middle management, and life was pretty dependable after the shock of the Kennedy assassination semiresolved itself. After a few trips back to the States when doubts and discomfort took over the pleasure of home leaves, we began taking our home leave from Brazil and Puerto Rico in Zürich where we felt more comfortable. My mother, who was now widowed, visited us in Switzerland and England, and my sister's family visited us in England instead of us going back to the States. Several American friends visited us in Spain and enjoyed participating in our simple lifestyle there. Then we retired in Canada and found ourselves able to stay for two months each winter in Tucson, helping out with the grandchildren and getting more involved with my jewelry business while attending the gem show. We began accepting the reality of how the United States had changed to a more ego-centered, monetary-consumed NIMBY community, polarized by two strongly-held points of view politically. But we were always so relieved to leave that pervasive emphasis on money and prestige, money and status, money and phoniness, and go back home to Canada. We even considered changing our citizenship status because we were so much more in tune with the Canadian people and their more laid-back approach to everything. In the end, Fritz decided he could not give up the American citizenship he had fought so hard to re-establish, as described in another chapter. We tried to ignore the emphasis on money, politics, and me-me-ism, and were appreciative of the fact that we had another go-to place available.

Blaise Clement also made some comments in her book pertaining to private emotions. We feel sorry when we read about the death of a person who was killed by a drunk driver, shot by a drug-seeking teenager, or killed in some political terror act. We feel sorry that we belong to a species that includes beings who have lost their minds and souls to such an extent they can destroy another being, even little children. We feel sorry for the anguish the victims' deaths have caused their families and friends.

But the sadness isn't personal. It doesn't change my life. The feeling is pure self-centeredness. Joana has a very good friend she has known for many years (she also thinks of me as her mother) and gifts me with orchids on Mother's Day and gift cards at Christmas. But she has a fetish about owning name-brand items. Knockoffs just don't cut it. So one year, Joana gave her a clay plaque to hang on the wall. It says, "If I die in Walmart, please drag my body into Neiman Marcus." She loved it.

The year 2016 will go down in history as the most contentious, anger-inducing, frightening election experience Americans have ever gone through. And now with the strong emotions generated about immigration, terror threats, nuclear threats, possibilities of more wars, ignoring starvation in Africa, worldwide poverty, and lack of jobs, will Americans ever, ever regain their reputation of being a generous people, a welcoming people, a compassionate people who formed a nation where the Statue of Liberty symbolized a new world of opportunity for those arriving by ship from war-torn, poverty-stricken areas of the world? America used to take pride in being the "melting pot": That multiculturalism produced the delightful diversity that engaged us. When did our compassion end? Fritz thought it ended with the invention of Levis. I think it ended with Kennedy's death, when hardness and disillusionment engulfed our souls. Only time will tell.

18

Apologies to Erma

A great many people remember fondly the writings of Erma Bombeck, the humorist who wrote weekly columns, appeared on the *Today* show, and wrote books on everyday life as a suburban wife in Phoenix, Arizona, in the sixties, seventies, and eighties. Erma wrote *The Grass Is Always Greener over the Septic Tank* in 1976, and it became a bestseller in 1978. But I'd never heard of her because my husband and I left Phoenix in 1965 and lived abroad for forty-four years. Fritz had worked for Carrier Air Conditioning for thirty-nine years, but in 1971, while we were living in San Juan, Puerto Rico, he decided to retire to Spain.

Fritz had grown up in Barcelona, and kept close contact with his friends from the German school there. When one of his friends, Hans Hoffman, became the German consul in Malaga, we would always stop by the consulate for a long lunch with him on our vacations to Spain. On one of those visits in 1968, Hans sold us two acres of land in a finca (plantation) that he had developed over the years. It was called Finca La Cancelada, between Marbella and Estepona on the oceanside of the coastal highway, forty-five minutes from Gibraltar. The finca had been a sugar plantation: a large piece of land which Hans had divided into parcels; he outlined each parcel with oleander hedges and put in gravel roads, and our water supply was a freshwater spring up in the mountains which he had funneled down to the finca's water reservoir. Once the decision was made, we packed up once more, arranged to ship our furniture, and in early 1971 flew to Madrid, with our furniture going into storage in Malaga on the Costa del Sol.

192

After two months in Madrid, we received our residencia permit to live permanently in Spain and promptly moved to the finca, into a furnished apartment over the garage of an existing villa. There were twenty villas in the finca belonging to English, Belgian, German, and American expats. We even had a former Russian princess living there.

Using the floor plan of a house we had visited during an open house the previous winter in Tucson, we found an architect in Marbella who recommended a Danish contractor whom he felt would be reliable (because he spoke English) and started building our retirement villa. The contractor's truck had the motto painted on the side panels: "For peace of mind while building—Cunild." That motto obviously leads to a future story: Whether it turns out humorous, or one of those stark, raving mad "what were we thinking?" stories remains to be seen. Two months after we started, while pouring the foundations of the house, my husband got a call from Carrier asking him to come back to work as a consultant on a temporary project. None of the houses at the finca had any telephones; in fact, in 1971 we didn't even have television. Carrier had called a nearby hotel, and a messenger came to the apartment requesting that he call Carrier immediately. Fritz accompanied the messenger back to the hotel, where he found out that the consulting job was in England, not Spain, and would start immediately. Carrier had purchased a factory on the Isle of Wight; they wanted to turn it into a manufacturing entity for Carrier window air conditioners to ship and sell in Europe. It was to be a six-week assignment.

Being a workaholic, how could he refuse? Then began the rationalizing: "You love designing and building houses." And "You learned to speak enough Spanish in Puerto Rico to finish up building the house." No problem. Fritz rented a super studio apartment just off Hyde Park Square in London and traveled weekly to the Isle of Wight, getting the factory in operation. I coped with workmen, most of whom were former fishermen. I began turning my Spanish 101 into Advanced Conversational Spanish as Fritz took off for London and I was left at the finca to begin picking up great cuss words in Spanish, and construction words like *vigas* (beams), *techo* (roof), *azulejos* (tiles), and *posso negro* and *posso blanco* (septic tanks: poop and pee, in that order). Every two to three months he would fly down to the finca and deal with whatever crisis needed to be straightened out. The six-week assignment interlude turned into a year and a half. There would be the occasional messenger treading the by-now well-worn path from the hotel phone to my door, and a pleading message from my husband to join him in London for a few weeks. Eventually the villa got built, and we had the celebratory paella party for the workers when the tiled roof was finished and they hung the Spanish flag from the chimney. We hired a gardener who planted geranium clippings from the neighbors' gardens, hibiscus plants, bougainvilleas, and a lot of grass, little plugs by little plugs.

On September 14, 1971, we celebrated our twenty-fifth anniversary by going to a nursery and buying a large mimosa tree. We planted it in the front courtyard and christened the house *Villa Mimosa*. We enjoyed sitting on the porch with our neighbors with our gin and tonics, watching the ferries pass by on their way to Morocco.

When we began getting visitors from the States, mostly friends from Arizona, I had to begin explaining why there was one large square on our front lawn that was greener than the rest. And that was when they told me all about Erma Bombeck and her wonderfully funny wit. Erma died, beloved by all her fans, in 1996. Thank you, funny girl. And yes, the grass really is always greener over the septic tank.

Peace of Mind while Building

When we began building our villa in Spain in 1971, we found an excellent architect in Marbella who accepted our wish for a house we had seen in Tucson at a Sunday open house. We had taken the brochure with us, and the Spanish architect was able to draw up the floor plan in Spanish while changing the exterior to reflect the Spanish influence by adding some arches and curved tile roofs and whitewashing everything. Add a few bougainvilleas, and voilà, instant Spain with a touch of American practicality. When we asked about a responsible contractor, the architect had an immediate solution: a Danish man who had built a lot of the architect's houses for foreigners, because he spoke English; I would be able to communicate with him while Fritz was up in England, establishing a factory for Carrier on a consultant basis, which was supposed to last only a few weeks. And to clinch it, Cunild's motto printed on his construction truck was "For peace of mind while building." What could be more reassuring than that? Fritz took off, the architect came out to supervise, and the workmen dug the trenches for the foundation of the house. Then Cunild arrived, followed by three slowly revolving cement trucks ready to release their mixture into the reinforced excavations for our Forever House. (We expected to live out our retirement years in Spain.) Moving up the dirt road from the beach at a measured pace, the first cement truck drove straight off the narrow path down into a ditch while the other two trucks followed like lemmings so that all three full cement trucks were tilted on their sides with the left wheels spinning in the air. It is fair to say that at that point my "peace of mind" vanished into thin air. Cunild called a tow truck to get them righted. Eventually, the house did get built, and was known as the best-built house on the Costa del Sol, able to withstand a strong earthquake. The fact that the Costa del Sol had never experienced an earthquake was beside the point.

Double O-7

When we were living in Spain on the Costa del Sol during the 1970s, boredom was the most pernicious danger. Not for tourists, of course, just for those of us who had retired there. I compared it to the Brazil we had left behind in 1970: for the tourists who came during the two weeks of Carnival and thought Rio was so glamorous. But for us who lived there the other fifty weeks out of the year, it was living with the fear of kidnapping and holding American executives for ransom, the danger, and the poverty of the favelas (slums). Sometimes being a tourist and a resident were miles apart.

In Spain in the seventies, our life would have been considered idyllic. Our villa was located on the Mediterranean: two hectares of land, views of the daily ferry to Casablanca, sunshine every day, moderate temperatures. Fresh fruits and veggies cultivated on our own land. Our gardener very proudly informed us that he had gotten some *patatas californias* from another gardener and would be planting them. Turned out they were sweet potatoes. With fresh seafood brought in at seven every morning by the overnight fishermen and a shopping trip to the *mercado* where you bought it two hours later, the fish almost still flopping. And let's not forget that back then you could take your empty bottles into the *botega* in Estepona and refill them from the huge wine barrels for fifty cents. The intoxicating smell of the wine drips mixed into the sawdust on the floor. What's not to like about all that?

Our daily routine ran with a late breakfast and lunch at 2:30, followed by a two-hour siesta, and then we began our daily walk around the finca. Down the gravel paths, between the oleander hedges, over to pluck a luscious ripe fig from the tree of an absentee owner, down to the Eucalyptus woods, out to the beach, greeting the patrolling tricornered patent-leather-hatted Guardia Civils, and back up to the house until we saw someone waving at us from their porch or patio, inviting us to stop for a while. We enjoyed afternoon visits with the English, German, Belgian, and American neighbors; we even had a Russian princess living on our finca. (She wasn't all that interesting: She had received a settlement in her divorce which allowed her to buy her little villa, but it was mostly about those fifty-cent bottles of wine.) As it was, unfortunately, with two other residents: both Americans. All we had to decide was which language we felt like speaking that day as we sipped the G&Ts on whoever's porch we had chosen to stop at. The conversations were mostly gossip about who was coming or going. (The "goings" were important to know, because we would all scramble to write letters to family so that the person leaving for England, or sites beyond, could take the letters and mail them from there for quicker delivery.) Because we lived part-time in England, we became the unofficial postman for the finca. We were not only smelling the flowers in the sumptuous gardens the gardeners maintained for us, we had time to smell the sea, smell the eucalyptus, smell the garlic cooking somewhere, well, you name it, we had the time to smell it. What we didn't have was a library, a telephone, a television set, a daily paper, or English magazines. When we had occasion to visit our doctor in Marbella, you never heard us complain about his year-old magazines in the waiting room: He was English, so at least you got to read up on the royal family, even if the magazines were two scandals behind. You had to drive seven miles to the nearest town to buy a copy of the *Paris Tribune* or *USA Today* (which arrived two days late). There was Spanish TV but, in the evening, it consisted mostly of telenovelas which were popular soap operas and had the craziest, most unrealistic plots ever. Our English neighbors tuned to a two-hour radio program with a Cockney DJ on the Marbella station every evening. And certainly no internet or Skype; long distance was used only to announce a death, from a nearby hotel telephone. My mother (bless her!) would mail me rolled up magazines *Woman's Day* and *Family Circle* every month, an event I looked forward to eagerly.

But with all of that, I liked our trips to the finca. I have always enjoyed many hobbies, and during the finca years I was into silk-screening and calligraphy, so the peace and quiet of finca life was very pleasant. I silk-screened all our Christmas cards at the finca and then would take them up to England to be posted because we spent all our Christmases there. Fritz, on the other hand, was bored out of his mind. He was a business manager, and with no office staff to boss around, he couldn't stand it. Secondly, I think he had secretly expected to have more contact with his friend and schoolmate Hans Hoffmann, talking about the old days in Barcelona and absorbing the prestige of the consul's office. But Hans had become the German consul in Malaga and was far too busy to take time for lunches or visits with Fritz. Thirdly, since Fritz was the only resident at the finca who spoke Spanish as his mother tongue, the other owners would save up their grievances or problems until we arrived and ask Fritz to resolve them with city hall in Estepona, or with their gardeners, and he resented becoming their messenger boy.

For excitement, we had the luxury of pulling up stakes and leaving for London every couple of months where we took in all the new plays, gallery openings, and free museums, and of course, Fritz would go into the Carrier office and chat with the employees. In Spain we would drive into Marbella and head to the port called Puerto Andaluz, where we would meander slowly up and down the quais looking at the luxurious yachts moored there and play the game of which one would we choose if we had *Lifestyles of the Rich and Famous*, the Robin Leach TV program that was so popular in the States then. Further out in the harbor would be a ship the size of a small cruise ship, with a heliport on the top deck and a large tender anchored at its side, and we would know that one of the nouveau oil riche Arab princes was there somewhere on the dock enjoying the same fresh, hand-thrown pizzas we were enjoying. The contrast between the yachts in the port and our simple daily life at the finca was interesting and made for great letters back to the folks at home. In the hills surrounding Marbella were the second homes of famous actors, diplomats, and well-known celebrities. Willy Messerschmitt, who designed the planes named after him during World War I and World War II had a villa a couple of miles down the road, and invited Fritz to coffee and cake one time; they had met when Fritz was in Weimar. The location of Sean Connery and his French wife's villa was known by many.

Life went on calmly and serenely for us. Then, suddenly, came word through the grapevine: A movie complex at Plaza Andaluz was opening, and one Sunday evening a month it would show the latest English or American movie to all the English-speaking expats. Manna from heaven! We eagerly looked forward to our monthly date night, making it a special occasion with a leisurely stroll around the docks, starting out at the lighthouse and working our way back into the heart of the port, and people-watching while eating a delicious pizza with a bottle of Rioja in one of the outdoor cafés; then we would head to the theater. We had set-tled into our seats one Sunday evening when I noticed two tall male figures mak-ing their way across the row ahead and choosing to sit down directly in front of us. Fritz was indignantly whispering, "Oh, no, they're going to block our view!" I had been able to see the profiles of the newcomers as they crouched their way along the row. I glared at Fritz and whispered in a stage whisper, "Hush, it's Dou-ble-Oh Seven and Stewart Granger." The two actors were close friends: Granger was a popular English film actor playing heroic and romantic leading men. His second wife was Jean Simmons, whom he married in 1950. After their marriage broke up in 1960, he moved to southern Spain and invested in real estate. Sean Connery was at the peak of his popularity in the 1970s, having completed five of the James Bond films where his "roguish charm and cool sophistication" ranked him as the "sexiest man alive." His ability to do many of the stunts in the Bond films due to his earlier roles as stuntman paid off. Although the Bond films were the most commercially successful of all time, he personally tired of them and the notoriety they brought him and loathed being called James Bond. But who can forget *Goldfinger* (1964), *From Russia with Love* (1967), and my personal favorite, *Diamonds are Forever* (1971) and the famous phrase "shaken, not stirred." Which meant nothing at all to Fritz, so I nudged him hard in the ribs and leaned close to say, "The guy in front of me is Sean Connery, James Bond!" Well, that got his attention. He leaned around and peered closely, then nodded in agreement. At that moment Sean turned around and smiled at me (ooooh, that sexy smile!) and said in his delicious Scottish accent, "I hope I'm not blocking your view." I shook my head and said, "No, you're fine." The house lights dimmed and the film began. I studied the back of his head, and, by the way, he still had all of his black hair back then. When the house lights came back up at the end of the movie, Sean turned back around and asked, "Did you enjoy it?" I replied, "Yes," and he and Stewart nodded to both of us and made their way up the aisle.

Don't ask me what was playing that night; I haven't a clue.

19

The Pension

When Fritz decided to retire to Spain, he took the time to go to the financial division of Carrier in Syracuse on our home leave to discuss the details, then had me go with him to help sign the papers. He explained that they would be giving him a $566.52/month retirement pension for ten years certain and folded the contract into thirds so that it showed the amount and the line designated for my signature stating I had seen the contract. What I didn't see was the details of the contract. I found it out in a strange fashion many years later, after we had retired to Spain. While we were living there, my mother sent me rolled-up magazines every month of the popular *Woman's Day* and *Family Circle*, which I devoured. One night, we were reading in our electric bed before going to sleep, and I read a little paragraph in the *Woman's Day* that a lot of women in the United States were discovering that when their husbands died, they did not receive his pension because of what the big companies had put in the contracts in the early seventies. He could have taken $49 less per month, and I would have received 50 percent of his monthly payment. Or he could have taken $105.17 less per month, and I would have received 100 percent of his pension for my lifetime. I did not know of this arrangement until twelve to fifteen years after the agreement was made. Only his signature appears on the agreement; wives don't count. If he lived past the ten years, he would continue to receive the amount until he died. But, if he wanted to receive $105 MORE per month, he could get the additional amount added to the original figure, but upon his death the entire amount stopped. Nothing was carried over to the widow. At that time, he had already lived fifteen years, which is when we did most of our cruising. I gasped, and my husband asked me what I had read. I read him the article, and at the end, he was expressionless. I looked at him and said, "Fritz, that isn't what you signed for, is it?" He shrugged. "Well, I lived fifteen years after retirement, so we got the extra money." I was shocked and said, "But what is going to happen to me if you die before me?"

I'll never forget his answer: It was burned into my soul. He said, "Well, you're so much younger than I am, you can find another man to marry."

20

The Question

When friends and family heard we were emigrating to Canada, which we didn't know at all, from our villa on the Costa del Sol in Spain and the modern apartment we were renting in England, the inevitable question was an astonished "Why?"

It was 1979, and we were accustomed to taking off from London or Malaga on a moment's whim for a trip to some exotic place because fritz had suddenly discovered no pin there on the world map that hung above his desk at the Finca. No one could believe that we would give up sunny Spain, where the rain seldom fell on the plain or anywhere else for that matter, in favor of snowy, icy Canada. And they knew we loved England as well, from our enthusiastic reports of having just seen a new play or musical in the West End, or having popped down by train from Hitchin for a free performance of a TV show live at the BBC. Or visiting one of the outstanding museums or art galleries, all on one permanent ticket that let you get in to everything. To give all that up, and go through the trauma of moving internationally? Especially since this move would be at our own expense; no more Carrier to pay the costs. We were retired.

Yes, the house in Spain was magnificent: marble floors, marble baths, a kitchen large enough to ice-skate in, over three thousand square feet of pure luxury, two acres of land all overlooking the Mediterranean where, on a clear day, you could see Morocco. Were we out of our minds?

And Hitchin, that lovely market town thirty-five minutes by train to London, where history was everywhere. From the date inscribed on the bell tower of the church (1073) to the tombs in the church of the knights who had lived there. You could make your own golden brass rubbings, full length, of their suits of armor. Rubbings which I had knelt on, hung in our living room. The living room filled with transparent Plexiglas furniture from the London Design Center which was so different from the furniture down in Spain. What were we thinking?

The Background

Well, it boiled down to a few things: Franco had died in 1974, and it wasn't long before we began marking changes. Franco was seen as a dictator and had acted so back in 1936 during the civil war in Spain. By 1974, King Juan Carlos and Queen Sophia had been affectionately reinstated, and the country rejoiced in the normalcy of life once more. Franco ran the country, but all was calm and well organized. We had had four years of relative tranquility and a peaceful life, where our American dollars of a pension and Social Security went a very long way. Building the house had cost slightly less than $100,000 USD, even with the size of it and the marble floors, cork wallpaper, latest appliances, and all of the accouterments. Food was purchased at the mercado in Estepona, with fresh seafood caught that night. Our gardener planted a vegetable garden in part of the free land below the house. Wine was fifty cents a bottle. Restaurants were inexpensive. Cultural benefits were nonexistent, but as we were able to do those to our hearts' content in England, Spain was mostly R & R for us, a place to enjoy the simple life and relax.

Free elections came after Franco died. All along the coast, the small villages elected communist mayors and city councils in defiance of all the dictatorial years under Franco. Gradually, over the next few years, prices and taxes began to rise. But only for the "extranjeros" who had received their "residencias" (permit to live in Spain permanently). Not the Spanish residents. Every year the property tax rose significantly. Strangely enough, it was not the property tax which became the straw that broke the camel's back. No, it was the garbage fee. In 1977, the fee for the monthly garbage pail collection suddenly jumped from 400 pesos per month to 4,000 pesos. Fritz had a hissy fit. The exchange rate in 1977 was 81 pesos to the American dollar, thus $49. Never mind, it was the principle of the thing.

Especially when Fritz discovered that the residents in the *Pueblo* Cancelada were still paying 400, while all the foreigners in the *Finca* la Cancelada were being charged 4,000. That did it. He went to a realtor and put our house on the market. We decided we would finally move back to the States, even though we weren't entirely happy about the growing problem with the materialism we found so evident there every time we went back on our annual home leave.

Quite frankly, I think Fritz was getting bored with Spain. He did not make friends with any of the finca residents except for one English couple. All the rest came and went, sometimes when we were there, mostly when we were enjoying the English apartment. I would have been content to stay there, but then, I had my hobbies of silk-screening, painting, gardening, sewing, and knitting. And, of course, the seventies were when we began adding all those pins to our world map. But I didn't mind a bit moving back to the United States: We would be able to see Joana and her family in Tucson and my family in Auburn more frequently, and of course Fritz would be able to maintain contact with all his Carrier workmates.

But the question remained. Where?

The Search Begins

We decided in 1978 to take a three-month vacation and make it a "location" tour to check out the retirement choices Fritz's colleagues had made. We shipped our Volvo from Malaga to New Jersey while we flew to New York. Fritz's friend Rep, with whom he had attended the Deutsche Schule in Barcelona while growing up, lived in Newark. He met us in Kennedy Airport and drove us to his home, where our car was waiting for us. We discussed the fact that we had decided to sell the villa, and then started out on our long quest to find a place to retire. Again.

Piling the luggage in the trunk of our car, we started by visiting friends in

South Carolina (they had retired to Fuengirola, Spain, before moving back to the States). Down the east coast to Florida, we stopped in various places Carrier men had retired to: Daytona Beach, Vero Beach, St. Lucie (where my sister and husband spent their winters), Palm Beach. Boca Raton (where a Carrier vice president had retired; much too rich for our blood), Miami Beach, and then across the Everglades to Naples (where Fritz's boss in the London office had retired) to Tampa, and all the way up Florida's west coast. We didn't like the awful humidity of Florida and frankly found it dull. The beaches were not important to us; we had had them in Spain, Brazil, and Puerto Rico. We cut across to New Orleans and into Texas, taking a look at San Antonio, which we liked very much, especially the River Walk, before heading to our ultimate goal of Santa Fe, New Mexico. Fritz had figured that after so many years in Spain we would most likely enjoy Santa Fe because of the Spanish architecture, the art and culture it offered, and the lifestyle. We actually had a realtor show us around and check out what the houses were like and the prices.

Strangely enough, we gave it a thumbs-down. After all those years seeing the whitewashed houses in Spain and the window boxes of colorful geraniums, the blah of adobe Santa Fe depressed us. Everything was beige or brown, how sad. We shook our heads and headed west to Tucson. But: Arizona was hot, hot, hot, and if we bought a place in Arizona again, we would have to get a secondary place in San Diego or Flagstaff for the summers. We drove on to San Diego, looked around there, then went up to Los Angeles, where our tour ended. We drove our car into the Volvo dealership and sold it to them in a couple of minutes. As we took a taxi to the airport, we looked back at the beautiful bluish-gray car, and the workers were already adding pinstriping down its sides. Stupid.

On the plane going back, we talked over all the places we had seen. We came to the unanimous decision that we hadn't liked any of it. The United States just didn't cut it for us after all the years abroad. We preferred the ambiance of Europe. As we landed at Heathrow, we decided we would keep the apartment in England as home base and go to the villa once in a while when visiting somewhere else in Europe at the same time. We left the villa up for sale, but it would take two more years before we got a nibble.

And we still didn't know where …

Paradise Found

In December, 1979, we flew into Kennedy from London. As usual, Fritz's friend Rep drove to Kennedy to visit with us in the VIP lounge of American Airlines during the layover before the connecting flight to Syracuse. It was our plan to spend a few days with my family in Auburn and Syracuse, then to book a flight from Syracuse to Tucson to spend Hanukkah with Joana and Stan in Tucson. Rep asked us if we had had any luck in selling the villa, and we told him the harrowing story of having had an offer from an English couple. The price was all agreed upon, and when we flew down to Malaga to sign the contract with the lawyers and realtor, they told us at the last minute in the realtor's office that they had changed their minds. No compensation for the flights, the lawyer's fee, or anything. Just walked out on the deal. Bummer. We were back to square one. Then Rep asked what we were looking for, since we had not found anything on the tour through the States.

I jokingly replied and described our prospective "Paradise." "Well, it can be a small city but must be in a beautiful area, like we had in Zürich. Should be near a beach, like we had in Rio. Should have fresh food and good wines, like we had in Spain. And oh, yes, should run on hydro power, not nuclear, and have a good climate, like we had in Arizona." Well, we all had a good laugh over that idealistic premise.

But then, Rep grew serious and said, "You know? There might be a place like that! I just had a visitor from Kelowna, British Columbia. He is a member of an international club I belong to, and he was telling me about this place. It sounded so good that Herta and I are thinking of moving there ourselves. So, I subscribed to their daily newspaper and brought along a few copies to show you."

At which point my well-traveled husband asked, "Where is British Columbia?" thinking it was some place in Central America. When Rep answered, "Western Canada," Fritz exclaimed, "You think we should leave sunny Spain for snowy Canada?!" Rep said that apparently Kelowna had a population of fifty thousand, was on Okanagan Lake, had hydro power from the twenty-three lakes in the Okanagan Valley, was a continuance of the Napa Valley and had fifteen vineyards and orchards up the hills surrounding the lake, had a good hospital and library, had the all-encompassing medical system, and was multicultural so it had a European feel. And close enough to Vancouver for cultural adventures when we went there to take a flight to Europe. As for snow? The Okanagan valley was nicknamed the Arizona of Canada. Tucson has an annual rainfall of twelve inches; Kelowna has a total of twelve and a half! Well, that was a surprise.

As he said goodbye to us, he slipped three copies of the *Daily Courier* in our hands, saying, "Let me know what you think." When I glanced through the papers the next few days, I compared Kelowna to Auburn, where I had been brought up: same size, on a lake, with a small-town feel to the articles and ads, and yet a certain element of sophistication. Fritz and I were impressed, but there was a lingering doubt. Canada? We didn't know anyone there, had no relatives there, and it was so far away from everything. Why would we even consider it?

Fate stepped in.

Only in Canada, Eh?

It was a bitterly cold winter in Syracuse and Auburn that year, 1979. We were ready and eager to get to Tucson. But so was everyone else. Or to Florida. Anywhere to get out of the snowdrifts of Upstate New York. When Fritz called to book our flight to Tucson, the travel agent almost laughed in his face. Every flight out of Syracuse to sunnier climes was booked solid. What to do? Fritz was not dismayed. This was opportunity knocking. We would take the Greyhound up to Toronto, book a compartment on the Amtrak Via, and spend four days on the train going across Canada! That way we could get off in Kamloops, take the bus down to Kelowna, take a couple of days to look it over in the dead of winter, get back on the train, and continue on the last day to Vancouver, where, voilà, we could get seats on a flight to Tucson. What could beat that for a solution?

Ummm, well, four days riding across the vast wasteland of the snowy prairies did not thrill me the way it did Fritz, but as you must know by now, it was not the destination, it was the journey. He would be going somewhere. Did it really matter where? So that is why we found ourselves climbing aboard the Via cross-country train in Toronto a couple of days later. We were shown to our compartment with its two bunks by night and couches by day with a toilet and sink, all to ourselves. And because there were few passengers on board, we took the circular stairway to the Vistadome car at the head of the train and had front-row seats to the vision of Canada in all its winterland glory while listening to Christmas by Muzak softly playing through the loudspeakers. Fritz was in his element. While we crossed the prairies, we were amazed at the hundreds of miles in all directions of just snowy wasteland, with no houses or population. At night, sitting in the Vistadome after dinner in the dining car, we looked out at pitch-black darkness with the lights of the train glistening on the snow nearest the windows. But then! Way off in the distance, suddenly appearing like magic in the black, starry sky, you would see a single house, a farmhouse, all lit up with Christmas lights. Not another house around for a hundred miles, but they had all the lights on for themselves. It was heartwarming to see.

Some evenings, we would walk all the way to the caboose, past the dining car, while the train would slow down and stop for a few minutes. The rear door would open, and the chef would appear on the little platform and throw out bones and meat and food to the elk and huge white jackrabbits that would appear out of nowhere. That was fun for the passengers to see.

On the second evening we were introduced to an elderly lady traveling alone, and after that she sat at our table with us, telling us about Canada. When she heard we were using the trip to explore the possibility of moving to Kelowna, she acknowledged that her nephew was the premier of Alberta, and she was very proud of him. His name was Peter Lougheed, and he was a very popular premier and politician. On the third night we didn't bother retiring to our compartment because we would be arriving in Kamloops at 3:30 a.m., where we planned to get off the train, sit around the train station until the early morning, and take the first Greyhound bus down to Kelowna. When Mrs. Lougheed heard what we were planning to do, she said at dinner, "No, no, you must come with me! I live in Kelowna, my son-in-law is meeting the train, and we will be driving down.

You must come with us!" We protested that we didn't want to be a bother, but she said, "Nonsense, I'm hoping you will decide to come live there." The son-in-law was also pleased to have us as passengers. They recommended a hotel across from the park, downtown, and dropped us off there when we arrived at 6:00 a.m.

Kelowna had about three inches of snow on the ground, and I had to confess that the lake and park looked awfully cold that dawning morning as we arrived. The people at the hotel were very friendly and suggested we try some of the VQA wines the Okanagan is famous for. It stands for "vintners quality," and the Okanagan wines are famous, winning gold medals over European wines in blind taste tests. Especially two sweet after-dinner wines called Spätlese and Auslese. The spät means "late harvest," and these have been longer on the vine. The Aus means "out," meaning the latest harvest you can possibly get, after the first frost. These have a fascinating history. It was discovered that if you left the grapes on the vines, past the harvest time in September, they absorbed more of the sunshine and heat and became sweeter. But they also shriveled up on the vines, so there was less juice in them. The vintners waited until the nighttime temperatures dropped to 10 degrees Celsius (14 degrees Fahrenheit), alerting the many volunteer pickers that the freeze would come that night, and at 2:00 a.m. word is sent out; the pickers come, bundled up against the cold; and pluck the frozen, shriveled-up grapes and send them to the winery to be crushed. It takes fifty pounds of these frozen miracles to produce a liter of sweet wine that is out of this world.

The Okanagan terrain on the lake hillsides is ideal for all the well-known European wines, from Rieslings to Burgundies, Chardonnays to Pinot Noirs, and the wineries give tours and wine tastings in some spectacular mountainous settings. That is why we decided to buy a bottle and, in the evenings, have snacks of wine, crackers, and cheese in our hotel room in order to taste the various whites and reds. In Canada, alcoholic beverages were only sold in government liquor stores in 1979, when we were there, but in later years they did allow wines to be sold in grocery stores. So, in the interest of our investigation, we walked around the BC Liquor Store on the main street late in the afternoon of our first day there. After choosing two bottles, as we were checking out, the clerk asked if we were visiting the Okanagan. Fritz replied that we were thinking of emigrating to Canada and specifically to Kelowna. The nice young man at the register listened, then said, "Can you possibly wait fifteen minutes? I get off in fifteen minutes, and I'd like to drive you around Kelowna and show you everything."

We couldn't believe a stranger would be that kind, but that was typical, as we found out many times over the next three days. We sat down and waited, and he then started out in the downtown, pointing out restaurants, theaters, city hall, the library, hotels, the hospital, the lit-up bridge over the lake, and out to the residential areas. He drove by the Parkinson Recreation Center, which he said contained exercise rooms, a pool, a senior center, a football stadium, a park, and six tennis courts. Across the street from the rec center was a three-story apartment house advertising condos for sale. The apartment house (Tudor Manor) was nearing completion, and we liked the English Tudor design of it with its beams and white stucco finish. It reminded us of Hitchin, where many of the houses featured wooden beams in the outside walls. We wrote down the telephone number of the builder. We told our young guide that we would go back there the following day to get an idea of what the condos were selling for. He beamed with delight at our appreciation for the kindness he had shown us before dropping us off at our hotel. True to our word, the next morning we called the owner, rented a car, and drove back to Tudor Manor to have him show us the models. His name was Bob Spall, and his family was well-known in Kelowna, having had Spall Road named after his grandfather. We liked the building, which had a lounge for parties, a nice lobby, a large underground parking garage, and one- and two-bedroom apartments. We were impressed with the quality of the construction, and Bob said he was living in one of the apartments himself. We explained that we couldn't commit yet, until we had our "landed immigrant" status, but that we really liked Kelowna and his building. To that end, Bob said, "Let me make a couple of calls." A few minutes later, he asked us if we were free for dinner that evening. We said we'd be delighted. He replied, "Good! Because I just called the six couples who are already moved in here, and we're all going to take you to the racquet club and convince you to buy the apartment." Are you beginning to sense a trend here?

Everywhere we went the next two days, it was the same. Such kind, genuinely friendly people—in the grocery stores, in the mall, at the library, at the rec center. We explored the Mediterranean Market and the German delicatessen. We finally ended up in an office of a lawyer who would draw up the sale when we notified him from England if we decided definitely to emigrate, and he also would draw up the emigration papers. It was a relief that all would be left in such capable hands.

On December 20, after four days in Kelowna, we went back up to Kamloops by bus, took the train to Vancouver, got the flight to Tucson, had a wonderful holiday with the kids, and then flew back to England. We questioned each other about Canada and concluded that even though we had no family there, no relatives there, no friends there, we had never met such nice, friendly people in all of our travels. And based only on that, we went to the Canadian Consulate on Regent Street in London and applied for landed immigrant status in Canada. We had to give them a police report from the States showing that we had no criminal records, a financial report showing that we had sufficient savings that we would not become a burden to the system, and proof that Fritz was fully retired and would not be taking a job away from a Canadian. Also, a doctor's report that we were both in good health. With that, six weeks later we got the happy news that we had been accepted, and that we needed to enter Canada through Victoria, on Vancouver Island, to get our permit stamp in our passports. We notified the lawyer in Kelowna, who started the paperwork on the purchase of the apartment in Tudor Manor and arranged for the transfer of funds. Got a lovely welcoming letter from Bob Spall. We went down to Spain and started packing books, records, clothes, etcetera. We arranged with the movers to coordinate sending all the furniture and cartons in a truck up to England, where the moving company in England would add our personal items in Hitchin to the load of Spanish furniture, and get it all in one load for the ship to Vancouver. It would all stay in a warehouse in Vancouver until we arrived in Kelowna and had the apartment there ready to accept the furniture. In the meantime, we would live in the hotel at the end of the street where Tudor Manor was. We started on our quest on December 16, 1979. On the eighteenth of April, 1980, the stamp in our passports declared us to be legal residents of Canada.

A little footnote here: A year after we had moved into Tudor Manor, Rep and Herta finally took the plunge and joined us. They came for a visit, ended up buying a condo in the apartment building next to Tudor Manor, and kept thanking us for many years. (With some people, it just takes a little longer to make a decision.)

But inevitably, the what-ifs kick in. Often when we are faced with life-changing situations, we think afterward, Did we make the right decision? What if we had made this choice instead of that? What if we had taken this turn in the road instead of continuing down the highway? What if we had hesitated instead of taking a firm stand? What if we had settled for something less than what we really wanted? What if, what if?

After twenty-nine wonderful, happy years in Canada, my thoughts turn to, What if a young clerk in the liquor store hadn't asked, "Do you have fifteen minutes"?

Classes during the Winters in Tucson

We gave our landlord in Hitchin notice; after eight years of the best people ever to take care of his plastic furniture, he hated to see us go.

We flew to Victoria on Vancouver Island as our entry visa required (what a nice, warm, friendly smile as the immigration officer stamped our passport!), then to Kelowna, where we rented a hotel suite at the end of the street of our new apartment and waited out the finishing touches on the condo while our own furniture and personal clothing, etcetera, sat in a warehouse in Vancouver. In three months, the apartment was finished and we moved in. It was time to escape the winter and snow, so we made our first trip to Tucson from Canada and found it easy as pie to take an Alaska West airline from Kelowna, Seattle, Phoenix, and Tucson. It was a little unnerving to find the safety precautions in Portuguese, and the stewardess explained they had bought all their planes from Varig. That gave us second thoughts, but we put our fears aside. We stayed from early January through February till early March, an indulgence from Joana and Stan that we tried to alleviate as much as possible by cooking, chauffeuring the grandchildren to all their activities, and babysitting. Many years later, Joana confessed that after dropping us off at the airport for the return flight, she headed straight to Dairy Queen. While in Tucson I attended the International Gem and Mineral Show, beginning to turn my acquired knowledge of stones into purchases, as well as tools and supplies. Fritz protested that every year I managed to acquire one large machine along with everything else. The stonecutting machine did require an excess baggage charge, but how else could I "save" money by buying "rough" and cutting and polishing it myself? My reasoning had been refined by his when it came to taking extensive trips and purchases. I was able to sign up for ten-week courses offered by Tucson Parks and Recreation, and I loved getting professional advice on specific techniques and chatting with students who had their own businesses and others who sold their projects only at craft shows. I learned tons of helpful and useful information as well as learning an entirely new method of making something every year.

On turning an Ammolite into a piece of jewelry:

The fossil sits there
patiently waiting for me
for two million years.

When we returned home to our little apartment in Tudor Manor, I quickly realized that those machines weren't going to do me any good in a storage locker in the basement of the apartment house. I decided to cut down on my household needs and stored the vacuum cleaner and laundry soaps in a broom closet while taking over the utility closet for my jewelry. It was about four feet by six feet, no window, no ventilation, just a table and a chair and some beads hanging on the wall. Paradise.

21

Canada

I've written extensively about coming to Canada and how happy we were that we had emigrated, but this part refers only to the jewelry-making. When we exchanged Tudor Manor for the condo on the lake, I grew into a larger closet for all my supplies and worked on the table-workbench in the second bedroom on one wall while the computer desk was opposite. I usually worked in there while Fritz took his afternoon nap in the master bedroom; otherwise, I had to ask permission if he was on the computer. I managed to produce enough with my "play," as he called it, to participate in craft shows where I pulled in enough to purchase my beads, pearls, and tools at the next gem show. I loved selling my pieces, explaining the techniques used and where the stone came from. When I described going to Coober Pedy in Australia for the gorgeous opals, the customers loved looking through the colorful brochures and seeing the photos of the yellow Danger signs showing someone stepping backward into an opal mine-hole. If you fell down one, you had to be rescued by helicopter because Coober Pedy had no hospital. I loved telling them the story about the guide we had in Coober Pedy. He ended up taking us to his house, which, like all the others in Coober Pedy, was underground, to protect them from the extreme heat of the Outback. He showed us how they used huge drills to drill into hills, or turn the drill to drill down deep to then vacuum out the dirt and plaster each room until they had a very satisfactory apartment, all underground but with electricity and plumbing, with only a huge green water tank outside the front door to show a house was there. Our guide informed us that owners were allowed to have one opal mine on their property, which was fenced in. From the air, you could only see all these squares of desert land patchworked with chain-link fences and a green water tank. But if they luckily struck gold and found an opal vein, he laughingly confessed that you would then see a field with the "damndest, deepest fenceposts *ever!*"

Fritz was very happy with the condo on the fifteenth floor of the Lagoons and loved his walks all around the boardwalk, the park with its canals and locks, and the area where he could sit and watch the pontoon planes take off and land, taking the tourists on a flight over Okanagan Lake, the railway trestles, the vineyards, and the ski mountains. Sometimes he would stop on his walk and wave up to me on our balcony.

The Lagoons

When we moved into the Lagoons on the lake in 2000, it was a new beginning for us as well as for the new century. Fritz had fought the move, saying the condo on the fifteenth floor was more expensive than our townhouse, the taxes would be higher, the protests more vehement. When Joana came up for a visit, we took her to see the empty condo, and she ended up enthusiastically endorsing the idea. As she leaned against the glass balcony trying to point out the advantages to Fritz, I was almost ready to change *my* mind, and urged her to step back into the center. As she eloquently spoke of the beautiful walks we would have along the waterfront, and how convenient it would be to have all the cultural venues within walking distance, Fritz finally agreed that it did have some advantages. Before she left, he had agreed to purchase it, and over time, he came to absolutely love the views and the location. His favorite activity became taking the short walk along the boardwalk to where the float planes were anchored, sitting on the bench in front of the Grand Hotel, and watching the planes take off and come in for landings, with the diamond-glittered water spray enhancing the picture. As a pilot, he could live vicariously with each flight. From our balcony I could watch his expedition through the binoculars, and when he turned to wave, I would wave back. We had our breakfasts out on the balcony, with the beautiful view of the lake below, as we sipped coffee and read the paper. We watched the sailboat races every Wednesday evening and Sunday morning. We watched the exciting activation of the locks, directly below us, as the glistening yachts pulled up to the heavy panels on the lake side (lower) and waited for the water in the locks to drain out; then the gates would open, the boat would enter, the gates would close, and the water would slowly rise again. When the locks were full again, the other end of the lock would open, and the boat could turn on its engine and move out into the lagoons that surrounded the park. The owners could guide their boat right up to the mooring link in front of one of the townhouses of the Lagoons. The view from our balcony was like having a permanent reserved seat to whatever play was taking place in the park and lake below. We watched the triathlon as it took place every year. The swimmers could be seen approaching the sandy beach below from across the lake; they'd stand up as soon as their feet touched bottom, race across the beach after being clocked in by the monitors, run along the lines of bikes to find their own, hop on while spraying water off their wet suits, and race to the start line for the twenty-six-mile bicycle ride. The grandstand was right below our living room window. Along the route, they would drop the bikes and finish the run on foot, arriving back singly or in small surges of two or threes as they passed the grandstand to the finish line.

The Ladies Who Painted

When I lived in the Lagoons, the high-rise condo we bought in 1999 in Kelowna, Canada, a lot of things changed in our lives. Fritz had objected strenuously to the purchase at first because of the higher price and higher taxes and, I think, just because of the change it brought. Perhaps partly because it had been my suggestion and I had done all the financial accounting to prove it would be an excellent investment. He slowly came around and ended up loving the fabulous location right on the lake and the walks he took every day along the Boardwalk. If the day looked nice from our balcony, he would walk down to the Waterfront Park, sit on a bench in front of where the seaplanes were tied up, and happily watch the tourists pay their forty dollars for a twenty-minute flight over Okanagan Lake. Over the city, over the nearby vineyards and orchards, over the Kettle Valley Railway trestles, the plane would then splash down in front of the Grand Hotel and idle over to the dock to wait for the next tourist. Life for Fritz didn't get much better than that.

We soon began to appreciate that we could walk to everything. The big arena where famous artists performed was right across the street. From our fifteenth-floor living room window we watched the long black limos arrive and disperse Elton John, the Three Tenors, the Blue Men, and others. Behind the parking lot of the arena were the Kelowna Art Gallery, the Rotary Centre for the Performing Arts (now called the Rotary Centre for the Arts), and the Wine Museum. It was a block and a half to the community theater where we held season tickets for the Chamber Music Society and the summer theater. A block to the beautiful library and the big, new health center. A few steps to the senior center, the yacht club, and the casino. Two blocks to the Actors Studio, which gave musicals in a dining atmosphere; we held season tickets to that as well. A seven-minute walk to downtown to the restaurants, bank, grocery store, and shops. Everything at our footsteps. And always the lovely boardwalk to walk around at night with the red and green lights of the boats reflected in the lake. On Wednesday evenings and Sunday mornings we would watch the sailboat races from our balcony. In the summers we sat on the balcony and could hear the pops concerts drifting up from the island stage just below us. We walked around the park and the boat locks, always hand-in-hand, living in the moment. Shortly after moving in, at one of the pleasant summer outdoor potlucks, we met a couple who owned one of the lakefront townhouses. The lady told me that there was a painting group that met every Monday morning in the third-floor lounge. It consisted of ladies who had taken painting courses together. I asked if I might join them because I had painted a bit. She generously invited me to attend the following Monday at nine. I told Fritz how exciting it would be to have the opportunity to paint right there in my own building. He agreed, with the proviso that I was back upstairs at noon to make lunch.

I showed up with my watercolors and oils, and was immediately welcomed into the group. The lounge was an ideal painting studio: lots of north-facing windows, tables already set up for entertaining, folding chairs, oilcloth covers to protect the tables from paint splashes, and a full kitchen. We made coffee in the big urn and took turns bringing cookies. There was also a powder room. What more could a painter ask for? Good conversation! Helpful advice! Suggestions about techniques from the more experienced painters! Those were in abundance. I learned so much. We all got along tremendously well.

We usually sat in the same places around the tables I pushed together so we had a nice conversational grouping. There was Nancy, the lady who had organized the group. She and her husband spent the winters in their condo in Hawaii, where she painted flamboyant watercolors of exotic tropical flowers. Her husband Frank was an accountant, and his claim to fame (for me) was that he managed the accounts of the fellow in the sixteenth-floor penthouse, an internationally renowned geologist who had discovered large diamond deposits in the frozen North. His three separate mines were putting Canadian diamonds on the map and competing in quality with DeBeers. Occasionally I would find myself on the elevator with him, and once I even got up the courage to confess I was a jewelry designer. Hoping for a free sample? He wasn't particularly impressed. There was Doreen, the youngest of the group; she and her husband, Stan, loved to travel, but to strange, out-of-the-way places. Usually to jungles or to remote mountainous regions. They would mingle with the natives even when they didn't speak the language, and her stories when she got back were always interesting. She painted mostly in oils. Then came Jane, who had a wry sense of humor and was near my age. A former nurse, she had lived for a time in England, so we shared many good memories of life there. "Do you remember Max Bygraves' shows on the telly?" "Of course! I've got some of his tapes." Jane did beautiful watercolors of scenes. I remember one in particular: a delicate landscape of Chinese fishermen in junks on a lake. Jane eventually moved to Calgary in November 2006 to be with her two sons and their families, but she and I have remained close and exchange emails almost every day, discovering to our extreme delight how many things apart from painting that we share in common. And lastly, next to me at the table was Jean. She was older, had white hair, was very gentle in her speech, lived alone, and didn't chatter as much as the rest of us, but painted seriously and quietly. I was the Experimenter, switching from watercolor scenes from our travels to oil abstracts to a very colorful acrylic of the showerhead in my bathroom, whatever appealed to me at the moment. So, five of us sat there every Monday from nine to twelve, chatting away, talking about our families, grandchildren, and experiences. Occasionally, a resident would wander by on her way out to the swimming pool and poke her head in to see what all the laughter was about. We became known as the ladies who painted. We met for eight years. We held an art exhibit in the lobby of the Lagoons once a year, on a Sunday, and invited all the residents to view what we had painted. We were more prolific than we were professional. But we *were* good. The residents enjoyed the art and punch and cookies, and looked forward to the nice social event.

The End

Late one night after we had gone to bed, Fritz woke me saying he had terrible pains in his shoulders. This time when I said I was calling an ambulance, he didn't object, so I knew it was bad. He was rushed to the hospital. The next morning, he was paralyzed from the neck down. He was devastated. After he had been in ICU a few days to control the pain, he was moved to a private room. and received wonderful care from the nurses, helping him eat and bathe. Every morning Dr. Warrender, his doctor for twenty-five years, stopped by to chat with Fritz and then accompanied me out to the corridor, explaining in detail what would be happening, preparing me for it. They put a Barcalounger chair in the room so I could stay nights.

It was during this period that Joana flew up to be with him a few days, and Andrew and Adriana called him and had good conversations. Then he was moved to the hospice unit at Cottonwoods. I brought paintings and photos from home and hung then on the wall so he could see them and played CDs of his favorite music. We could wheel him out to the patio, but not far because he was hooked up to transfusions and painkillers. I could take walks around the outer limits. As I was tying my tennis shoes to take a walk about a week after he was in hospice; the nurse was taking his vitals. She looked up and quietly said, "Perhaps you should wait a few minutes, Janice." I removed my shoes, and a few minutes later, she said, "He's gone."

Even though we knew it was coming, those few words were a shock. I sat there as she gently removed the wedding ring from his finger and handed it to me. "You'll want this." The various specialists were called in to verify the time and do their work as I sat there, not speaking, not crying. I was numb. When they were ready to move his body somewhere else, the nurse turned to me and asked, "Will you be all right to drive home, or would you like someone to take you?" I replied that I could drive. We took all the photos down and packed all personal things in some sturdy brown bags and took them out to the car. As I drove back to the house, I did everything mechanically, realizing I would have to call Joana right away. It was a difficult call.

I don't recall ever crying during the days that followed, talking to the funeral directors and arranging for the memorial service two weeks later. The church was full. My son-in-law and their children all gave eulogies. Many said it was the most beautiful service they had ever been to. I played the record "Con ti partiro" at the end. It was the song the *Crystal Symphony* entertainers always sang at the end of their last show the final night of a cruise. "It's time to say goodbye." I touched the urn before walking up the aisle.

When Fritz passed away in 2005, the sympathy and support the ladies showed me was very comforting and helped me get through. I continued to attend the painting sessions.

I had not been able to participate in any of the ladies' social activities (birthday lunches) because Fritz didn't like being left alone. They encouraged me to join them on their annual summer camp, and since I was now able to go anywhere, I decided to attend my first session in July.

Each summer in July, we shut down the lounge painting sessions because Nancy and Frank moved across the lake to an area called Fintry Landing. They owned a "cottage" there, complete with boat dock and sandy beach. The so-called cottage was actually a very large old house; it had five or six bedrooms. It was deemed "heritage" because it was over a hundred years old; therefore, it could not be radically renovated. Fortunately, the plumbing had been updated and the kitchen modernized. Nancy always invited the painting group to spend three or four days with her when Frank was visiting elsewhere. We painted from morning to night on the large porch which encircled the house. We all brought casseroles, salad makings, desserts, and Okanagan wines. Since we were so far north, it stayed light until 10:00 at night.

Of course, a heritage cottage came with a resident ghost: the owner who had been killed in the First World War and always appeared correctly in that uniform. Stories of his sightings were told with great relish by Nancy, quoting various guests who claimed to have seen him, usually at the head of the stairs. She embellished one story about how the ghost had knocked all the jars of preserved fruits and vegetables off the pantry shelf once while she was in the kitchen doing the dishes and no one else was around. (He left the peanut butter jars intact.) It raised goose bumps on our arms.

Fortunately, he kept to himself during *our* annual visits, but I have to add that we all learned to hold our pee during the night rather than chance running into him on the way to the communal WC.

It was enough that we had to hear the whoosh of the large colony of bats who lived legally in the attic, as they left through the window right on time every night. They were under wildlife protection because the colony numbered over a hundred. And boy did the guano smell when the temperature reached the nineties! Our summer camp was always a lot of fun because each of us was required to come up with one unique idea to try out. Once it was doing wet-on-wet watercolors. We thoroughly wet the watercolor paper, dropped wet splashes of color on it, and let them spread into each other, creating more colors, sometimes tilting the board to let them run downward, then adding crumpled pieces of Saran Wrap to the wet paper. After it had dried overnight, we peeled off the Saran and painted a scene over the pattern it produced, a white birch tree forest, for example.

One summer I gathered up all of my extra pearls of every size, shape, and color and some Swarovski crystals, gave each lady a ten-inch square of canvas, and had her paint in oils or acrylics, leaving some areas thicker with paint, and placing the gems with tweezers into the thickened areas. They loved it. Most hung the small paintings in their guest bathrooms.

After I had renovated my condo in late 2005 to early 2006, I decided to do two large canvases in oil for the dining room wall over the table. I was mostly into abstracts by then, realizing that I didn't have to explain what they depicted (the way I occasionally had to explain my watercolor scenes). I found some beautiful, striking paintings in an anthroposophical calendar that year, which would look good in the dining room. The canvases each measured three feet square, and I intended to hang them next to each other. A rather daunting project for me to tackle, but I looked forward to it. I have the huge advantage of being able to envision painting, decorating, or jewelry projects in their finished state, so the process was clear in my mind.

Since the pictures referred to anthroposophy, I explained to my ladies as I rough-drafted them that they were of a religious nature; they represented the search by the Knights of the Round Table as they rode their horses throughout Europe and England searching for the Holy Grail, the chalice which would contain all the wisdom of the world. The first painting on the left would portray a royal blue chalice on a stark maroon background, filled with a bright yellow light which represented the Christ Spirit. The painting on the right would show a larger blue chalice (cup) that was overflowing with the Light, to indicate the wisdom of the Christ Spirit flowing down onto us mortals below. The yellow light would transform into viridian green (in anthroposophic paintings, viridian green represented Wisdom) as it transparently mixed with the blue of the chalice. In response to the ladies' somewhat skeptical looks, I laughed and said, "Well, if that doesn't work for you, at least the paintings are so abstract, I won't have to explain anything."

I actually enjoyed painting them. The colors were so strong that they made me happy. Finally, after several weeks, I decided one morning that I was done, and as was our custom when we had finished a painting, I picked up the two canvases, leaned them against the wall on two long tables used for buffets, and invited the ladies who paint to make their comments or suggestions. They all gathered around in front of my masterpieces, gazing seriously in silence. Doreen went first. "I love the bold colors." Nancy agreed; she felt I didn't need to add anything more. Jane concurred. Then Jean remarked quietly, "That is the biggest yellow penis I have ever seen."

There was a stunned silence. Slowly, all eyes turned toward Jean. Had she just said what we thought we heard? Suddenly the room erupted in laughter as we all saw the painting in a different perspective. I raced over to my place at the painting table, grabbed the long-handled inch-wide stiff bristle brush, dunked it in turpentine, rushed back to the painting, and began frantically scrubbing the yellow dribble, scrunging the royal blue into it, turning it green.

And there it stayed. To this day.

The paintings no longer represent a religious concept to me. Instead, they are symbolic of good times, good friends, a gourmet ghost, and gales of laughter.

Fritz's Death

My husband died on May 11, 2005, at the age of ninety. He had had prostate cancer since 1990, but the radiation and chemo had never shown any sign of the disease until the fateful night when he woke me at midnight saying he had a bad pain between his shoulder blades. In a few minutes I could see it had gotten worse, and I decided to call 911 for an ambulance. He didn't make a protest, so

I knew it was serious. The paramedics were there within five short minutes be-cause the hospital was only a five-minute drive from our condo. It was my first experience with calling 911, and the young men responding to the call could not have been more courteous and respectful to Fritz. They maneuvered the stretcher in the elevator, reassuring him on the way to the hospital. He was given a cur-sory exam in the ER, but because tests would be necessary in the morning, he was given a sedative, and I was urged to return home to spend a sleepless night, wondering what had happened. The next morning at the hospital, he started get-ting tested, and the MRI showed a large tumor pressing on his spinal cord. That day he became paralyzed from the shoulders down. Our doctor said that the prostate cancer had finally metastasized into the tumor. I wanted to have Fritz receive radiation and hormone treatment, which had worked so well over fifteen wonderful, travel-filled years, but he admitted to me that the paralysis would be permanent, and I begged to let him come home.

I explained that I would install a hospital bed and a lift over the bed so he could be lifted up and transferred into a wheelchair. I could take him out for walks along the boardwalk, and he could watch the seaplanes taking off and landing. Our doctor quietly explained that even with the lift, I would not be able to handle the deadweight. The question was resolved when Fritz became some-what comatose, drifting in and out of consciousness. With the pain medication, he slept a lot through the first week in his private room in a special care ward. The doctor came by every day and spent a lot of time with Fritz. He had been his doctor for twenty-five years, and we could not have had a more caring physician. Fritz's pain was controlled by morphine drip. The nurses came in when Fritz was awake and lifted him into a wheelchair; they took him to the special pool for hot-water relaxation and bathed him. By the end of the first week, our doctor took me aside one morning and explained that the time had come for him to be moved to a hospice, as there was nothing they could do for him in the special care unit. I cannot put into words the fear that the word gave me as the meaning swept over me. From that moment on, I had to allow the professionals to make the necessary decisions, as they were the experts. They knew what was best for Fritz.

The hospice is in my opinion the next best place to Heaven. The jury is still out on Heaven, but the hospices of the world are Here and Now. My gratitude for the angels who work in those places knows no bounds. I watched them care for my dying husband. Their kindness to me as I sat for another week, holding his hand and talking, gave me strength. I reminded him of things we had done and the places we had gone to, which gave him some solace. I had called Joana and Stan, and Joana was able to cancel some of her patients and fly up to Kelowna. She arrived the day after the ambulance took Fritz to the hospice. She was there for three days, and some of the time he was alert, aware of her presence, and obviously grateful that she had come. He took phone calls from Stan, Andrew, and Adriana, and they even had him laughing as they recounted funny stories on the phone. The hospice encouraged families to bring paintings from home, so I brought over one of my large watercolors, creating a warm personal environment in the large private room that was more like a hotel room than a hospital room. Photographs of the family adorned the wall next to his bed, and a table held a music system for playing his favorite tapes and CDs. A Barcalounger for me to sleep in overnight was next to the large window where there was a bird feeder so he could watch an occasional cardinal landing and feeding. There was a patio on the days when he could be taken in the wheelchair for a few minutes in the fresh air to sit by the running fountain and enjoy the flowers and budding trees. There was a pathway all around the complex for the relatives and visiting friends to use, and I would take a break for a few minutes' walk when he was being bathed or sleeping.

The fifty-nine years were ended. What would be the next chapter?

How would I spend the empty days? That was when the studio in the arts center became available to rent. Was I up to it?

Part 2

22

Studio in RCA

When I was adjudicated and selected out of twenty-four candidates for the studio on the second floor of the Rotary Centre for the Performing Arts, it felt like the world's biggest challenge had just dropped in my lap. Can you picture a seventy-eight-year-old lady who had never worked, was very insecure, who had doubts as to what the studio would entail, who was shy about talking to strangers, who simply didn't have a clue how to proceed, and had only been a housewife all her life?

But I was determined to find out if in all those years of making jewelry, I had learned enough to be professional and respected by colleagues. So, I blindly plowed ahead. I found out quickly how kind people can be to someone who has self-doubts and how encouraging my fellow artists were. First, I think I surprised them when I had the entire interior painted aubergine—eggplant fuchsia. Then I began adding furniture from my apartment: a studio couch for visitors to sit on, a coffee table, beautiful shelves which I filled with some of my more unique pieces. I attached spotlights to the top shelves and aimed them on the jewelry so that at night until eleven, the jewelry shelves were illuminated although the studio lights were off. Audiences to the theater could stroll by during intermission and decide to come back to see the jewelry up close. I bought a microwave, coffee machine, and small fridge for the back wall because I was already thinking of giving classes rather than just making jewelry in the studio, like the painters.

The potters-and-weavers studios gave classes and were always full. Kelowna had people eager to learn.

I plunked my own workbench smack in the middle of the studio so that people walking by to get to the balcony of the theater could see me lit up and working, and the door was open so they could come in and watch for a few minutes. That was when I made the discovery that I wasn't as shy as I thought myself to be. I enjoyed explaining what I was soldering and how to do it. And the funny thing is that when you find out you know more about something than they know, you tend to sound confident. And with that *comes* confidence. Then, when I detected a German or Swiss accent, I would switch to German, and they were delighted! They didn't mind my grammatical mistakes: They knew what I was saying, and loved the opportunity to relax for a few minutes in their native tongue. One time I received an email from some Belgians who said that because I had made the effort to mix my French with German, their visit to my studio had been the highlight of their trip to Kelowna. You can't beat compliments like that.

I loved that studio so much that every morning I got up early so I could take care of household chores and be free by 11:30. I could walk over to the Rotary Centre and enter *my* studio. How I loved that simple act. And on days when I was giving a class, it was a joy to welcome the four or five students who arrived with smiles on their faces. On nights when the theater was active with a traveling play or a concert, I would stay open until after intermission so that people could wander in and have a look around. The executives of the Rotary appreciated my willingness to participate in any of the city's presentations, and especially when I donated special pieces for silent auctions. Some of the pieces were ammolites (the fossils found only in Canada) and the fabulous cultured pearls, rare because of their size and unusual shapes, and some with shapes of fish or parrots which required a lot of handwork. One piece was called *Heaven and Earth*. It consisted of an unusual silvery meteorite which had broken off of a star, traveled through the atmosphere, turned molten when it entered Earth's friction, and showed the silvery streaks. Then, below that, set in a silver bezel, was a colorful ammolite, which is the fossilized shell of a snail that was alive seventy million years ago. Crawling along the bottom of the ocean which still covered British Columbia and

Alberta in Canada, it speaks to me about how long some life has been in existence and gives us hope that our present troubles will disappear, given time.

My students loved using scrap silver to make unique broomstick castings. When the students "created" a work of art, it was the equivalent of when they had their Wow moment at the polishing machine and brought their first ring to its shiny finish. I still correspond by email with some of my students from those years. One of my larger challenges was that I soon realized that if I were going to teach classes, I needed to have manuals they could follow. I discovered that manuals back then seemed to preclude that you had already taken classes and would simply say: "Solder the bezel to the backing." Well, that was ridiculous! To not describe that there are three different degrees of solder? Three different hardnesses of metal? How much flux do you add? What kind of flame on the torch? My goodness, you needed to know and to have practiced so many things. So, I wrote manuals as if the reader had never known a thing about jewelry production. I explained all the meanings, I drew diagrams. I took photographs of works in progress to demonstrate. I printed up copies of each technique and then, when I was teaching a class in that, I included the manual in a free notebook so they could make notes of their own project for the next time.

It was during this period that one of the oil painters in the Rotary talked me into going pro. She kept prodding me to open up a website or pay to join an already established website. She belonged to one called Ruby Lane and featured artists in four categories: Art, Jewelry, Antiques, and Vintage. It was very well run and advertised in creative art magazines. I paid the fee and the advertising coverage, and I was off. I was moderately successful, selling eight to ten pieces the first year. Ruby Lane showed the photo and description of the piece, and when a piece sold, they took the payment and immediately let me know I could mail it out to the customer.

I started with them in 2008 and discontinued in 2019. I had decided to sell at craft shows, where I sold many more pieces, instead of online; the customers paid cash or by check, and I saved all the advertising and postage costs. So, I not only learned to write manuals, I also learned how to photograph jewelry for listing online. That's a *lot* of technology to learn for an eighty-five-year-old! While all of this was going on, I started getting well-known. Enough that the weekly writer for a spiritual column in the *Daily Courier* called and asked if he could interview me. I assumed it would be a line or two in his weekly column. But he stayed for over an hour, and you can imagine my astonishment when I opened the Sunday paper, and there on the front page of the entertainment section was a two-page article about me, with a photo of me at my workbench and a headline in big black letters proclaiming, "Janice got her first job, at the age of 78."

After that came notices in the paper of my showings in other galleries, two beautiful articles in the Okanagan Arts magazine, speeches to the Okanagan Arts Institute, and then, finally, winning the trophy for Best Designer of the Year in 2008.

I truly marveled at how all of my doubts and insecurities had been answered so positively, and it is why I spend so much time now encouraging other older women to take a chance. After all, what can you lose?

23

My Epiphany Moment

A couple of years ago I was attending the American Gem Trade Association show at the International Gem and Mineral Show held annually in February in Tucson, Arizona. It is the main source of jewelers' materials and supplies. The AGTA is the most prestigious of all the organizations represented at the show and the source of the latest trends and newest discoveries.

That year as I made my serendipitous route through all the aisles and booths, I found a Japanese pearl dealer offering a bowl of half-drilled Tahitian black pearls for the price of $8 each. Since I had only allowed myself to purchase half-drilled pearls in the $2 to $3 range, I was tempted but decided to pass. However, I continued to see in my mind the large size, rich color, and luster in several rings and kept going back, walking past the bowl while trying to decide whether to splurge or not. While eating my brought-from-home chicken sandwich in the food court of the show and listening to a classical guitarist playing over the loudspeaker, I noticed a couple who sat down at my table and were examining their purchases: rubies, sapphires, and emeralds, wrapped neatly in individual tissue packages. He was holding them up to the light while she recorded each one in a notebook. Suddenly I heard him ask her, "I see this in an eight-thousand-dollar ring; what do you think?"

I have to confess I was stunned. You look at a beautiful stone and only see its monetary value? Not how you are going to set it to bring out its greatest beauty? Not showing it in a *creative* way? Just to sell it for the largest amount possible for that size? I had an Epiphany Moment—wrapped up my sandwich and walked quickly back to the pearl dealer where I purchased three of the $8 pearls. I later made them into very beautiful rings, each one different in its setting, but each setting designed to show off the pearl, nestled into a textured, oxidized silver ring—as if that particular pearl had been intended all along for *just that design*. When you are passionate about your craft, your pieces reflect that, and those pieces become favorites of your customers. I often told this story to my students in order to teach them what true value is. But I wondered if they really understood. Until one day after a class in fabrication, one of my students added a garnet, polished her ring, put it on her finger, and proudly held it up for everyone to see as she pranced around the room, saying, "Look at my eight-thousand-dollar ring, everybody!"

They all smiled. They understood what true value was.

The Gem Show

What is called simply the "gem show" is actually a group of twenty-six organizations which have banded together and fill every hotel room in Tucson, Arizona, annually, the last week of January till the second week of February, in order to serve commercial jewelry stores, jewelry designers, wholesalers who sell in bulk, and wholesalers who reduce sales to custom designers with superb specimens for one-of-a-kind samples.

The International Gem and Mineral Show is the largest in the world. It attracts millions of visitors to Tucson every February and September. The show is one of the single highest revenue-producing events for the Tucson economy. The estimated economic impact in 2018 was $120 million. That figure is not only the sales of gems but also what the dealers spend on hotel rooms and restaurants while they are here. The jewelers, designers, and big-name stores that attend the gem show are professionals: manufacturers, custom designers, and buyers for Tiffany's and high-end stores across the country as well as dealers who resell the stones to smaller companies that don't need to buy in bulk. There are also dealers who sell finished pieces to buyers from stores. It is only available to wholesale buyers, not open to the public. For the most part, this area of the gem show is in the higher-end hotels in the city center and in very large, sturdy tents (air-conditioned) around the Tucson Convention Center and the downtown hotels. These shows are put on by organizations such as the Gem and Lapidary Wholesalers, Gem and Jewelry Exchange, the American Gem Traders Association, and the Tucson Gem and Jewelry Show, otherwise known by the trade as the G&LW, the GJX, AGTA, and JOGS. There are many more gemstone dealers all around the city. These dealers sell precious stones, rubies, sapphires, and diamonds, but far more business is done by all the cutters and dealers who mine turquoise, amethysts, opals, tourmalines, jaspers, agates, meteorites, fossilized stones, and, need I add, pearls of every size, shape, and color, freshwater, cultured, Tahitian, and manmade. The dealers and companies represented there come from every corner of the globe, and for three weeks you have a perfect example of how the world can get along, buying, selling, and trading in every language and dialect. I am a jewelry designer and learned the trade in Zürich in 1967. I told my husband it would be a good way to learn to speak German. But my heart led me down the rabbit hole called making jewelry, and I became addicted to it. To be able to attend a show where the most beautiful and unique stones are offered at wholesale prices is nirvana. After thirty years of making jewelry to sell at craft shows and in galleries, I had my own studio in an arts building and added teaching to my résumé. I wrote manuals for every process. I discovered the joy of teaching and giving classes in every form of jewelry-making. I designed a website and sold online.

Attending the gem show every year in Tucson plays such an important role in my life, I look forward to it all year. It's a major event, and the statistics are convincing that Tucson hosts a unique kind of convention, one no other city can even come close to achieving. Sure, other cities have gem and mineral shows, and they might fill up a convention center for three or four days, but Tucson fills up the convention center with two full shows, held on different dates. Every hotel room in the city is booked from one year to the next. For a jeweler, whether from Tiffany's or JF Designs (my company), the dealers welcome you to have a look around. (If your badge says Tiffany's on it, you may get offered a glass of champagne!)

A bit of background: The first Tucson Gem and Mineral Show was held in an elementary school in 1955 and was put together by an enthusiastic group of rockhounds. It then moved to a Quonset Hut at the Tucson Fairgrounds. In 1973 it moved to the Tucson Community Center, and the Tucson Gem and Mineral Society took over managing it. The show began to draw the interest of the gemstone community around the world and expanded. After the completion of the Tucson Convention Center in 1990, the Tucson Gem and Mineral Society moved there, and even the Smithsonian began to exhibit.

There is another aspect to the gem show, the part that deals with minerals, crystals, fossils, and collectibles. It consists of over forty different organizations which are represented each year, usually in the same hotel or tent. All of the organizations relate to some aspect of jewelry-making *or are for specialized collectors.* But aside from the long-established groups that reach out to the professionals, there are hundreds more who spread out skulls, fossils, dinosaur eggs, and freshly mined eight-foot geodes, split apart to show their amethyst crystals inside the green stone exterior. These displays are mainly for collectors or for the person who enjoys just wandering around to "find something pretty" for their shelves. The Tucson show has the mineral and fossil exhibition mixed in with the gem pavilions. The gem shows are wholesale and closed to the public. To get in, you have to register in advance, giving a sales tax ID number and business license, and pick up your badge at the entrance to the tent or ballroom. Hanging the badge around your neck is the equivalent of getting your high school diploma. The mineral and fossil show is open to the general public, and unless you are the Smithsonian or a well-known museum or gallery, the prices are retail to the general public. No badges required.

And therein lies the controversy. Some people who claim they attend the gem show every year belong to the group of collectors who are searching for a newly discovered rare crystal, or a newly uncovered cache of dinosaur eggs (you can own a nest of them for $25,000). These shows are in the hotels and motels along the I-10 frontage road in Tucson and in smaller tents in the spaces between the motels. They even sell out of the backs of their trucks parked along the freeway. The "exhibits" usually have some treasure on display from the Smithsonian. And in another room, they have new machines and tools being demonstrated. It's not just boys and their toys: girls can love acquiring tools, too. Many manufacturers of machines and equipment offer their products in tents down near the Kino Sports Complex area. In the early years of building up my equipment, my husband used to complain that we were always lugging a big carton containing a polishing machine or a new drill press back to Canada.

When you enter the arena of AGTA or the immense ballroom of a big hotel, you are overwhelmed by the brilliant lighting, as each jewelry showcase is illuminated to bring out every nuance of the gems displayed. The first year I attended (thirty-one years ago) I was dazzled by seeing large brandy snifters filled with cut diamonds, sapphires, emeralds, and rubies. I asked the dealer from India, "How am I supposed to buy them?" He reached under the table, pulled out some little scoops and Styrofoam plates, and handed them to me. "Scoop out some sapphires onto the plate, then start separating the ones you want over to the side. When you are happy, give the dish to me, and I will weigh them and give you the price." Well, I have to confess I would have loved to have bought some diamonds or sapphires by the same method I buy a pound of chops, but unfortunately the budget never allowed. They are sold by the gram, and fifteen sapphires would cost a thousand dollars, and each one resold for between two and three hundred each depending on their color and cut. I should point out here that the gem shows are all covered by a lot of security personnel. The off-duty police augment their income nicely by walking around under cover while uniformed police are hired by the organizations for a visual presence. Nevertheless, every year there is an article in the newspaper about a naive dealer who put his square sample case down on the curb while waiting for a taxi and found it missing when he went to get in. What impresses the dealers more than wearing an expensive piece of jewelry is to show them photos of what you made from one of their stones you had purchased from them the previous year. They love seeing the results.

No Guns

When we were living in Canada, if we re-entered in our car from the States, the customs official would look at the landed-immigrant page in our passports, smile, and say, "Welcome back! You don't have any guns with you, do you." Not a question, just an affirmation. (If we had, we'd have been asked to check them with him till we made the next trip out.) Because we wouldn't have felt the need to carry while there. Ever. That is why they have such a low rate of "accidental" killings.

Artists @ Work

Another memory of my time at the Rotary Centre for the Performing Arts in Kelowna was when we decided to have a monthly Art Crawl, like larger cities in Canada and down in the States. All the artists in the studios held a planning meeting and decided to keep their studios open at night the first Thursday of every month, and we called it Artists @ Work. We held meetings each month to think up a theme and followed through with costumes, food, and music to correspond to the theme. We held demonstrations in the studios to show the public what the Rotary Centre offered.

Well, I believe the public did enjoy themselves—but not half so much as the artists. On Greek Night, some of us draped sheets over our shoulders, wrapped our heads in grapevine wreaths, and served feta and filo pastries. I bought a Greek music CD, and if I never hear Melina Mercuri singing "Never on Sunday" again, it will be too soon. On the night we did Renaissance, a friend downloaded a CD of harpsichord music for me, and in a long gown, I served cream puff swans which were floating on a mirror "lake." How did that relate? Well, the thinking process was convoluted, but it had to do with Renaissance being manor houses which had ponds or lakes with swans floating regally on them. And it beat having to roast a boar for three days.

On the night we did the Fifties, I hate to conjure up the vision of me, at eighty-two, going as James Dean: with jeans rolled up, white tee shirt with rolled-up sleeves with a pack of cigarettes—borrowed from the maintenance man—tucked in one, and a bandana around my head. The laughter emanating from studio 203 that night when the visitors figured out who I was, was raucous. Then there was the night we had to come as our favorite artist: I spent a lot of time thinking about it but finally decided that I should give up on coming as Toulouse-Lautrec, because hobbling around all night on my knees didn't sound all that fun. I finally decided on Grandma Moses, which didn't require as much Method acting.

The Theater

I was privileged to be one of eight artists to have a studio at the Rotary Centre for the Performing Arts in Kelowna, British Columbia, Canada, between October 2005 and October 2009. Kelowna is a beautiful city on Okanagan Lake, idyllically surrounded by vineyards and orchards. The Rotary Centre, funded and supported by the various rotary clubs but managed by the city, contained a music hall, dance studio, restaurant, and 350-seat theatre with splendid acoustics. The Chamber Music Society held its concerts there. It also had eight studios for artists, ceramists, sculptors, weavers, and one jewelry studio—mine. It was ideally located between the Kelowna Art Gallery and the Wine Museum and was across the street from the huge Skyreach Dome, the 6,500-seat arena where hockey dominated the local sports scene and was the site of big-name concerts. As I walked to work every day, it was always fascinating to stop for a few minutes and admire the huge motor homes lined up at the stage door entrance, next to all the vans containing sound and lighting equipment, and wonder who was performing that night. When a pamphlet on the ten-year anniversary of the Rotary Centre was being prepared, the director requested the artists in residence to submit any events or memories of their experiences they had had that might be of interest to the residents of Kelowna. I found it difficult to choose one specific thing because the four years I spent at the Rotary were the happiest years of my life. They gave me the opportunity to find myself, and the road to discovery was occasionally bumpy but gratifying as my jewelry studio became a destination for the tourists and my students.

Eventually one memory kept resurfacing, and I finally selected this story to recount for the Centre's pamphlet: an event that was life-changing. One of the more pleasant things made available to the studio tenants was the opportunity to enjoy complimentary performances in the Mary Irwin Theatre if seats were still unsold shortly before the doors closed for the performance. I attended a number of excellent plays and concerts by keeping my studio open past the normal 6:00 p.m. closing time, thus providing the early arrivals for the theatre the chance to browse in my studio. Then at 7:30, I would leave the lights on but lock the studio, walk down the corridor, and slip into the auditorium to an evening of wonderful entertainment. Some of those performances had a profound effect on members of the audience.

One play which stands out in my mind as a life-changing experience was a touring company of just two actors: a young man and an older man. The play was called *Visiting Mr. Green*. It was about a crotchety old widower who survives his loneliness by clinging to his religious beliefs and a successful young man who insulates himself against his isolation by burying his emotions and focusing on his career. When the young man almost drives into the old man, he is charged with reckless driving, and six months of community service is imposed. He has to spend a few hours every week helping the old man. But the young man is homosexual, the old man intolerant, and the old man goads the younger one with unkind and thoughtless remarks. Little by little, throughout the play, they break down the barriers each have built around themselves and developed their relationship into a strong friendship. But what held me spellbound was the end of the first act, when the old man taunted the young man with the remark that he had made his choice to be gay. The young man turned to him and in a tormented voice cried out, "My God, do you really think anyone would CHOOSE this life?" And with that anguished cry the curtains came down. No one moved. The silence in the auditorium was deafening.

After a few minutes, some people stood up and moved to the lobby, murmuring to their friends. It was already generating discussion.

I had always considered myself a tolerant, if ambivalent, person, and in fact enjoyed a close friendship with a gay couple who were members of the Spinners and Weavers studio, across from mine. They would often stop in my studio for a comfortable chat, and both had a great sense of humor.

But since that evening in that revealing moment, if I hear anyone saying the gay lifestyle is a *choice* they make, I tell the person about that play and the effect it had on me. Science has indeed established that the only "choice" that is made is when the sperm hits the egg.

After that, you learn to live with it, perhaps adapt adequately, perhaps not, *maybe celebrate it.* Even now, when I listen to the interminable debates on the subject, in the guise of religion, I hear that cry echoing through the auditorium—and my heart.

24

The Move to Tucson

In 2009, when I turned eighty-three, I made another life-changing decision. As happy as I was with the wonderful lifestyle I had created in my studio, I began thinking about what would happen if I had a heart attack or a debilitating illness. Joana and Stan were both doctors, and they had their patients to attend to down in Tucson. How could they take the time to come up to Canada, get me settled in a care place, sell all my jewelry, cancel the rent on my studio, get rid of all my midcentury modern furniture (which was collectable), sell my condo, and close out my business (JF Designs)? I felt that I owed it to them to do all of that while I was physically able to do it myself. It was time to make a major change. Again.

While I was in Tucson for my winter and gem show sojourn in February, I started looking at housing. I found a lovely townhouse, reasonably priced, in a gated community, fairly near to Joana and Stan's house in the Foothills. When I went back to Kelowna, I had put money down on it with two months to conclude the purchase after I figured out the Kelowna part. I put the Lagoons condo on the market. When my rent renewal lease on the studio came due, I wrote my resignation. Sadly, so sadly. I held a huge closeout sale with all my supplies in the studio and gave away a lot of equipment (workbench, several expensive machines, etcetera). I sold some equipment to the new renters of Studio 203, who turned out to be three of my former students. I was so proud of them. The day of the sale, I counted up $1,700. After all, I was moving to Tucson; it wasn't as if I couldn't replace all those beads and pearls! I rented a storage locker and moved all the studio furniture and equipment into it to incorporate into the moving van.

As the moving date of October 29 approached, I booked my airline flight, with one suitcase. I called Mayflower, who gave me an estimate of $4,000. They wanted another $4,000 to hook my Honda on the tail, which I thought was seriously overpriced. Then, magically, I heard about a retired Air Canada pilot. He and his wife had a hobby of driving peoples' cars wherever they were needed for $1,200, delivering them to the destination airport, and emailing the owner to say where the car was parked, and when the owner flew in a few days later, there was their car, fully gassed and ready to go. And the chauffeurs got a paid-for vacation, because being retired Air Canada employees, they got free flights home anytime they wanted after spending a few days' vacation there. My pilot guy spent winters in California, Arizona, and Florida, or visited relatives all over the States. Not a bad retirement!

Mayflower came in on the twenty-fourth and did all the packing: cartons of dishes, clothing cartons, everything boxed. I drove for the last time to the cemetery to say goodbye to Fritz. That was difficult. The pilot and his wife came by on the twenty-fifth with their suitcases and drove off with my car. They would email me on the twenty-ninth, telling me what letter and number the car would be in at the long-term parking lot at the Tucson airport. On the morning of the twenty-sixth, Mayflower pulled the huge van up and loaded all the large pieces of furniture and the big cartons on the van first, then went on to two other locations whose belongings would be disposed of at earlier destinations on the way down to Tucson. With a big gulp and enormous sadness, I left Kelowna on October 20, 2009. I've never been able to go back.

Lucky in Tucson

When I landed in Tucson, I took the parking lot van and had no trouble at all locating my car exactly where the pilot had written it would be. Unlocked the door with my key and found the keys he had used in the glove compartment.

Drove off to Joana's, where I would spend a few days till the moving van arrived. I met the van at Miles Circle, my new home. I had paid in full for the house, having enough savings, but my condo in the Lagoons had not sold yet. The real-estate market was still depressed from the disastrous 2008 collapse. The house on Miles Circle was one of forty in the gated complex. It consisted of four streets reaching out from the center, which contained a club beach house with a sauna and a hot tub. There were three tennis courts, a picnic area, and a heated swimming pool. My townhouse was directly across from the swimming pool, which I thought would encourage me to do walking exercises in the pool. I did go from time to time, but not as often as I had intended. Ah, well, you know what's paved with good intentions …

Each of the four streets had ten houses supporting that area, but strangely, you never saw people outside much unless they were walking their dog. Then, it was only a quick "Hi, how are you?" Or, "Nice out, isn't it." I only became acquainted with the folks at the end of the circle because the lady had a gorgeous garden out in back and loved to talk flowers with me. Her husband was on the council. We functioned with a homeowners association, and all decisions were made by the residents on the board. I later served two years as a board member.

Since the residents were so reclusive, I decided I had to take my passion for jewelry elsewhere and begin teaching again. I had heard of the Oasis organization and enjoyed reading their catalog of classes and realized that was exactly what I wanted to do. I applied, I was accepted, and right from the beginning, my lectures were well attended. I started out giving lectures on how to identify pearls and natural precious and semiprecious stones, and then graduated into teaching classes on how to knot pearl necklaces, how to make beaded necklaces and add professional-looking clasps, and how to make your own earring wires. When Oasis decided to close their Tucson facility a couple of years later, my students decided to stay with me for classes in my house. I had been in Tucson seven years and enjoyed selling my jewelry in two galleries, but decided to branch out. My realtor found a beautiful, large house, the middle one of three, set back on a long driveway into the center of a quiet, well-located block, near shopping centers, doctors, a bank, and a Trader Joe's; it had four bedrooms and a two-car garage.

Oooh, one bedroom for my exercise machines, one bedroom for my computer workroom, one for me, one for guests, and I turned the big garage into a huge jewelry studio. I bought a four-ton heat pump, added ten spotlights, extra outlets all across one wall with continuous workbenches, a complete wall of pegboard holding all the strands of beads and tools, and two long tables for my students to work on. *I loved it!* All my students from Oasis came with me; in fact, several of them helped me make the move. One couple took all the clothes over and hung them in the new master bedroom closet; another one and my cleaning lady moved the delicate glass china cabinet over on his truck, and many brought over all the cartons holding my jewelry supplies. I was so touched. I bought a beautiful gazebo for the large patio; installed a flower planter, a running fountain, and a large table-and-chairs set; and began teaching all-day classes in the former garage. (I built a shady carport for the car.) We had wonderful lunches with wine out on the patio, and then, refreshed with food and happy conversation, would go back into the studio and finish up our soldering, stonecutting, art clay metal fusions, all the complicated things that required us to get down and dirty. We had a ball! They enjoyed my funny stories about living in strange places and the things that had happened there, and my stories often coincided with the funny stories my male student, Myron, told. He was so good with all the ladies, loved joking with them, the jokes always in good taste. I called them "Myron's Harem." As a treat for them taking all my classes, I always invited them to attend the gem show with me, and I would lead them to my favorite dealers, then point to all the natural stones, teaching them to recognize them and to learn their value; then they could buy individual stones which they decided to set or wire wrap in a future class. It tickled me to see them wilt and drop around two or three in the afternoon while I, the old lady, was still rarin' to go when the shows closed at seven.

Sometime around then I received an unusual telephone call from Nova Scotia, eastern Canada. The caller said she had seen my work on my Ruby Lane website and liked the designs and wondered if I gave classes. I said yes, but not in Canada anymore, just in Tucson. That was okay, she would come to me! Her name was Chris, and she would fly to Tucson and stay for a week and I was to teach her everything I knew that the week's time permitted. Well, she was so determined that it was the most intensive week I think I've ever had, as we flowed from designing, measuring, sawing, fitting, soldering, finishing, polishing, stone setting, bezel setting, prong setting, stonecutting, shaping and polishing cabs, pearl knotting, adding clasps, and even working in some silver art clay. Total immersion. Chris soaked it all up like a sponge but was a very outspoken person, expressing what she liked and other things she couldn't be bothered with. The following year she flew back, and I had a great comrade during four days at the gem show. She was an X-ray technician in a hospital but was consumed with a desire to make jewelry. She decided to concentrate on just one thing: ammolite fossils. The insides of snail fossils, found only in Alberta, Canada, seventy million years old. She decided not to waste a lot of time fitting settings herself for the shaped and polished fossils, so she eventually found websites offering settings which the stones would fit in, and her business took off. Eventually she had her own website on Etsy and last year was able to retire from her hospital job and make jewelry full-time. Her sales on Etsy have reached astronomical heights, and she generously credits me with having changed her life. Actually, I am *very* proud of her professionalism and what she has accomplished. We are good friends and exchange emails all the time. A few years ago, she came down for the gem show and offered to give a lecture on ammolites to all my students, which they enjoyed tremendously.

Eventually, the large house on Glenn Street became just a bit too difficult to maintain, even though I loved the garage studio and all the facilities it offered. It was getting expensive to maintain the gardens, the irrigation, and the taxes. I was also falling prone to the various health problems of being in my nineties. I had my aortic heart valve replaced with a pig's valve, and died on the operating table before they made the incision. They injected me and resuscitated me, replaced the valve, and then I suffered a stroke in the intensive care unit. I was there for eight days, and the family did not think I would survive. But I did, and was well enough to even continue driving. A year later, I suffered a second stroke and lost half the vision in each eye, which ended any thought of driving. I made the sorrowful decision that it was time to cut my losses and move into an "independent living" facility. I chose Atria Bell Court Gardens, a hundred-year-old mansion

which had been turned into a retirement community, featuring beautiful Spanish-style arches and red tile roofs that reminded me of our years in Spain. I chose
a one-bedroom apartment, rented two storage lockers, and taught jewelry classes every Saturday morning to thirteen students in the activities room with the
Engage Life director. But I discovered in the two years I was there that I did not
enjoy being part of such a large community (160 apartments), living on the third
floor, and not being able to walk around the grounds very well. When they raised
my rent for my one-bedroom to $4,000, I decided to move again.

Dear Abby (Holiday 2017)

Back in the fifties, a strange phenomenon began making itself known. It was
the ubiquitous Christmas Letter, which let you write one generic letter about your
past year to tell all your relatives and friends how things were going. There was
no internet then, so you typed out the letter, took it to the copy shop, chose some
cute Christmasy paper, and had a hundred copies made. Which you then mailed
to everyone on your Christmas List. You wrote about your husband's promotion,
your kids' all-As report cards, a new car, and your good health, which allowed
all of you to enjoy a week in Atlantic City. The letters got so prolific and so bad
that people began writing to Dear Abby to complain. Then came computers, and
Christmas letters became the norm. Unfortunately, they did not change their for-
mat; it was just a lot easier to write and a lot cheaper to send.

Thanksgiving, 2017

Hi, Everybody,

Greetings to family, friends, and those acquaintances who only get an Update once a year, and whose first reaction probably is, "My gosh, is she
still alive?" Yes, she is, though the gait is slower, the vision stops at the
middle of her nose on the left side, the willpower to get up in the morning
wanes, the jewelry-making gets done tenaciously, and most of the thought

processes are still working adequately. On June 23, we were all excited when Andrew flew to Washington to accept an award from Rod Rosenstein, head of the Justice Department, for Special Prosecutor of the Year. So proud.

As for me, I continue giving classes in jewelry-making, having taken a brief hiatus during July and August, while everyone with any sense was on a beach somewhere away from Tucson. During that time, I became a little jewelry machine, turned out sixteen pieces to put on my website, which resulted in a few sales. I enjoyed the creative whirlwind. My volunteer drivers are a lifesaver, taking me to doctors' appointments, banking, and grocery-shopping. I'm gradually training them to read the backs of all the cartons for carbs and sugar, but sometimes they sneak a snack into the grocery cart. That's my story and I'm sticking to it. The hobby that is giving me the most fun (and challenges) is writing. I joined a Writers Group at the library and once a week present another chapter in the memoirs I am putting together for a possible future book. I'm inspired in the project by the other writers, several of whom have already been published. They speak tenuously of their self-imposed deadlines, and I scurry home, and write furiously on the computer, knowing that my deadline has a more macabre meaning than theirs. But with all of Fritz's and my travels and our living in several different countries where strange, funny, and curious things occurred, it is exciting to dredge up a lot of those memories and put them down on paper. When the shocking terrorist attack on the Ramblas in Barcelona occurred, I wrote about how beautiful our visits to Barcelona had been and the article was published in the Sunday Edition of the *Tucson Daily Star*. I'm also including my thoughts on life in general, and since so many of them came to me as we were flying long hours overseas, the book is tentatively titled *Life as Observed from the Middle Seat*.

I can't help but express my sorrow and sadness for what is happening in the United States, but since this will go out to some who don't share that concern, I can only say that having lived so many years abroad in countries where being an American meant something honorable, perhaps

I tend to look at things globally, the bigger picture. Maybe things will get better by the time I push Send on this message the week after Thanksgiving. No, if anything, things are only worse. As I head off for Thanksgiving Dinner at friends' today, I see only darkness and despair ahead. I have always been a person who sees the glass half-full, even better if the first half was a decent wine. I have just finished another Erma Bombeck book which makes me so thankful to have a sense of humor. At the end of the book, which came to be written over a year of reading self-help books, she noted that it's our Constitution at fault: that the Life and Liberty are a piece of cake; it's the Pursuit of Happiness that's the problem. She quotes Gail Sheehy, author of *Passages*, that sums up a flaw most of us have when we pursue happiness: "Would that there would be an award for people who come to understand the concept of enough. Good enough. Successful enough. Thin enough. Rich enough. Socially responsible enough. When you have self-respect you have enough, and when you have enough, you have self-respect." My wishes go out to you all, for a Merry Christmas, a Happy Hanukkah, or whatever you celebrate. May 2018 bring us good health and optimism, time to spend with our loved ones, less reliance on material pleasures, and contentment with what we have. Put down the iPhone, gather the grandchildren or, as in my case, great-grandkids, and go catch a firefly, build a snowman, or let your kids jump over a sprinkler. Happy New Year!
Love, Janice

P.S.: I wrote this year's Christmas letter a little bit tongue in cheek, in re-membrance of all those Dear Abby letters, but trust me, every word is true.

Time Well Spent

Clichés become clichés because they are so true. They are clichés because they happen so often. They become clichés because they are so prevalent. A cliché is an overused, overworked word and should be avoided at all costs. According to Wikipedia. When you decide to write on a subject of what you want but can't have, clichés tend to take over the article. So, please excuse all the quotations I have saved over the years in the hope that eventually I might find a use for them. Today is that day.

What I want are a bunch of things: youth, lots of money, wisdom, courage to take chances, happiness, more time, good health, and the ability to speak in public.

Now that I'm ninety-two, I realize and accept I can't grow younger, only older. But birthdays are good for you. *The more you have, the longer you live.* And it's okay if at class reunions, you feel younger than everyone else looks. Good health follows the ability to find humor in everything and finding something to be grateful for each and every day.

Money can't buy happiness. But somehow it's easier to cry in a Cadillac than in a '94 Honda. If you lend someone $20 and never see that person again, it was probably worth it. *Money will buy a fine dog, but only kindness will make him wag his tail. He who dies with the most toys is nonetheless DEAD.* To acquire Knowledge, one must study; but to acquire Wisdom, one must observe. Some mistakes are too much fun to make only once. *It's easier to get older than it is to get wiser.* Being courageous means nobody cares if you can't dance well. Just get up and dance. *It may be that your sole purpose in life is simply to serve as a warning to others.* Besides, when you think about it, *the only failure you can have is the failure to try.*

I wish I had more time. When you begin thinking that you must make every minute *count*, and you look at five boxes all labeled Future Projects, you don't want to waste a minute. So why do I sit and watch a Hallmark movie for the sixth time? I guess because my mantra has become *Procrastinate NOW!* Anyway, *a Creative Mess is better than Tidy Idleness.*

I used to be painfully shy. Then I learned that you should always Be Yourself. *Because the people that matter don't mind … and the ones that mind don't matter.* So now I find that I can even speak in public before a hundred people, and when they laugh, I find that it's FUN. Agreeing on religious differences, or finding common ground, *can* be difficult. My husband thought he was God and I didn't. So we became Unitarians. Problem solved.

One thing I want, and can't figure out how to get, because it evades me, is the Forgiveness that I feel so desperately in need of. All the years I had to spend out of the United States, because of my husband's business; being unable to connect with my daughter and family. I can't get back those years, nor can I change them. Not knowing about their illnesses, not being able to share their sorrows or worries, not being there for birthdays, Christmases, and achievements. Not hearing about my daughter's activities, her boyfriends, her honors. All the hugs, compliments, and comforting I would have been able to give, had I only been there. I paid for it in the lonely nights, crying, wishing I had a friend in whom I could confide, but there was no one. Internet, Facetime, and Skype didn't exist. Letters could never say what I wanted to convey. Unfortunately, I couldn't find a single cliché to cover Regrets. It's a burden you bear alone, in silence and shame.

Fear of Falling

Last Monday I shut down the computer, turned off the ceiling light, and felt my way around the corner of the bed. Patting the thermal blanket, I started up the side when my bare foot stepped on one of the silk decorative pillows which had fallen to the floor. Just that tiny touch threw me off balance and I slithered to the floor, the blanket slowing my fall. I ended up sitting on the carpet next to a high electric bed, unable to put my hands and arms on the top of the mattress and push myself up to a kneeling position.

I wasn't hurt, just feeling the adrenaline racing. To calm down, I assured myself that if I could "hump" myself back around the bed, over to the treadmill, I'd be okay because surely, there, I would be able to draw myself up and get on my feet. I wouldn't need to call the night security man to come and lift me up.

Ever since I lost half my sight as a result of the second stroke, I've had to face the fear of falling. The pandemic hasn't helped because I'm either sitting watching Hallmark movies or sitting staring at the computer. I've lost a lot of muscle strength from atrophy. Note to self: Get back on the PowerPlate vibration machine to build up your muscles. Well, I couldn't even get the strength to push up on the low treadmill. Using logic, I decided that maybe it was time to call Bruce, but the bathroom was now closer than my night table where the telephone was charging, so I decided to "hump" myself there instead of returning to the head of the bed. When I got on the hard floor of the bathroom, I began regretting my choice, as every bounce hurt my tail where I had broken a couple of vertebrae and they had glued me together a few years ago. I wiggled around and put my hands on the step-in area of the walk-in shower, but my arms still had no strength to push me up. I pulled the emergency alarm bell cord hanging behind the toilet paper holder. A minute later the phone on the counter rang. I was sure it was Bruce in security, but I couldn't reach the phone; it was near the back of the counter on its charger. I scrounged the toilet bowl brush out of its holder and tried to poke the handle around the back of the phone to push it nearer to me, but each push shoved it further away. The phone stopped ringing. Finally, I knocked it over and grabbed it when it fell over the edge. When I dialed what I thought was Bruce's number, I got the message the number was not in service. Note to self: Wear your med-alert bracelet night and day.

By that time, Bruce had unlocked my patio door and was calling out to me, "Janice, are you okay? Janice, where are you?" He found me huddled on the bathroom floor at the same time I answered. I assured him I hadn't broken anything, nor had I hit my head; I just needed him to lift me up under my shoulders. He was already dialing 911 as he explained that the rule at all Atrias was "Don't TOUCH the person who has fallen! Cardinal Rule Number One! Only *firemen* can lift the resident who is on the floor." Ah, the power of lawsuits. Bruce handed me his phone. "She wants to talk to you."

A lady asked if I had bumped my head, if I hurt anywhere, and I assured her I had slunk to the floor, not fallen or tripped. Then she asked me how much I weighed. I thought that was pretty fresh, till I realized it was for the benefit of the arriving firemen. She hung up, satisfied, and Bruce told me she was located in Toronto! Good heavens, I was the cause of an International Incident.

Bruce said he was going to leave me for just a few minutes in order to go out to the street and wave the firemen in. Is this the moment to tell you I realized I had chosen to wear a very short tee shirt to bed? Bruce was back in five minutes with four of the cutest firemen I ever saw. They knelt around me, asking more questions, and then one of them asked if I could bend both my knees up. OMG. I hadn't thought of that! I was so grateful I had kept my panties on! Thank you, God. Two firemen put one arm under each of my shoulders, the other arm under each knee, and counted in unison, "One, two, three!" and up I flew, light as a feather. They held on to me for a minute, could see that I was steady on my feet, smiled, and left. The Fireman Dating Service is not a long-term thing …

25

The Great Fantasy

Often, when I'm trying to get to sleep and can't, because my mind is going around and around, I find myself thinking about a larger social problem and I force myself to work on a solution. After all, when the men pondering the same thing toss it off as "impossible to solve" or "would cost too much" or "it just wouldn't work," the saying goes, "Just give it to a couple of women; they'll figure it out." So, I lie there in the tangle of sheets and thermal blanket and resolve a couple of questions, then drift off to sleep. Over time, I usually come up with a solution. The challenge is that the solution has to *make sense*, be *financially viable*, and *solve a lot of side issues* as it resolves the main question.

Thus it came to pass in 2015 when the problem of homelessness hit the newspaper big time, there were a lot of discussions and letters to the editors. There were almost three thousand homeless in Arizona in 2015, with the highest density in Pima county. After all, the winter tourists are not the only ones attracted to Tucson because of the climate. Photos showed cardboard cartons in which the homeless slept on the sidewalks of downtown Tucson. The park named Veinte de Agosto, favored by the homeless, was closed by the city because of health and safety problems after a death occurred there. It had been filled with tents and pilfered shopping carts piled high with clothing and personal possessions, and littered with cooking equipment. It was declared unsanitary due to lack of toilets. The city suggested putting porta-potties on the streets, but that was met with disgust from the public who claimed an equal right to the sidewalks. There were photos of encampments under bridges, people sitting on the sidewalks with cups or bowls in front of them, begging for food money. It got so bad that the city passed an ordinance stating that the homeless had to leave a five-foot walkway through the maze of boxes and litter for the public to be able to walk on the sidewalk. That's government for you: write another law that is impossible to enforce to take care of a problem that you make no attempt to fix. So, then they closed the park and *no one* could use it. Charities like Primavera Shelter for Men, located south of Tucson on the Benson highway (hard to get to), the Salvation Army, and various churches had shelters filled with cots and serving meals, but that did not meet the needs on a permanent basis.

The homeless had a spokesman, Jon MacLane, who spoke at length about the problem but never had any actual solutions that would alleviate the situation. His main suggestion was that the city of Tucson should build twenty "homeless parks" with large tents and public toilets, one in each voting district so that the public would be aware of the problem. Would building more of the parks help, or just add to the problem? He gradually drifted out of the news when it was seen as just a political ploy. He obviously enjoyed the notoriety. The problem of the homeless was huge and had a lot of diverse elements. Most attempts to solve it attacked only one or two of the problems, but they were Band-Aid solutions and didn't really go to the heart of all the various reasons for the homelessness. Something like that intrigued me to see if there was anything that could be done in totality.

To understand the problem, I needed to itemize the various causes:

- The economy, obviously: So many working men and women had lost their jobs because companies downsized when the market crashed in 2008.
- Funds had been cut drastically from social programs that people relied on by the state government when the new governor took office.
- When people could no longer make the payments on their homes, the banks foreclosed.
- They also could not afford rental payments.
- They had health problems and could not afford medical care, nor could

they hold down a job, if they found one, because they couldn't afford health insurance.

- Living in various parts of the city, they couldn't get to jobs on public transportation, and the bus company solved the problem of lost riders by raising the fares, compounding the problem.
- There were a number of people on the streets with mental problems such as schizophrenia, who could not get the medications to control them because they did not have a general doctor.
- Many of the homeless had worked in construction, and when the housing boom collapsed with construction almost nil for over two years, they could no longer find any work.
- Many were addicted to drugs, and panhandled to get money for their next fix.
- There were also the veterans, who came home with PTSD and couldn't cope.
- And some just did not want to improve their lot, preferring the random life on the streets. They had no incentive to change their lifestyle.
- For the ones who did want to get back to what they had had before they became homeless, the challenges were many: They did not know what resources were available to help them, and many could not qualify for help simply because they had no permanent address when applying for it. They had no way to get to those organizations. Just the simple fact that they had nowhere to live meant they were helpless to get help.

There was no coordinated help or organizations that worked as one unit to resolve the larger issue. Stan Kozachik on the Tucson City Council was the only one heading up several homeless committees. But the lack of funds strangled his efforts. And the fact that nothing was attempted on an all-inclusive basis meant that the problem remained intact.

At the same time the problem of homeless people was growing, there was another problem rearing its ugly head: shopping malls were dying. Most shopping malls are "anchored" with a Macy's or a Sears, and slowly we began to read that

Macy's was closing seventeen stores across the nation and that Sears's profits were down for the third year in a row, and they were closing the less profitable stores, thus adding to the unemployment problem. Without the big stores to draw the customers into the malls, the shopping centers were losing customers to the big box stores, to the discount warehouses, and especially to online shoppers as the popular Amazon expanded its merchandise line.

In 1996, Hillary Clinton had written a book called *It Takes a Village* with the subtitle "*to Raise a Child.*" The Republicans derided it, saying it takes a family to raise a child, but that was the entire point of the book. When a family hasn't the resources or means, the whole community needs to get involved. You need to have an *inclusive* economy as well as an *inclusive* society. And that is where my racing mind took off. As I tried to fall asleep each night, my mind would think of all sorts of possibilities. Possibilities that might just work and become probabilities in the process. I gradually organized some ideas, and it became The Great Fantasy in my mind.

The Great Fantasy started with the malls in cities all across the land. Where the huge three-story department stores had closed and lay empty, unleased, the corridors and parking lots showed a decrease in customers.

Why not take the large stores and renovate them into low-cost housing units? What was needed was a comprehensive approach. I began to think outside of the box. Or the cardboard carton, if you'll forgive the pun.

I imagined the city of Tucson leasing a Macy's or Sears, and turning the ground floor into a showroom for all the items they carried with a sample of each which could be ordered and shipped from one super warehouse somewhere in the state. This showroom would have the advantage of the customer seeing and touching an item in person rather than ordering it from a picture. A picture doesn't always show you how much you can squeeze in that freezer. It would employ salespeople to explain the features while allowing Sears or Macy's to compete pricewise with the big-box stores because they would not have to fully stock each store with multiples of their merchandise. Apart from the department store showrooms, the ground floor of the mall would be refitted with a glassed-in day-care center, a walk-in clinic with drug counselors available, and a branch of SCORE, as well as the normal shops and boutiques. The upper floors of the former department stores would become low-cost housing.

Shoppers in the mall could drop their children off for an hour or two at the day-care center with trained teachers and retired volunteers (surrogate grandmas and grandpas) in attendance, and working people could leave their children there for the entire day, with tenants being able to stop in to play with their children on their lunch or coffee breaks. The bonus would be that the shoppers could glance in and see a bunch of little children happily playing together, and stop for a moment to watch. Take time to smell the roses.

A walk-in clinic would be available during the hours the mall was open, therefore until nine every evening. This way people with minor problems of colds or flu, cuts or falls, could be treated, and emergency rooms of hospitals left to handle more serious problems. Drug addicts could be treated with methadone or other medication prescribed by the doctors in attendance. Reasonable fees would be charged.

The organization which was previously known as the Service Corps of Retired Executives and is now recognized as Counselors to America's Small Business would have an office to provide business mentoring services to entrepreneurs and could guide the homeless people who used to have a profession to get connected again with the job market. They would get fees for seminars for existing businesses and offer free consultation for the jobless. It is funded by the Small Business Association. The consultants are retired business executives. My husband was a member of the international division and was scheduled to be sent to Argentina many years ago, when the request was cancelled.

Part of the ground floor of the mall would feature a culinary arts school, where the students could learn all aspects of hostelry, from cooking, waiting, housekeeping, and management. The school would feature a typical restaurant, open to the public, serving the various recipes of the day which the guests would evaluate at the end of the meal, along with the service. The students would gain experience which would make them successful candidates when they graduated and applied for jobs with local restaurants or hotels. With a steady job and an income, the turnover on the studio apartments would be frequent, to allow more single homeless people the opportunity to participate.

With plumbing, sewer drainage, lighting, air-conditioning, and other amenities already installed on every floor, the upper floors could be turned into one and two-bedroom apartments for low-cost housing at minimum cost. Just by adding plumbing pipes and electrical wiring to each individual drywalled unit, the apartments could be added in a square around a center court on the second and third floors.

There would be an attractive glassed-off entrance leading to the escalators in the stores which would take the tenants to the upper floors, with a sign stating that the escalators were for the use of tenants only. Each upper landing would be a courtyard where the tenants could gather, with comfortable patio seating and potted plants and trees.

The elevators to the second and third floors would be closed to the public and work only when the tenants inserted a card into a slot on the elevator door but would not work for the public. The escalator would remain the centerpiece, with the apartments being constructed in a square around it. The second floor would become dormitory housing with each studio containing a private bathroom but having a kitchenette niche with sink, microwave, and small fridge for single men and women looking for temporary housing with a permanent address, until they got on their feet again. The studios would be the size of a hotel room, with pull-down wall beds and a full storage space. The possible tenants would be vetted by a social worker, and also a psychologist (to find people with mental problems so they could be placed elsewhere and undergo treatment). The ones accepted would be directed to the building manager to sign a lease stipulating the regulations and conditions for receiving this beneficial housing. The second floor would have space for two lines of apartments going around the square: the inner studios facing the courtyard, and the outer studios opening on a corridor going all around the outside perimeter of the building. The backs of each row of apartments would contain all the additional plumbing and electrical connections, the kitchens, and bathrooms.

The second floor would also house a gently used clothing store solely for the tenants, with donations from the public, so that those wishing to apply for jobs in offices or with companies could purchase items at a small cost and be well-dressed when they were interviewed, giving them a greater air of self-confidence, something an employer is looking for in an employee.

The third floor would be turned into more permanent one- and two-bedroom apartments, allowing children. They would be entered from the courtyard but extend all the way back to the outer perimeter of the building and include a small balcony. School buses would pick the children up every day at the mall entrance and bring them back in the afternoon. They would be walked to the day-care center by the mall security guards, giving their parents peace of mind until they could collect them after work.

The mall would continue to offer the usual shops and facilities: a pharmacy, a dry cleaner, a mini-mart or gourmet grocery store, a bank branch, a computer store with tech support, boutiques, fast-food specialty stands, restaurants, and the usual movie theater assortment. With bus lines serving the mall, tenants would have more access to jobs outside of the mall, thus making them more independent once they were back on their feet.

With many of the tenants living and working in the retail shops, boutiques, garages, offices, and restaurants at the mall, they could put aside savings, and eventually move out into the community as responsible members. These simple solutions could turn their lives around and give them back their dignity. It gives a leg up to those who want to help themselves.

It would make the streets and parks of Tucson as safe and friendly as they used to be, especially in the growing, popular downtown area, where some of the graduates from the hostelry school would find jobs in the growing number of restaurants, and make the tram ride a fun destination for our winter tourists.

But what of the die-hard vagrants? I prefer to keep my fantasies on a wistful premise, so I would set aside a substantial fund to have a roving van with two social workers on board. Each night they would patrol the streets looking for these people.

Because the Tucson City Council would have passed an ordinance saying that the streets and parks must remain clear and the sidewalks left open to the public *at all times* and not be subject to sleeping carton accommodations, these vagrants would be taken to a large empty warehouse somewhere near the airport, heated in winter and swamp-coolered in summer. Supplied with only the necessities of water, porta-potties, and an area to cook in, it would give those who are picked up a place to sleep out of the cold, rain, or heat—with space to unroll their sleeping bags, as they would have done under the bridge.

The social workers would question them to determine if any had any desire to improve their lot. For those who appeared amenable to the suggestion of further help, they would have a follow-up talk the next day about the possibilities available to them. And for those who were indifferent or not interested, they would spend the night. In the a.m., free to go. No breakfast; nothing different than a night under a bridge.

The last question is, how can all of this be funded?

Which brings us back to Hillary's book. It has to involve the entire city. The joint decision to make all the different charities and organizations *want* to solve the problem and coordinate their resources. That means that the city council would have to make some profound changes, changes that would be a benefit to the citizens as a whole.

First, the money that is currently being spent just on bandaging the problem could be allocated to solving the problem of the store renovations covering the apartments in the empty department stores. Because many of the charitable organizations or churches would find their services lessened somewhat, more of their funds could be allocated to the low-cost housing needs. Much of the day care, hostelry classes, financial counseling, and walk-in clinic would be covered by the fees and with eager volunteers. Rio Nuevo could contribute some of its generous funding and endorse the concept with enthusiasm, changing it to a downtown business association. And the tenants themselves would be paying rent, minimal though it was, responsibly accepting their own liabilities.

Is *the Great Fantasy* so unrealistic that it is doomed to failure without giving it a chance?

Mostly, as I try to fall asleep, I fantasize about being loved.

The deepest, truest love. Eternal love. The kind of love that turns and smiles, just at you. The kind of love that shows in his eyes, "I'm so glad we're together." The kind of love that sighs with contentment. And as I pull the rumpled sheets around me in my warm comfortable bed, the kind of love that empathizes with those who have less.

26

No Regrets

The topic in our writing group this week was "Something I had never done, but would like to try."

Now I would not like to pretend I have been everywhere and done everything, but what I have done and the places I've been have proven to be quite satisfactory, and if there's something I've not yet put on my Bucket List, I'm not aware of it. So, I come to the end of my life quite content and without regrets. I don't worry about being one of the women who passed on dessert that last night on the *Titanic*.

But as I was desperately searching for something I would have liked to do, it suddenly occurred to me that I had never written a song, and I love to sing. Seventy-six percent of my brain is taken up with lyrics, so why not try?

Two hours later, I've decided I'm no Hammerstein. The lyrics, the cadence, the rhyming, deciding if it should be country or western, or whether to just be romantic, doesn't come close to the decision about which comes first, music or lyrics? And then there's the problem of whom to record it with: Barbra Streisand or David Prouty.

Decisions, decisions. I guess I'll just book a cruise to the Galapagos. Always did want to see all those little baby turtles waddling off to the surf. And if I can save one from being snatched up by an hors d'oeuvres-seeking hawk, I'll cross it off my Bucket List.

A Mother-in-Law Joke

My son-in-law Stan is an oncologist. He retired three years ago, so I should probably say *was* an oncologist. But Stan is a people doctor, so he *is* an oncologist, *was* an oncologist, and will always *be* an oncologist. He has years of Christmas cards from patients testifying how he helped them. When he was doing his internship at M. D. Anderson Cancer Center in Houston, Texas, they asked him to stay on and continue doing research. But Stan's goal had always been to treat patients. So, he returned to Tucson and became a partner in the cancer clinic on the grounds of the Tucson Medical Center. This expanded to a complete clinic with eight doctors, labs, chemotherapy, and radiation. Whenever there was a breakthrough on a new drug to fight cancer, Stan was the go-to guy on the ten o'clock news to explain it. When he finally retired at seventy, we wondered what this dedicated doctor would do with his time. Well, he has taken up the cause of literacy, coaching young students in south Tucson once a week. He walks miles on the river walk three times a week, plays tennis, donates platelets, and offers advice at several health clinics.

Before pulling the plug on my dead hard drive, he had resuscitated it by taking it to some experts who brought it back to life and saved all my chapters. I was so grateful. Afterward, following my orders, you should have seen him beat the heck out of it with a hammer on the cement driveway, so no one could retrieve anything before we buried it in the garbage bin.

When Stan retired, Joana threw a party for him at La Paloma resort. The ballroom was filled with colleagues, friends, and family. Andrew and Adriana flew in from Los Angeles and Denver. It was an Event.

The microphone was passed around the hall as several of his colleagues made speeches saying what a great doctor he was and how they had been privileged to have known and worked beside him. They spoke of how much they had learned from him. The accolades poured in. Andrew gave a very funny speech about his dad.

In a lull, I suddenly stood up and asked the microphone guy for the mic. I could see Joana cringe, sinking down in her seat, wondering what on earth I was going to say in front of all their friends. I didn't know, either; I didn't have any notes to read from.

I smiled at the audience and said, "For those of you who don't know me, I'm Stan's mother-in-law." There was a titter of laughter.

"I've been sitting here enjoying all the comments from Stan's colleagues. But the thought occurred to me just now that no one has said how it was like to be his patient. So, I thought I should tell you.

"Shortly after moving here from Canada, I developed a very bad case of pancreatitis. The pain was excruciating, and Stan and Joana took me to the ER. After seeing the appropriate doctors, I was moved to a private room while they waited to remove my gallbladder. For a whole week, I couldn't move. I couldn't have anything to eat, I could not even have a drop of water to drink. The nurses moistened my lips with a wet sponge. I had oxygen tubes up my nose, an IV drip in one arm to feed me, and a morphine drip in the other arm to control the pain. I kept thinking this must be like being caught in an earthquake buried under tons of cement, unable to move, but still alive. I passed the hours listening to Michael Bublé singing old Frank Sinatra songs on the radio, the CDs repeating over and over.

"Every morning after making rounds of his own patients. Stan would stop in my hospital room with a cheerful 'Hi, Mom, how you doing?' then head straight to the computer by the side of the bed to see what had happened overnight.

"One morning he was standing there reading the doctors' notes, when suddenly the door flew open and two nurses rushed in, their faces panic-stricken. When they saw Stan, they came to an abrupt halt and looked at each other; then one said, 'Dr. K? Uhhhh, you're standing on her oxygen tube!"

The ballroom exploded with laughter.

"Well," I continued, "that story was too good to be ignored. It went viral all over TMC. I told Stan that he had hit a new low in mother-in-law jokes."

As I sat down to the applause, Joana looked relieved.

Later, as we were getting ready to leave, a man came up to me and shook my hand. "Hi," he said. "I'm Dr. So and So. I just wanted to tell you that if I had had a mother-in-law like you, I wouldn't have divorced my wife."

He turned to Stan. "Congratulations, Stan."

I wondered if he was congratulating Stan on his retirement or his choice of a mother-in-law.

Whatever.

It Takes a Long Time to Become Young

Pablo Picasso

I had a hard time waking up this morning. I so wanted to lie in the warm covers and just relax. But Thursdays are Bacon Day at Atria, so I grudgingly hauled myself up and out. I used to say that I would plant bacon but couldn't find any seeds. While brushing my teeth, I asked myself, "If it's bacon day, that means it's also Writers Group Day, and what were we supposed to write about?" Oh, yes, they agreed to write on the subject of the Picasso quotation, even though no one knew what it meant.

I pondered it and decided that I would have to first come up with a description or definition of what it's like to be young. Okay. Young is three or four. Young is feeling happy. Young is running around the yard chasing butterflies. Young is having enough vocabulary to be able to express your feelings. Young is having a Mommy or Dad who is there to take care of you, cook food that will make you grow big and strong, cover you up at night to make sure you are warm, read you stories that make you want to learn to read yourself, and kiss your owies and dry your tears. To be young is fairly easy, I think. But to BECOME young, after you've become old, is maybe not so easy. How do you dismiss the disappointments in life, the disillusionments, the betrayals, the meanness, the hurts that no kiss can make go away, the struggles to survive, the hypocrisy, the egoistic ways of thinking, the strong emphasis on materialism, the stress, the rush, the domination of the iPhone. Can you really regain that carefree happiness of youth?

Yes, perhaps, but you have to work hard to achieve it. You have to admit that certain things you thought were important, aren't, really. Dismiss them. If you can't forgive and forget something your best friend did to you, don't. Forgiveness is not very easy, so why bother? Just stick that memory in a Brain File, and when something similar happens, open the drawer, remember the pain, vow not to let it hurt you again, and close the drawer. If corruption of public officials bothers you, be sure to exercise your right to do what you want, and make the effort to vote the buggers out. You'll feel good. Help others who don't have the good life you have; gratitude is the surest way to gain the happiness of youth. When you share your toy with your little friend, you smile.

Mostly, when you have become old, you have learned to become suspicious. A child doesn't even know what suspicious means. Or cynical. Or selfish. They are usually empathetic, even if they don't know the meaning of that big word. So, stop and think of what life was like for you before you learned what life is *really* like. Feeling happy? Take time to think of one thing to be grateful for every morning before you get out of bed. Bacon? That'll work. Chasing butterflies? How about sitting in the patio gardens, watching the butterflies sip nectar from the flowers surrounding us. Being able to conjure up fancy words when writing articles for the writing group. Instead of Mom and Dad, we have our children who take care of us, friends who love visiting us, and a staff of people who knock on the door every morning if you haven't released your upper lock. Being served a nice choice of food which is designed to keep you healthy, but now you know enough in your second Youth not to turn up your nose and push the plate away. You get to share your owies with other friends at lunch or dinner and have a receptive ear. Even if the conversation turns to *their* owies.

Oh, yes, the best way to become young again? Learn to laugh like you did when you were three or four. Carefree, joyful, where everything is fun or funny. A sense of humor is the fastest route to growing young again. Cultivate people with deep laugh lines. It will be time well spent.

One thing to laugh about is Pablo Picasso's art. Only someone young at heart could paint women with two eyes on one side of their faces, or an eye in the middle of a forehead, or a contorted body shape depicting sex. Was he only trying to see if we were still young, or young again, and could laugh?

The quality of mercy is not strained ...

... it droppeth as the gentle rain from heaven. Upon the place beneath. It is twice-blessed. It blesseth him that gives, and him that takes ...

With this week's writing assignment, I was left sitting in front of the legendary "blank page" of my computer screen. "What is the quality you value most in others?" My goodness, how much time have you got? To begin with, anyone I spend my precious time on had better have more than one quality, I can tell you that right now. It got me wondering about my friends and family and which qualities they exhibited the most. I did my usual exercise in drawing the circle in the middle of the paper with "Quality" inside the circle and the radiating lines going out from the circle, doing north, south, east, and west first and then adding NNE, NNS, ESE, and ESS; you get the picture. Then I started listing the *general attributes* of what I expect from *everybody* and wrote those qualities above the lines emanating from the circle. As I jumped in my mind to the next person, I found a different reason for valuing that person. My mind started moving faster, and more lines were drawn, I realized I was running out of space. Well, at least I was making a good start. After numbering each thought as to its importance, I was ready to start writing.

The most important quality I seek in *everyone* is Integrity, which to me is another way of saying *genuineness*. I admire a man who respects his wife and remains loyal to her through the years, as she does to him. Empathy is an important quality, and not everyone has that ability to project themselves into the soul of another person. Hospice nurses come to mind. And, sometimes, doctors. Our doctor was so kind to me as Fritz lay dying, explaining what would come next, trying to prepare me. Gentleness is another form of empathy. Being an optimist is such an important quality. I'm an optimist and always see the glass half full. My husband was a melancholic and always saw the glass half empty. But instead of looking at the glass of wine that way, all you need to remember is that *it can be refilled*! A person who is an optimist is usually someone who wants to learn something new every day, open to ideas and a new way of looking at things. Someone you enjoy being around because they are exciting. With that comes a sense of humor. How can you NOT like someone who makes you laugh at a witty line that portrays the topic so perfectly? Someone who can leave to your imagination how what they just said relates only to you and that person, like a special in-joke. A remark that leaves you feeling warm and fuzzy. Special.

How about the qualities of being helpful, thoughtful, suggesting ideas because they know you so well? When I moved into Atria, my friend Ann came over time after time and was as excited about my move as if she were coming herself. It was Ann who suggested where to place this or that painting, or hanging the beautiful grapevine woven screen from the ceiling so it could be seen more fully in front of the window. And it was Ann who confirmed that my special shag rug would fit over the living-room carpet space by suddenly lying down on the carpet and telling me that the rug was six feet wide, and she was five foot three. It would fit between the furniture perfectly. Finding out that we shared the same interests, the same background, spoke the same foreign languages, held the same political beliefs.

As to the human characteristics, I value the ability to listen, not for the chance to break in and tell about *their* story, but because they care about you and want to *help*. Being *kind, courteous, considerate, and concerned*; maybe that's just another way of feeling empathy, but all are qualities I admire and need to keep me going each day. Some values I admire in a friend are ones we sort of take for granted, and maybe they deserve more appreciation: Frankness, without hurting your feelings because they know that first and foremost, you value *truth*. Promptness, because they know you don't like to be kept waiting. Maybe that is an old-age thing, but it's something you appreciate. A sense of fairness that generates nondiscrimination, tolerance, and the belief that everyone should have an equal chance at happiness. A sense of trustworthiness that gives you security, knowing that your friend or family member can be depended on and will always be there for you, whatever.

And, finally, the quality of accepting you just as you are, warts and all.

And you being able to accept that acceptance with the *humility it deserves*.

27

I Finally Luck It Out

I went back to Atria Valley Manor, a facility which was much smaller (sixty apartments), which I had visited at the time I saw Bell Court Gardens. Valley Manor had been built in 1962 to house the commanding officers from Davis-Monthan Air Force Base in south Tucson. The apartments were therefore larger than most found in retirement communities, all on the ground floor like townhouses, and had a more midcentury modern look. I liked it: two bedrooms, huge patio, my furniture looked good in it, and in the second bedroom, I had a jewelry studio again! To top it off, it would cost a thousand dollars less per month than at the former Atria. Was there any question? In the year and a half I have been at Valley Manor, I have made several friends, have started giving jewelry classes, and have written most of the chapters for my memoirs, all while also coping with being quarantined for Covid-19, wearing masks and being required to sit apart, and then getting fully vaccinated and gradually "freed up." What a year! The staff is wonderfully friendly here, the size of the apartment just right, the patio a delight to sit in and watch the six rosebushes all blooming. The dining room is small and intimate, the food is multiple-choiced, the activities include nice concerts, and it's located nearer to my daughter's house. A van takes me to doctors, shopping, the bank, and Trader Joe's. I have a complete large room to make jewelry in and to teach classes in air-conditioned comfort.

Over time, the enthusiasm cooled somewhat, Personnel quit, and we went five weeks with no laundry or cleaning done. No office manager for a long time. Other negatives. Atria Valley Manor lasted only a year and a half.

Holiday Greetings 2020

Hello, Everyone!
Family, Friends, and Fellow Survivors,

2020 will go down as That Was the Year That Was. Or Wasn't. If you are reading this, you are one of the "lucky ones," as is the Writer. Who ever imagined back in March when the disaster was first becoming known as a potential Pandemic, that it would be part of a political game plan by those in power, and ignored or dismissed to an irrecoverable crisis. I suspect there will be a flood of orders for "I survived 2020" tee shirts. For those of you who only get this one email for the year: Briefly, I moved again on January 9 into an Independent Living establishment called Atria Valley Manor, from its larger sister, Atria Bell Court Gardens. I have two bedrooms and an enormous terrace. I've turned one bedroom into a large jewelry studio. I was happy that I made the move before all the pandemic took place. I'm perfectly content being by myself, and have never been busier. The staff delivers meals and snacks to our patio doors, I have a cleaning lady who fixes my computer (how great is that!). That doesn't mean there have not been crises this year: no. Every day brings a new crisis you hadn't foreseen: changing insurance companies, straightening out mail order prescriptions, updating my Will, classes being canceled, the list is endless and time-consuming. But overall, I'm glad I moved and grateful for the security—and put up with the inconveniences. I Zoom my Writers Group every Friday, picking up pointers on how to self-publish. My book of memoirs is still a long time away from getting published: I recently went through two cartons of manuscripts only to discover that I had a lot more unrevised chapters than I thought. The *Tucson Daily Star* published a poem I submitted in October which was picked up by David Fitzsimmons (a local cartoonist and columnist) on his Facebook page which went viral with his 5,000 followers. I tried to answer as many as I could find addresses to.

I can empathize with those who are suffering. Having lived in so many places where normalcy is hunger, poverty, and no medical care, I feel there is no excuse for it to be happening here. But I have confidence that if these problems can be solved this late in the game, the new administration has the people who can do it.

I'll be 94 in January. Everybody is sending me jokes about "Do you remember?" listing all the things we used to do and use, and of course, I remember every one. But I also remember when America was admired all around the world, when politicians respectfully listened to their opponents, and when we didn't have mile-long bread lines and everyone had the job they enjoyed doing. Do you remember?

Stories from Atria

Two nights ago, I sat at the dinner table with three other ladies. You never know where the conversation will go. One of them had had a massage that afternoon and was extolling the virtues of massages and pedicures. The others concurred, but I mentioned that I couldn't do either because I was so ticklish. I was uncomfortable having another man, other than my husband, rubbing my bare back with rose oil, and as for a pedicure, the moment the woman reached for my foot I'd be kicking her in the chin from the tickly reflex. The massage addict quickly responded that I should do reflexology. She went on to explain that with reflexology, the masseur starts at the knee and works his way down, pressing and prodding all the tight knots in your muscles.

"When he gets to the foot, he hits the pressure points in the foot which control various parts of your body, like your back, and puts pressure on the area. Your pain in the shoulder, gone." One of the other ladies agreed, and they waxed harmoniously about how great you felt after a reflexology session. She wrapped it up definitively by declaring sotto voce, "It's the closest thing to an orgasm."

Well, I certainly hadn't seen that coming!

In return, I lowered my voice and asked, "Who do I call for an appointment?"

The Writing on the Wall

I don't like clutter, so you won't find photos of my family, work, or travels on every end table, the coffee table, the night tables, or just tables in general. Nor bookcases, or desks. I have photos of my family on a shelf in the master bedroom closet, where I can say hello to them every morning. Other photos of significance in my life's journey are all gathered together in one section of the master bedroom wall. They are of places I've been, goals I've accomplished, and people who have influenced my life. Mostly they hold truths I've learned over the years which I'd like to share. Lying in bed contemplating them the other day, I decided they deserved a chapter in my memoirs.

The first one was taken on a trip to Africa in the late nineties. It was originally a pencil sketch. I made notes of the colors and painted it after I got home. It is one of the innumerable villages of Ghana showing small mud huts with thatched roofs, communal baking ovens, women working with babies tied to their backs, and little kids waving to us and our tour bus. So why is this village special? Because our guide-driver pulled up all of a sudden on the side of the road and told us this jumble of mud huts was the birthplace of Kofi Annan. At that time, he was secretary-general of the United Nations. I sketched furiously as the guide told the history of this famous man who had accomplished so much from such humble beginnings. Annan was born there in Kumasi in 1938, managed to get an education in Ghana, graduated from Macalaster College in the United States in 1961, did graduate studies in Geneva, Switzerland, and was a fellow at Massachusetts Institute of Technology in 1971 and 1972. He served his first term as secretary-general between 1997 and 2002. He received the Nobel Peace Prize in 2001 for his work in the United Nations Assembly on education, AIDS, immigration, and multiple problems. He was held in high esteem. And he came from such humble beginnings in this tiny village of hundreds of mud huts. What an inspiration.

The second picture is a colored photo of the *Sails*, a stunningly beautiful statue at the foot of Bernard Avenue in Kelowna, British Columbia, Canada, where I lived for twenty-nine years. The sculpture is symbolic of the many sailboats out on the blue Okanagan Lake. A different kind of life from Kumasi, but the *Sails* reminds me of a place I still feel so deeply connected to and the genuine people there. It was sent to me after I had moved back to the States in 2009 by my former neighbor, a very kind gesture because he understood how much I was missing Kelowna.

Waterfront Park had locks which allowed the Chris-Crafts to enter from the lake, raised them eight feet in the locks, and released the yachts into the lagoon level to dock in front of the townhouses, ready for the next run around the lake. The bridge over the lake would lift to allow the sailboats to pass under it. From my balcony I watched the sailboat races from the yacht club each Wednesday evening and Sunday morning, enjoying the whisper of the fountain and the pots of flowers on the balcony. Good times.

The third row has a photo of Michael Bublé, a large formal portrait of Joana in her wedding dress, and a photo of me at my workbench. Michael Bublé, the famous Canadian singer whose voice was a perfect match to Frank Sinatra's. I had attended two of his tour concerts and loved them. The guy has a tremendous rapport with the audience. He can fill a stadium of ten thousand people and make every person there think he is singing just to them. So I thought, "Why not?" He played a major role in my life. In 2010, I lay near death from pancreatitis at Tucson Medical Center. It was so severe, I had to lie completely still, without moving, for an entire week, and couldn't eat or even drink anything; they just moistened my lips with a wet sponge. A friend of Joana's brought in her radio, and Joana brought in several of my Michael Bublé CD's. They would put one in the CD slot, tune it to Low, and push Repeat. His compassionate, warm voice kept me calm and carried me through the long days to recovery. He deserved the spot.

It was funny, really, how I got that photo of Michael. I had bought a monogrammed cap and a mug, and a couple of CDs from his online shop, which had made me a member of his fan club, I guess. Anyway, they must have gotten my birthdate from the information, because after I moved to Tucson, a day or two before my birthday, I received an envelope which said, "Photo—do not bend." It had a return address of Burnaby, British Columbia, and I thought, "The only person I know from Burnaby is Michael Bublé, and it couldn't be …" But it was: a photo of Michael showing him doing a kick with a red-soled shoe (I found out later they were famous Louboutins). In big black Sharpie it said, "To Janice, Yours, MB," his signature letters done with a flourish. I was ecstatic. That same day, in the same post, I received an envelope from the IRS containing a refund check for $4,000. (When did I ever overpay that much?) That evening, I was talking to Joana on the phone, raving about the autographed photo from Michael, and then said, "Oh, yeah, I also got a refund from the IRS." Don't tell me I don't have my priorities straight.

Next comes my pride-and-joy photograph of Joana in the wedding dress I had made, taken in the synagogue between two large pedestals of white roses and greenery. Such a beautiful picture of her on such a wonderful day. I have written an entire chapter on how I came to sew the dress after we had retired to Spain while our villa was being built on the Costa del Sol, so I won't go into the details again. Just have to say that Joana never saw her wedding dress until two days before the wedding.

Talk about trust and faith! She and Stan will celebrate their forty-seventh anniversary this year.

The third photo was taken of me working at my workbench in my studio in Kelowna. It was taken to accompany a full-page newspaper article about how I had had the courage to try out for the studio after my husband had died and I was left wondering at seventy-eight what I would do with the rest of my life. The photographer from the paper was doing that photography thing of clicking away while constantly moving, but as he crouched down on the floor and aimed his camera up at my face, I leaned over the bench and yelled, "Don't you dare!" He laughed when I explained I didn't need a photo of all my chins. He grinned and then asked, "You want me to get a ladder?" Funny. Oh my, but I had some wonderful times in that studio. It opened up a whole new life that I never dreamed was possible.

The next row is interesting from an antiques viewpoint. It contains two round tintypes of a little child probably about two years old, and the middle picture is a photo of a bronze trophy.

The first tintype shows a little blonde in overalls holding a small garden shovel, ready to help her grandpa plant some flowers. The other one shows her sturdily standing in shallow water in the lake, dressed in a full old-fashioned swimsuit with a belt and buckle, holding a trowel to dig up some sand. The tintypes are rather rare. I checked them out on Google, wondering what the difference was between tintypes and daguerreotypes. Daguerreotypes were always held under glass to keep the silvery finish from tarnishing. Tintypes contained iron and can be authenticated by the attraction they show to a small magnet. Mine practically jumped off the wall to the magnet. My sister claimed they were of me, but the eyes look different to me, and I think the one in the swimsuit was of her, but I never could figure out how both pictures could look like the same age. Then I noticed they both carried the imprint of Columbia Medallions Studios Chicago on the back of the gold frame, and the good old internet came to my rescue. For several decades the Chicago-based studio was the world's largest purveyor of hand-painted photo medallions. *The medallion business was founded in 1888 as the Columbia Portrait Company, a name it retained in an official capacity, even after it started using the "Columbia Medallion Studios" name in more of its marketing after World War I.* It hit its peak of popularity in the 1930s.

Don't Let Memories Grow Dim! That tagline was from the company's 1919 advertisement in which the customer was encouraged to send in a photo of a loved one, mostly children, but also veterans of the Spanish War in 1898 and World War I. The photos were then reproduced on a six-inch celluloid button medallion, and for an extra price would be hand-colored.

So that was the answer: My parents had sent in photographs of my sister and me, both taken when we were around two years old. And they splurged for the hand-painted version which cost $3.25 each. (In today's value, $66.)

The major legacy Columbia left behind, rather morbidly, are the hundreds of six-inch medallions now floating anonymously through America's antique shops and eBay listings—perfectly preserved, as intended, but mostly robbed of their historical significance and emotional resonance. Since these portraits rarely included any printed descriptions of the people or places depicted, we're left to consider the irony of the situation. The medallion was purchased to keep someone's memory alive, but the memory itself was always dependent on the customer being around to remember it.

I suppose that this is going to be the future norm for mankind, now that nearly every picture we take is digitally stored in some intangible cloud, impervious to degradation. Label those old JPEGs unless you want to be remembered someday as "unknown child in garden with shovel."

"Pictures fade—Columbia Medallions last forever. ... They are made from any photograph, copied on non-corrosive metal and the surface glazed. Thus, they become works of art ..." They are still very sharp photos, and I was sure cute. Somewhere in the article it refers to these tintypes as "relics." Really? Vintage I am, antique, gettin' there, but *relic*? Come on!

The photograph in the middle was the bronzed trophy I had won for Best Designer of the Year. I was nominated by one of my students, seconded by the director of the Rotary Centre based on the many civic activities I took part in during my years at the arts center, and voted in by the judges. The night at the university where the awards were given out to the best actor, actress, musical director, artist, dancer, etcetera was one of the happiest and momentous events of my life, a night I will never forget. A far cry from the little tyke with a garden shovel seventy-nine years earlier.

So many childhood memories are stored in that house. Christmases with a huge tree in the corner of the living room and the excitement of wakening early and rushing down to see what Santa had brought and if he had eaten the cookies left out for him. He was actually a bit messy: always left a few crumbs in the dish and the empty glass of milk.

The huge Thanksgiving dinners my parents gave every year, which included as many relatives as could get there as well as lonely people from Dad's office who were always invited.

The annual dinner of everything venison each fall, which my dad threw for his male companions who went hunting with him. They skinned the deer, tanned the hide, and had a butcher freeze the various meat sections. Those gourmet dinners had to be introduced with a colorful menu card in front of each place setting, detailing each course. I was proud that Dad thought so highly of my artistic ability that he always asked me to paint the picture on the front. I particularly remember one year the picture he drew was of a jaunty fellow heading out with a fishing pole in his hand, and I added the color. I was good at painting inside the lines.

At Easter, we went to church dressed in our new finery, patent leather Mary Janes with frilly white socks and hats. And before church, the Easter egg hunt all through the house and out in the front lawn. The Easter baskets always held an enormous chocolate bunny which lasted several weeks. One year we actually received a live white rabbit, with red eyes and long pink ears. He succumbed three months later after finding the cellar door open and eating a whole bag of onions stored down there. After that fiasco, there were little baby chicks, who, cute as they were, soon became chickens and got moved out to cages in the backyard.

The dancing and singing performances we always put on for Aunt Maudie, who came up from Long Island to visit and thought we were the most talented kids ever. The ice cream socials every summer for the Methodist church, when Dad strung Japanese lanterns all over the backyard. Catching fireflies in jars and jumping over the revolving sprinkler with the neighborhood kids.

Having my first boyfriends come calling. They were so gauche. Except for the sophisticated ones who came in from all over New York State as part of the Army Specialized Training Program. Those guys knew all too well how to entice a small-town girl, and the kisses were breathtaking.

The other two pieces of art in the last row were pencil sketches I made of my grandma and grandpa. They are both looking down because I copied the portraits from a photo taken of them on their sixty-fifth wedding anniversary as they were about to cut the cake. My grandparents were such basically good people, and set such a fine example by the simple way they lived, that it formed in me a lifelong desire to emulate them. It is because of them that I disdain the fakeness and insincerity so prevalent today. Instead, I value good friends and a hearty laugh, and every day I find something to appreciate in my life.

Charging Batteries

Someone asked me the other day how I liked socializing at Atria, since we do that every day when we go to the dining room to have either lunch or dinner. I had been painfully shy in my younger years, and felt comfortable being alone, I had to think a moment to examine how I had changed.

I think of myself now as the Energizer Bunny. He gets plugged in every night and recharges himself. Lately I find myself with his funny little waddle and banging a drum to make a point.

But, I'm wondering, now …

When I'm tired, where do my ideas come from? How do I form my thoughts? How do I keep on writing when I'm "dry" or staring at a blank computer? I don't think it's from being with others as much as it is from quietly thinking by myself. Long ago, I decided not to be a whiner or complainer. Instead, I charged myself with coming up with solutions. So, I sit and think of the origin of the problem and then figure out how best to resolve the issues surrounding the problem.

When I work out several solutions, I find I'm happy again and raring to go. Then I seek out my friends to share my wonderful thoughts with them, energized and batteries charged!

On Turning Ninety, or,
I Thought Getting Old Would Take Longer

Honestly, I thought getting old would take longer. But somewhere along the way, either Einstein's theory of relativity, the speed of light, or the speed of sound kicked in and suddenly I went one day from being sixty-eight to having my daughter ask me how many friends I wanted to have at my ninetieth birthday party. I think all my seventies and eighties went down some of those black holes we keep hearing about.

On Friday, December 30, 2016, Joana planned a lovely family birthday celebration for me since the kids were all here between Christmas, Hanukkah, and New Year's and wouldn't be on the actual date of January 13. We met at an old favorite Mexican restaurant, Casa Molina, where many family celebrations had taken place over the years. Around the table were my daughter, son-in-law, grandson, Andrew's wife, my two great grandchildren (five and two) from Los Angeles, and my granddaughter, Adriana, from Denver. When I arrived, Cameron kept yelling, "GG, boons! Boons, GG!" I had decided with Don's arrival that I was not going to be Grammie, but GG sounded good for Great Grandma. And yes, indeed, there were several balloons on the table proclaiming "90" to the whole world, as well as a pretty silvery centerpiece also with the numerals "90" all over it.

We had fun and good food and then the waiters arrived with a sparkler, bearing a plate of nut-covered fried ice cream and singing "Happy Birthday," and the whole restaurant joined in.

We went back to Joana's for more ice cream (Dilly Bars), also a tradition, and my grandson suddenly blew the little paper bag that it came in and slammed it hard so it made a big bang, also traditional because Fritz (Papa) always did that; the great-grandchildren then had to pop theirs. Stan was ready to take me home, and as I was going out the door, I mentioned that I still didn't think of myself as ninety, and Adriana said, "That's because ninety is the new sixty, Grandma." (She has a possible future in the Diplomatic Service.) Joana dryly remarked, "As I was ahead of you walking out of the restaurant, carrying the balloons and centerpiece, everyone was wishing me a happy birthday."

Made my day.

On Turning Ninety-Two

Whenever I tell someone my age
They look in wonder and say
"Wow, you don't LOOK 92!"
That usually Makes My Day.

I tend to guide the conversation
Around in such a way
That I can work in my age somehow
just to hear them say

"Wow, you don't look 92"

I wonder what 92 looks like
Bent over, wrinkly and such?
Using a walker and grumbling?
Watching Hallmark too much?

Not for me, after all this time
Having fun with all of my friends
Telling jokes and writing my story
I hope it never ends.

But Reality looks back from the mirror
Each morning when brushing my teeth
I look at the image projected there
And it's not the image I seek.

There are wrinkles I call "laugh lines"
And blotches that shouldn't be there
And my hairbrush contains samples
of what used to be colorful hair.

The smile that looks out at me
is amused by all it surveys
I think of the chores awaiting me
And the friends who are waiting to say

"Wow, you don't look 92!"
They don't know how they've just
Made My Day.

But, really and truly, it's not how you look
That makes such a difference, you know,
It's not the number of years in your life
But the life in those years that will glow.

I counted the tears that went with those years
And prayed to the Powers that Be
To let me enjoy one more year to come
So my friends could say, "Hey, not bad—For 93!"

The time has spun by in a whirl,
the balloons all say 95.
The look that I get when I tell them,
says "You're lucky to be alive."

But Grandpa lived to 100
and I promised I'd better his goal.
It's a promise I'll keep
If I could just get some sleep!
And writing is good for the soul.

I'll finish the book, by hook or by crook
and stop talking about it, I swear.
When it's on my coffee table, I'll gaze at it
And, with you, my pride I will share.

On getting a life

I moved into Atria
Thinking with joy
That no more cooking
would be my next ploy.

I ordered the bracelet called Life Alert
to wear on my wrist all the time
and now I feel safe because I know
I'm no longer in my prime.

I explained it to friends and even to strangers
And they all acknowledge the fact
that it lets people know wherever I am
that I'm Okay and intact.

But one friend wrote back and gave me the truth
that the bracelet is merely a way
to acknowledge what everyone knew except me.
It's called Life Alert for a reason, they say.

Atria has many events to enjoy
and time enough if you're not a dunce
So, whenever I get a life again
They'll let me know at once.

Satire

Dear Readers,

I'm a stickler for good grammar; even in grade school I loved spelling contests, and always did those vocabulary tests in the *Reader's Digest*. Because of my three years of Latin in high school I was able to select the correct word of the three choices, based on the Latin derivative.

So, when I belonged to the writing group in Tucson, I decided one week to play a trick on them. I got out the list of rules about what NOT to do, stood every rule on its head, and wrote each sentence as wrong as I could make it, just for the fun of it. You can't imagine how hard that was to do and the hours it took to make EVERY sentence incorrect! Then on Friday I printed out eight copies and stood up and told them what I had done, and to please not feel that this week they had to correct anything. I TOLD THEM IT WAS ALL SATIRE. Every single sentence.

I expected them to laugh all through it.

The room went silent. Then out came the pens.

I was speechless. I had written it SO WELL, so believable, that they accepted the entire thing as my weekly contribution. (I was shocked to think that my NORMAL writing was so lousy.)

ONE lady had left her page pristine white and wrote, "Good Job, Janice" across the top. All the others were covered with curlicue e's, meaning eliminate, or underlined phrases, or crossed-out words, punctuation marks, and grammatical errors.

FYI: Rules for Writing.

1. Don't use adverbs. (Unnecessary.)
2. Don't start sentences with conjunctions; so, and, but, when, now, well, etc.
3. Don't end sentences with prepositions
4. Don't use too many exclamation points.
5. Don't use hardly ANY punctuation marks, only periods.

6. Don't use capital letters except at the beginning of sentences. Not to emphasize.

7. Don't quote other writers; you have to pay a lot of money to get the right to quote. They're all copyrighted.

8. Don't make paragraphs too long. Tighten, tighten, tighten.

9. Don't make paragraphs too short. Change paragraphs every time you change a thought.

10. Don't make a sentence too long with many different points.

Here it is. Put away your pens.

How to Write Satire
(Pay attention to everything!)

When I woke up (awakened) a half hour ago, I found myself contemplating a kind of phenomenon and thought it best to get up and write about it, then maybe I could get back to sleep for another couple of hours.

You see, I belong to this writing group which meets every Friday afternoon at the Dusenberry-River Library. It's a wonderful group of people: They're all so intellectual. They've been everywhere, done everything, it's fascinating to read their essays. I listen to them, engaging with the other fellow writers, and I think, "Someday, Janice …" I mean, some of them are actually **published!**

It's a group of about 10–12 (oops, ten to twelve) women and one man. Poor guy. Every week he has to sit and listen to yet another version of *The Vagina Monologues* but he has developed a tolerance for what women talk about and is as stoic as they come. What he goes home and tells his wife is probably interesting, although a bit vague, I would imagine.

When I joined the group. I never divined that the learning curve to writing one's Memoirs would be so steep. More like a suicidal cliff, really. Well, before joining them, I would never have used the word "divined" to express conjecture or to find out by intuition. I don't know where to find Spell-Checker, so I still refer to *Webster's*.

They have this thing, you see, about grammar and punctuation, and they are adamant about not using adverbs. I mean, actually, Who made up that rule?

What we do is: we write an essay every week. Or, as in my case and several others, a Chapter. (Makes it sound more professional.) Like it might actually get published one of these days. Or, as is likely in my case, at 91 (oops, do you still have to write out ninety-one?) posthumously. I doubt if my daughter would go to all that trouble. But I digress. Then, we make 12 (oops, twelve) copies of the piece, which has now become our Baby, and six (got it!) lucky people get to present it to the group for critiquing.

Wow, what can I say! This critiquing thing has the ability to turn these nice ladies, and gentleman, into monsters. It's the strangest thing! The POWER just goes to their heads, and they tell you to leave entire paragraphs out (paragraphs that you have shed blood over). Out! Or at least move it up to the first, or last paragraph of the essay; they never seem able to make up their minds about that. Now, the rule is that you can't start sentences with conjunctions; conjunctions are those connecting words that hold thoughts and sentences together: and, but, or, because, if, when, so, and as. At my age I like anything that can hold my thoughts together.

They cover the pages with little curlique e's all over the place which means "eliminate." One time there was hardly anything left, I kid you not. They don't much like Capital Letters except at just the beginning of a sentence. And of course, there's always that cardinal rule that you must never use a preposition to end a sentence with. I mean, there are so many rules to follow, it's a wonder we can write anything at all. I forgot to mention punctuation, but that's in a class by itself. They're constantly critiquing me that I use too many punctuation marks. My problem is that I write like I talk. I hesitate, I put a comma; I ponder something, I put a question mark. I'm astounded, I use an exclamation mark, so what's the problem? They want everything to end with a period, for heaven's sake....... (And all those periods there mean "Just think about it.")

Oh, yes, then there's that thing about last sentences. I LOVE last sentences. I try to end every chapter with a humorous last sentence. I mean, Erma Bombeck did it, David Fitzsimmons does it, why can't I do it? Aren't my chapters worthy of funny last sentences? I guess that's a rhetorical question. But, last sentences, OUT. Leave the readers hanging.

If it weren't so damn much fun, I'd forget the whole thing. But the Friday meetings are so stimulating I'm drawn to them like a magnet. On the last Friday of every month, after the meeting, where these brutal people have just torn you to shreds again, we break and take a short walk to Whole Foods for a social hour, getting an iced latte (You can do that in Tucson in January) and one of their sinful desserts.

And now comes the strangest part: During the walk over to Whole Foods, the ladies must shrug off their critiquing robes, because once inside the store, they chatter, and joke, and become the sweetest people you ever met. I think we have the plot of a new version of *Dr. Jekyll and Mr. Hyde*. I mean, they're almost NORMAL.

I googled *satire*. (What would Writers do without Google?) Here are some examples of political satire.

99 percent of politicians make the other 1 percent look bad.

Anyone can become president of the United States I didn't believe this until this year. (Written in 2018.)

I concluded that I had been too subtle; satire requires you to make the entire piece reflect the main joke (all the rules of grammar), and to exaggerate a strong point of view.

Maybe I should have mentioned how long it took me to think up all those mistakes.

By the way, one of the suggestions posed by Google in How to Write Satire, was:

Join a writers group, so you can ask them if your articles are funny.

Murphy's Romance

Last week the fixed subject to write about in my writers group was "A movie you love, and why." We had to write extemporaneously for ten minutes.

It didn't take me long to figure that one out. The movie I love (and the only one I ever recorded) was one filmed in Florence, Arizona, and starred Sally Field and James Garner.

It's called *Murphy's Romance*, and is a romantic comedy about a May-December romance between Emma (Sally Field) and an aging pharmacist (Garner), Murphy Jones. She is a divorcée with a twelve-year-old son and has inherited a run-down horse ranch, which she hopes to renovate and make a living with. He befriends her by buying a horse and paying her rent to take care of it for him. Some of the dialogue is priceless. When she bakes him a birthday cake, in order to find out how old he is, she asks him how many candles to put on it. He replies, "Just set the damned thing on fire." In a funny scene when she is in a hospital after crashing her old truck, she is walking down the corridor in a hospital gown and he moves inauspiciously behind her.

A lot of the success of this movie is not what they *said*, but what they left unsaid. After they realize they love each other, in the last scene, she asks him, "Stay for supper, Murphy?" He replies, "Only if I'm still there for breakfast." She slightly hesitates, then asks, "How do you like your eggs?" Then, as they walk up the steps, holding hands, he murmurs, "I'm sixty." With those few words, they convey their love for each other and their confidence in the future, and he shows how much he trusts her by telling his age. Beautiful writing. Leaves the interpretation to the viewer's own experiences. The movie's title song is called "I'm in Love for the Last Time," sung by Carole King. Sets the stage perfectly for Murphy's romance. Love, love, love it.

28

And Then He Kissed Me …

A couple of years ago I belonged to a writers group when I lived at Bell Court Gardens, and we chose different topics which we would each write on and see how different people approached the same theme. One week someone suggested we write a piece of fiction. I said I had never written any fiction and hadn't a clue how to start. One lady said, "Janice, just pick the least likely thing that could happen and embroider it."

This chapter is a work of pure fiction.
(Partly)

Jan hit the turn indicator as she saw the "Special Tour Today" sign in the middle of the street and turned left into the long driveway for Bell Tower Mansion. The sign was a permanent fixture; you could get a tour any day you wanted.

She felt the pleasure and satisfaction of being a resident in the hundred-year-old Spanish-style home and gardens. Then, before reaching the steps to the lobby, she hit the turn indicator again, this time to the right, even though no one was behind her, just force of habit. She slowed down over the hump, thinking as usual of her time in Spain where humps in the road were called "policia durmiendo" (sleeping policeman) and smiled at the analogy. She parked her car in the back of the building on the gravel area and walked to door C, which led to elevator C, which led to the third floor and directly to her apartment.

Breathing a sigh of relief, she felt the coolness of the apartment after the ninety-plus-degree heat of winter in Tucson. At least she had taken care of the screwup by the bank which had deducted the last Visa payment two times from her checking account. Good thing she still had the wits to check each month's statement line by line and found the error. The personal banker had acknowledged the error and corrected the balance. She gave him a small piece of her mind about all the stupid apps they were constantly coming up with instead of making the Accounts page clearer about payments and confirmation.

She headed to the kitchen, filled a tall glass with ice cubes, and poured in the leftover coffee from the morning. With a biscotti slice in the other hand, she eased onto the padded office chair, mindful that it was on a hard-plastic carpet protector and could easily slide out from under her. She clicked on the Inbox to see if any new emails had arrived during her absence.

Seeing nothing urgent, she looked at the monthly program of activities and then confirmed any changes with the weekly Update recorded on her own calendar.

She discovered that this month, January, everyone with a January birthdate was invited to a party in the chapel that afternoon. It would feature a guitarist by the name of Darell. Jan decided to go, since last week she had turned ninety-two and had written a funny poem about it. When she walked in the chapel, she mentioned to the hostess that she had written a birthday poem, in case they would like to hear it. Mary took her up to the entertainer and told him that somewhere in his program he could introduce Jan, and she would read a humorous poem. He smiled and agreed.

Jan began feeling a little nervous, because she had never read anything she had written out loud before and wasn't sure that the audience would think it as funny as she did.

The entertainer introduced himself and said he had a list of birthday celebrants, which he would read later. He finished tuning his guitar, then began singing along with his strumming. Medleys of golden oldies, all of which Jan hummed, having learned all the words back in the forties every Saturday night on the Lucky Strike Hit Parade. She thought ruefully, "If only my memory of all the new people I've met at Bell Tower was as clear as the lyrics to the old songs."

She became aware of the clever phrasing the singer demonstrated with his smooth voice and the fact that he appeared to sing all the songs without taking a breath. No matter what request he got, he instantly began playing the song by ear. Remarkable, she thought. She loved the way he sang John Denver's "Today."

Darell mentioned that he had played in nightclubs and bars for forty years in New York City and that his wife had been a Rockettes dancer. Then he read the list of birthday names, and when he came to Jan's name and recognized her, he called her up to the mic to read her poem. It was titled "On Turning 92" and was all about how happy she was when telling someone her age, and they exclaimed, "Wow, you don't *look* 92!" She was delighted that the audience laughed all through it, and when she finished and took her seat again, Darell grinned and said, "Wow, you don't *look* 92," which got another laugh.

By the end of the concert, Jan had made up her mind that she wouldn't miss any of Darell's performances. She highlighted the dates when he would be performing, and whenever she heard a song she liked on the Easy Listening channel, she would make a note of it and request it the following month. He always mentioned how much he liked her choices. He was so easygoing that she looked forward to each month's performance. She admired his professionalism and liked the intimacy of his smooth voice.

One night as he was packing up his equipment and she was walking out, he waved his hand, indicating for her to stay behind. As she came back to the guitar stand, he motioned for her to sit down and then joined her on the couch. They made small talk about some of the songs she had requested, and the conversation turned to the places they had both traveled to, surprising themselves with what they had in common. She mentioned her large world map with all the pins in it. It was very pleasant.

A few months after the birthday concert, he again suggested that they continue their conversation, and they walked around the gardens, chatting comfortably, with Darell laughing at Jan's funny stories of what had happened in some of the foreign countries where she and her husband had lived. This became their routine, sometimes for just a few minutes' catch-up, sometimes for longer conversations.

After one evening concert he asked if they could go to her apartment and sit on the balcony. Jan was a little flustered and blurted out, "Darell, that might not be a good idea; your wife probably expects you home soon."

He looked perplexed. "I'm not married."

"But you're wearing a wedding ring, and you speak of your wife every once in a while, during your concerts …"

He quickly removed the gold wedding band and placed it in his shirt pocket. "I was divorced fifteen years ago."

"I don't understand …"

"Oh, Jan, if I tell you why I wear it, you will think I'm bragging or, worse …"

"Please!"

"Okay. But don't laugh!" She promised not to.

Darell took her hand, and they walked around the softly-lit patios.

"You see, a few years ago when I came back to Tucson, I began to give concerts in several senior living facilities, and at one of the places there were two older ladies who began flirting with me and making suggestive remarks, and honestly, I didn't know how to handle it. A friend suggested I pretend I was married, because with *their* generation, they still respected the sanctity of marriage. I dug out my old wedding band and started wearing it to the concerts, and every once in a while, I would mention my "wife." It worked like a charm; I never had any more trouble. So, I just decided to keep up the charade."

Jan couldn't help it. She covered her mouth and began giggling.

"You mean, you were being *stalked* by two old ladies?"

"Hey, you promised not to laugh!"

"Oh, you are such a gigolo!" She hesitated, then took his arm and said, "I'm on the third floor."

She opened her eyes slowly the next morning and was startled to see his tender smile and his eyes looking deeply at her as if trying to memorize her face. He whispered, "Good morning, Jan."

"Good morning. Have you been awake long?"

"Since six." He finger-combed her hair away from her face, then leaned closer and kissed her. He tucked her head under his chin, tightening his arms around her. She relaxed and kissed the hollow of his neck.

The Easy Listening channel played softly in the background. It was playing John Denver's "Today."

29

The Dance

Anne Murray's song "Could I Have This Dance?" is so apropos in relating my story. The song is a favorite, played at weddings for the newly married couple to dance to since the next line was "for the rest of my life."

But the song which resonates more with me is "The Dance," written by Toni Arata and recorded by Garth Brooks, the song that made him famous. It talks about the first dance, the dance when a couple holds each other and knows at that moment that they want to be together forever.

But you don't get to pick and choose how your life turns out, and the song goes on to explain how perhaps that's good. If we had a choice to "delete" everything bad, the actions that brought pain and sorrow, we would also have to wipe out the events which brought moments of joy. Music marks those moments in our lives. When we feel love ignite, how could we know what the future holds?

As I reach the final pages of my memoirs, I look back over my life and question many of the things I did which I shouldn't have done, or didn't do, which I should have. Most were done wrongly, or not done, ignorantly unaware. Back in the forties and fifties there wasn't the widespread information that is available to women now. Back then it was different. Women were chattel; there is no other way to describe it. *Webster* describes chattel as "movable property, not real estate." Bearers of children, keepers of a house, and owned by husbands who provided for them, they accepted this as the norm, believing it was infinitely better than becoming an "old maid." Marriage vows back in the forties called on men to love, honor, and cherish while women had to promise to love, honor, and obey, and they were pronounced "man and wife." Not "husband and wife" as they are today. For the most part, they lived comfortable lives, and the majority had good relationships and enjoyed many advantages they otherwise would not have had.

Slowly things changed. Women had gained the right to vote in 1919, but the glass ceiling was unknown. They had few choices if they were on their own: teacher, nurse, secretary, or salesperson. A few distinguished themselves as business leaders, but they were oddities. Some became famous in special fields, like science, but that was the exception. I lived in locations where this activity was unheard of, and books with information about possibilities not yet written. I had no mentor. I was left three or four decades behind in my approach to life and marriage.

I am left with deep regret, sorrow, and chagrin in not having known how to manage my life better. But I acknowledge readily that all of the things I experienced in living abroad for forty-four years under different conditions and cultures did result in forging me for the final years, when I finally — actually — realized my potential.

There is the loneliness of being alone, and the loneliness of being with someone. When your husband becomes the only person you have contact with, you become totally dependent on him for everything, all decisions. But inwardly, you are becoming stronger and self-reliant, even if you don't realize it. You hold close to those rare moments of complete surrender or affection and approval. And surprisingly, you begin to acknowledge the wisdom of that famous instruction on an airplane, "In the case of an emergency, place your own oxygen mask on first."

At the end, memory is all we have. It's imaginary and fictional, painful and triumphant.

It's what books and songs are made of.

As Toni Arata wrote so eloquently: Looking back on your first dance together, you see it as perfect and wish all the events in life could be so wonderful. But then you realize that if you could delete all the pain and sorrow that happened, you would also lose all the happy moments that came unexpectedly and in the end, it is better if Life is left to Chance.